T3-BLC-574

Crossing Barriers

CROSSING BARRIERS

People Who Overcame

MARY ELLEN SNODGRASS

1993
Libraries Unlimited, Inc.
Englewood, Colorado

For my daughter Deborah,
who makes crossing barriers look easy.

LIBRARIES UNLIMITED, INC.
P.O. Box 6633
Englewood, CO 80155-6633

Library of Congress Cataloging-in-Publication Data

Snodgrass, Mary Ellen.
    Crossing barriers : people who overcame / Mary Ellen Snodgrass.
    viii, 248 p.   17x25 cm.
    Includes index.
    ISBN 0-87287-992-5
    1. Biography--20th century. I. Title.
CT120.S588   1993
920'.009'04--dc20
[B]   92-39789
                                                          CIP

Contents

Introduction

Obstacles, whether minor annoyances, major setbacks, enduring prejudices, or lifetime sentences, confront all people. Most have a choice: Ignore the obstruction, bypass it, or tackle it. *Crossing Barriers* includes some examples of admirable courage and determination and delineates the source and makeup of truly heroic character, the kind that becomes legend. Sequoyah, for example, overcame the superstitions of his people and created an entire writing system so that the Cherokee could communicate as easily as the white settlers who surrounded them. Likewise, Louis Braille, who lost his sight early in childhood, evolved a method of coding text so that the fingers of blind people could become as efficient at reading as the eyes of sighted persons. And Ishi, last of the Yahi, chose to become a living example of a way of life that disappeared with his tribe.

Many of the people who overcame handicaps achieved in vastly different fields. Claude Pepper, a victim of old age, became a spokesman for the elderly. Plantation slave Frederick Douglass not only escaped bondage but warred against slavery's inhumanity. Former vice president Nelson Rockefeller, a victim of dyslexia, rose to positions of authority in business, art, and politics. Hervé Villechaize, a dwarf, achieved a respectable career in the entertainment world. Jack London, born to an unstable home, compensated for his insecurity by challenging rough Klondike trails, which he used as backdrops for his novels.

An impressive number of people who overcame handicaps have been women. Black singer Marian Anderson took a stand against racism to help victims of discriminatory practices, and Quaker scholar Elizabeth Blackwell trounced opposition to become the first woman to practice medicine in the United States. With similar courage, Golda Meir challenged sex discrimination and led her adopted nation, Israel, during a crucial time in its history. Carson McCullers, invalid Southern author, battled paralysis to write books, stories, and plays about courageous characters. And Marvella Bayh, another strong woman, used her final moments during a fight against cancer to bring other victims hope.

In numerous stories of barriers crossed, the hero defeated an internal demon. Notable survivors of substance abuse, particularly Bob Welch, Betty Ford, and Johnny Cash, have used the public's interest in their private battles to benefit addicts. Chris Sizemore, central character in *The Three Faces of Eve*, has lifted mental patients from ignominy and despair. Joan Baez overcame paralyzing fear to sing songs of liberation; Mel Tillis used the voice that he failed to control in speech to achieve a singing career.

In contrast to these sufferers, the handicapped whose bodies lack normal muscles and bones have succeeded despite crippling diseases, trauma, and birth defects. Among these are Charles Proteus Steinmetz, genius inventor for General Electric; Max Cleland, legislator and former director of the Veterans Administration; and Joseph Merrick, beloved "Elephant Man." More problematic, perhaps, was the affliction of Chang and Eng Bunker, whose birth defect turned them into a single being, the world's prototypical Siamese twins. They coped with farming, travel, family life, and other normal activities in ways that set them apart from most handicapped people who have only the afflictions of a single body to cope with.

The range of handicaps this book sets before readers varies from the emotional trauma of Everett Alvarez, Jr., prisoner of war in Vietnam, to the religious ostracism suffered by Christian Science founder Mary Baker Eddy, and from the stigma of poverty that marked the early years of both Anwar Sadat and Jesse Stuart to the marital abuse that threatened to overwhelm rock star Tina Turner. Whatever the difficulty—whether the child neglect and abuse faced by Gloria Steinem and Christina Crawford, the sexual misidentification of Renée Richards, the deportation of Esther Hautzig, the inhuman incarceration of Elie Wiesel, the libelous inquisition that labeled Dalton Trumbo a Communist, or the homophobia that stigmatized Malcolm Boyd—the challengers who dared to overcome them leave behind a legacy of courage inspirational to all.

Everett Alvarez, Jr.

For any soldier, the possibility of disfigurement, imprisonment, or death awaits in the background of wartime experiences. For Everett Alvarez, a handsome navy pilot and one of two million soldiers to fight in the unpopular Vietnam conflict, the nightmare of capture came early in the war, and lasted until the end. Appropriate rewards—a Silver Star, two Bronze Stars, two Legions of Merit, the Distinguished Flying Cross, and two Purple Hearts—honored him for his determination to survive savage treatment while refusing to aid the enemy.

Since returning to the United States, Alvarez has completed a law degree and worked for both the Peace Corps and the Veterans' Administration. He has traveled, made speeches, and shaken hands with the style and appeal of a true hero, a man whom future Americans can look to for leadership. Despite his sufferings as a victim of what many think was an unjust war, he continues to represent himself and his country with dignity and pride.

At the age of fifty-two, after the passage of two decades, Alvarez, with the aid of veteran newsman Tony Pitch and cellmates Barrett, Berg, Carey, Coffee, and Metzger, penned his autobiographical account of wartime imprisonment and torture. In this work he focuses on his effort to stay alive and sane, speaking dispassionately of beatings, isolation, and cruelty. Entitled *Chained Eagle*, the work was dedicated to fellow Vietnam POWs along with the dead, their loved ones, and "those who still wait" (Alvarez 1982, v.).

BOYHOOD IN CALIFORNIA

Born December 23, 1937, in an ethnic neighborhood of Salinas, California, to Lalo and Chole Sanchez Alvarez, Everett "Alvie" Alvarez, descendant of two generations of working-class Chicanos, grew up on Pearl Street with his sisters, Delia and Madeleine. The three Alvarez children were conditioned by firm discipline and grounding in the Catholic faith, a foundation that served Everett well during his captivity. Shy, studious, and soft-spoken, he learned early to ward off attackers by studying boxing and wrestling. Lalo, an eighth-grade dropout, encouraged scholarship and inner strengths by giving his son a personal treasure—a bookmark featuring a reprint of Rudyard Kipling's "If."

1

Alvarez grew into a handsome, well-rounded adult. He enjoyed the friendship of his cousins and pals; his favorite recreation was camping near Big Sur. A high-school honor-roll student and outstanding track athlete, he applied himself fully to two years' worth of makeup classes at Hartnell College to work off deficiencies so that he could enter Berkeley. His junior year, he changed his plans and enrolled in electrical engineering at the University of Santa Clara, a Jesuit men's school.

A chance airplane ride during his teens changed the course of his ambition. Filled with the wonder of flight, he immersed himself in movies about flying, even though his father advised against his career choice. Determined to fly, Alvarez persisted and signed up to become a navy carrier jet pilot.

BECOMING A FLIER

In the winter of 1961, Alvarez began flight training on T-28s at Whiting Field in Milton, Florida. By summer, he was flying F-9F jet trainers in Kingsville, Texas, where he received his wings. Navy training offered fringe benefits, filling in the social graces he had missed in his early years. He studied survival skills at Florida's Eglin Air Force Reservation, never suspecting that someday his plane would be downed and he would have to draw on all his resources to cling to life. Following his marriage on December 15, 1963, and a honeymoon in Carmel and Las Vegas, he took charge of a crew of pilots at Cubi Point, Philippines, expecting further missions in Hawaii and Japan, but not Vietnam.

CAPTURE

On August 4, 1964, eight days after posing for a photograph on the flight deck of the USS *Constellation*, twenty-six-year-old Lieutenant Alvarez, Captain John "Nick" Nicholson, and the rest of Attack Squadron 144 cut short their leave time in Hong Kong to be catapulted from the carrier toward an historic mission—the initial assault inside North Vietnam. The squadron was placed on alert to halt torpedo boats jeopardizing destroyers in the Gulf of Tonkin. As a part of President Lyndon Johnson's retaliation for unprovoked assaults on the *Maddox* in international waters, the sortie included Alvarez's two strafing runs over PT boats at a naval dock 450 miles away.

The stormy weather hampered visibility during the second mission. Just as Alvarez's guns either jammed or ran out of ammunition, his A-4 Skyhawk fighter-bomber, capable of flying 500 miles per hour, bobbed out of control after being peppered by flak on the port side over Hon Gai Harbor. The hydraulic system failed; controls were useless as fire engulfed the disintegrating plane. Barely clearing the bluffs overlooking the Gulf of Tonkin, he bailed out, landed in saltwater, and inflated his life jacket.

As the battle raged overhead, Alvarez swam near enemy sampans, where six fishermen picked him up at grenade and gunpoint. They gestured to the smoking wreckage as though blaming him for the damage. Following an inconclusive interrogation by an English-speaking officer, he declined a greasy, unappetizing meal of water-buffalo meat and followed guards to a seven-by-ten-foot cell in a farmhouse, where he was washed and manacled and allowed to sleep.

Alvarez was at first blindfolded, yet not unkindly treated. The officer, nicknamed Owl, supplied him with a Vietnamese-English list of essential terms so that he could communicate pain, hunger, and needing to use the toilet. He could look outside the window at normal village activities, which steadied his nerves and raised unfounded hopes that he would soon be released into a diplomat's hands. Later, the prime minister of North Vietnam questioned him.

FAMILY REACTION

Back in the United States, reports of Alvarez's capture reached his wife and family. His parents and sisters, the first to realize that Everett was missing in action, went about their daily routine with heavy hearts. Married only seven months, Alvarez's brown-eyed, black-haired bride, Tangee, in contrast to Laio, Chole, and Delia, reacted hysterically on the afternoon of August 5 when she talked with officers bringing news of her husband. She had dreaded his wartime involvement and feared the worst.

Officers later confided to Chole that there was hope that her son was only missing, not dead. The whole family exulted when Reuters news agency relayed the first evidence that Alvarez was alive in a North Vietnamese prison. Later, a smeary photo from a Chinese Communist journal confirmed to Chole that her firstborn, nicknamed Hijo, did survive the downing and was still able to walk. In time, the family's cheerful outlook turned sour after televised clips of North Vietnamese mistreatment terrorized her with glimpses of her son and other POWs being assailed by a rabid mob.

PRISON CONDITIONS

On August 11, Alvarez was transferred to a regulation prison. At first, along with local thieves and prostitutes, he was locked within rat- and roach-infested mortar walls, twenty-one by twelve feet, in room 24 at Ha Lo Prison, derisively named the Hanoi Hilton. He was allowed courtyard privileges by day; his keepers returned at 5:00 P.M. to lock him in for the night. For his pain, resulting from injuries sustained when he ejected from the plane, infrequent visits by medical workers brought questionable remedies. The Viet Cong, who were at first reasonably humane, tempted him with promises of immediate release in exchange for confessions of war crimes and collaborative letters to Ho Chi Minh. Alvarez rejected their offers.

For the first six weeks, Alvarez lived on substandard rations and cold water from a faucet. Sometimes the rancid food caused fits of retching, followed by his pathetic attempts to eat the vomit-flecked servings. Owing to bouts of dysentery and diarrhea, he lost 55 of his normal 165 pounds and feared that he might die of malnutrition. His jailer, a taciturn middle-aged man, took compassion on him and began bringing edible food—eggs, chicken, vegetables, bread, and fruit. He also returned some of Alvarez's warm navy-issue clothes. That winter he got his first hot bath.

Hungering for reading material as much as for food, Alvarez persuaded his captors to give him what they could furnish, mainly English versions of local Communist newspapers. From these he learned the names of new inmates at the prison. By the end of the first year he had identified Storz, Guarino, Butler, Morgan, Lockhart, Shumaker, and Harris.

At first the newcomers thought that Alvarez, with his swarthy skin and long mustache, was an Oriental. Then they recognized him as the first Vietnam War POW. The men, both navy and air force, formed a cherished camaraderie and exchanged nicknames. In a limited show of contempt for their captors, they called the guards and the different areas of the prison compound by a private list of satirical names such as Rudolph the Red-nosed Guard and the Zoo.

STAYING ALIVE

In November 1965, Tom Barrett joined Alvarez as his first cellmate from the United States. The two caught up on home culture and events as well as developments in the war. Though their tempers flared from ennui and stress, they bolstered each other's spirits and kept in touch with the goings and comings of other prisoners through the prison grapevine. The group toned their bodies by playing basketball and renewed their faith by saying the rosary. At Christmas, they chased depression by singing carols, unaware that their captors were photographing them as a propaganda device.

Discipline for POWs called for polite bows to all captors. Lack of respect resulted in beatings with rubber truncheons. Manacles held wrists painfully close. Torture took numerous forms, such as sleep deprivation, psychological manipulation, and ropes binding the neck as near to the ankles as possible. The Viet Cong pulled back the prisoners' arms, sometimes tying restraints so tightly that restricted blood flow caused extreme pain.

At their lowest, POWs, including Alvarez, signed a dictated confession and apology to the North Vietnamese. The men suffered depression and deep regrets of betrayal yet realized that they had had no choice but to comply. In later years, officials of the high command concurred that they had done all that was humanly possible to remain loyal to their country without jeopardizing their lives.

Whenever possible, Alvarez maintained an observation post behind any available peephole so that he could keep up with the movements of the staff and his fellow POWs. Communication, a necessary measure to maintain morale and to warn of danger, depended upon the American Sign Language Manual Alphabet, wall taps, notes, scratches on food bowls, and whistling. As a further unifying effort, the men recited the Lord's Prayer and the Pledge of Allegiance in unison. They celebrated a mutual holiday when Ho Chi Minh died.

Alvarez wrote letters to his family on regulation seven-line note forms. On November 24, 1972, his airmail message from Gu'i May Bay to his mother contained plans for a long vacation and a trip to Europe. He kept up a pretense of cheer, asked for long underwear, and reported good health despite regular infestations of parasites and a severe bout of hepatitis. His letters received infrequent answers. Some of the best surprises from the outside world came in Red Cross packages containing corned beef, towels, chocolate, playing cards, and cigarettes. In the final year of captivity came a reply to his demands to know the truth; Tangee had divorced him, remarried, and had borne a child.

RELEASE

On February 12, 1973, 102 months after his capture, Alvarez led the line of prisoners who boarded a transport plane headed for Travis Air Force Base. On landing, he shed healing tears when he grasped his squadron-operations officer, Nick Nicholson, who had reminded him in the last radio communication he had heard that Alvarez knew what to do. Alvarez also revealed his deep devotion to Robbie Risner, the senior-ranking officer who had helped him through the darkest times in Hanoi.

Four days later, looking fit and happy, Alvarez, supervised by a hospital psychiatrist, posed for family photos with his parents and sisters at Oak Knoll Naval Hospital. His behavior, as demonstrated by his lack of emotion and inability to select from a menu card, indicated how deeply he had been affected by confinement. At the family reunion he learned of his family's long years of support for POWs, Delia's opposition to the war, and the whole family's efforts to set him free. Also, he learned of their personal adjustments to Lalo's drinking problem and to the deaths of Everett's grandmother and uncle. It wasn't until years later that the family revealed the inmost thoughts and fears that had plagued them throughout the war.

Alvarez made no complaints about his physical condition, but medical examinations confirmed the toll of his years in captivity. He had parasites and unidentifiable rashes and needed extensive dental work to replace or cap teeth broken during interrogation or from rocks in his food. His jaw and the nerves near his elbows were permanently damaged.

Public notoriety kept Alvarez in the spotlight. Bags of fan mail poured in. Groups invited him to address their gatherings. Phone calls from old friends filled in the gaps left by years of separation from home and community life. By March, he was ready for a public reception at a Santa Clara city park named for him, where 100,000 people lined the streets and cheered. He accepted an award from old friend Joe Kapp of the Minnesota Vikings.

STARTING OVER

While traveling around the country shortly after his return, Alvarez met Tammy Ilyas, a thirty-three-year-old passenger service representative for United Airlines at Dulles International Airport. She was drawn to his swarthy, well-groomed looks and compact muscularity and admitted that she would like to see him again. Because his invitation to the May 24 White House POW dinner-dance called for a date, he remembered Tammy and began a relationship that led to their engagement. The new start required facing old wounds, lawyers, questions of an annulment of his first marriage, and his mother's disapproval.

In spite of the obstacles, the wedding took place on October 27, 1973, at St. George's Eastern Orthodox Church with the Alvarez family in attendance. A smiling Tammy and sterner-faced Everett posed beneath crossed military sabers on the church steps. In the couple's honor, a flag was flown over the Capitol.

Alvarez opted to finish his naval career. He returned to flight training for a refresher course. No longer gung ho about flying, he moved on to postgraduate study in Monterey, where he could be near his first son, Marc Ilyas, born in 1974. Two years later, a second child, Bryan Thomas, completed the family. While enjoying his wife and sons, Alvarez pursued his education at George Washington University Law School. In June 1980, having begun a legal career, he retired from the navy with the rank of commander and settled with Tammy and the boys in Rockville, Maryland.

Honoraria continued to fill Alvarez's calendar. He was inducted into the California Hall of Fame and had buildings named after him. By the end of 1980, he accepted President Reagan's offer of the directorship of the Peace Corps. From there he advanced to VA deputy administrator. In this capacity, on Veterans Day, November 11, 1982, Alvarez addressed a mass of visitors at the opening of the Vietnam Veterans Memorial. He stated that the monument was symbolic of healing, then appended a word of warning about the responsibility that freedom places on a democratic society. As he faced his fellow veterans, his words expressed his warmth and optimism: "With this long overdue week of activities, with this parade today and especially with this dedication, America is saying, 'Welcome home!'" (Alvarez and Pitch, 1).

SOURCES

Alvarez, Everett, Jr. "An Eternal Touchstone." *Nuestro*, November 1982, 17.

Alvarez, Everett, Jr., and Anthony S. Pitch. *Chained Eagle*. New York: Donald I. Fine, 1989.

Garcia, Ignacio. "America Says 'Welcome Home.'" *Nuestro*, November 1982, 15-21.

Pitch, Anthony S. "A Prisoner's Tale." *Reader's Digest*, August 1990, 39-42.

Marian Anderson

Being the first Negro to sing with the Metropolitan Opera Company required concerted effort and many years on the concert stage. To overcome the poverty and racism, Marian Anderson pursued various avenues that would allow her to express her prodigious gift. She developed a richly warm and interpretive contralto that moved effortlessly through a varied repertoire, from Negro spirituals to the folk songs of Schubert and Brahms to Italian opera. For each of her early performances she earned a meager fifty cents, but she eventually commanded large fees, which she often donated to black schools and other charities.

Anderson did not spring into international fame overnight; nor did she always believe that she could achieve greatness. Rather, she made her way one increment at a time, crossing the most immediate barriers that lay in her path. She traveled world-wide and toured the United States annually, expressing her love of music. She sang on radio and recorded many kinds of music, including "Ave Maria," which sold 250,000 copies. In 1935, she sang for Arturo Toscanini, who exclaimed, "A voice like hers comes only once in a century" (*Encyclopedia Americana* 1, 808). Others have chosen stronger words of praise: "the consummate artist" and "the world's greatest contralto" (*Current Biography*, 8).

EARLY YEARS

Marian Anderson was the first child of impoverished parents and was born in a rented room in an integrated neighborhood in South Philadelphia on February 17, 1902. Her father, John Anderson, worked at a variety of jobs, including selling ice and coal. Her diminutive mother, Annie, a schoolteacher from Lynchburg, Virginia, stayed home to raise Marian as well as her younger sisters, Alyce and Ethel, and worked as a domestic only when she had to. For a short time in 1904, the family lived at Grandmother Anderson's house, then later found a suitable small residence they could afford.

At age six, Anderson got her musical start in the Union Baptist Church junior choir. Soon she was singing duets and performing with the adult choir. Early hand-bills dubbed her "the baby contralto," although her astounding vocal range allowed her to sing high C. Her father, pleased with his child's early display of talent, bought a piano for her when she was eight. Later, she gravitated toward additional instruments, particularly the used violin she bought from a pawn shop with her savings.

After John Anderson's death from a brain tumor in 1912, life changed for Marian. She returned to the house of her grandmother, a strong-willed matriarch who surrounded herself with children and demanded their respect. Annie Anderson helped out with expenses by taking in laundry, which Marian often delivered. At William Penn High School Marian struggled with shorthand and other business courses before transferring to South Philadelphia High School for more intensive music training. With the help of actor John Thomas Butler, she sang for Mary Patterson, a voice coach, and received free lessons.

As Anderson became better known, she sang at religious and secular meetings, traveled to numerous performances at Negro colleges, and joined the Philadelphia Choral Society. On her first forays from home, she encountered Jim Crow cars on trains and ate her meals behind a curtain at the far end of the dining car where black waiters were fed. Because hotels and restaurants refused black patrons, she had to stay in private homes. She often received donations from individuals interested in furthering her career.

LEARNING THE SINGING TRADE

During her teen years, Anderson studied with a series of local coaches. When she was nineteen, her church put on a concert to raise money for her voice lessons with Giuseppe Boghetti, a noted singing teacher who strengthened her vocal technique through rigorous exercises and developed her sense of professionalism and stage presence. Boghetti also introduced her to operatic roles, which she was not to play for many years. Because Anderson was so promising a pupil, after her money ran out, Boghetti taught her for a year free of charge.

Early in her training, Anderson selected William "Billy" King, a black pianist, to be her accompanist and sometime manager. Although others took his place in later years, he remained devoted to her throughout her career and helped increase her fees from donations to $100 per performance. In her early twenties, Anderson used her savings to buy a dream house for herself and her widowed mother, who worked for Wanamaker's Department Store until respiratory problems forced her to retire. Eventually, sister Ethel and her son moved into the house next door and completed a supportive family unit.

Following an unsuccessful engagement at Town Hall in New York City, Anderson responded to bad reviews by withdrawing from her singing career. She lost enthusiasm for lessons. Mired in doubt, she wondered if her dreams of stardom were fantastic. Later, after her mother and coach convinced her to accept the sour with the sweet, she asserted herself to do better, particularly in the area of foreign languages, which she knew only through phonetic rote memorization.

At the age of twenty-three, Anderson sang "O Mio Fernando," an aria by Donizetti, and bested 300 contenders in a local competition. Her reward was an outdoor concert with the New York Philharmonic under the direction of Eugene Ormandy at Lewisohn Stadium. The *New York Times* review reassured her with a polite appraisal: "Miss Anderson made an excellent impression. She is endowed by nature with a voice of unusual compass, color and dramatic capacity" (Anderson, 106-107). This encouragement helped her regain self-confidence, retain an experienced manager, and increase her booking fee to $500. Still, she experienced prejudiced treatment in public facilities and hesitated to accept engagements in the South.

At a turning point in her career, Anderson received the National Association of Negro Musicians scholarship for foreign study. In 1930, she boarded the *Ile de France* and was soon singing before the elite of Europe. On her return, she obtained a scholarship for six months of training in Berlin, where she improved her understanding of German. Two years later, she returned to the United States, sang in New York City, and set out on a tour of her own country.

AN APPRECIATIVE AUDIENCE

Later concerts in Scandinavia resulted in part from curiosity about a black singer, a novelty among predominantly blue-eyed blonds. She endeared herself to the people of Finland by singing in their language and returned to Scandinavia for a two-year tour. Among her fans were the kings of Sweden and Denmark, the widow of Edvard Grieg, and composer Jean Sibelius, who toasted her with champagne and sang a song in her honor. Critics referred to the enthusiastic European reception as "Marian fever" (Anderson, 148).

In France, Austria, Holland, Scandinavia, and the Soviet Union, Marian formed a firm bond with the audience, particularly with her favorite spirituals, "Deep River" and "Heaven, Heaven," which were ostensibly forbidden in Communist countries. In Moscow, Stanislavski invited her to sing *Carmen*, but he died before acting on the offer. As a result of her overall success, impresario Sol Hurok began managing Anderson's career with spectacular results. He took a personal interest in developing her talent and expanding her horizons.

Soon Anderson was singing to capacity crowds in Carnegie Hall and the Philadelphia Forum and touring South America, Japan, and Africa. Critics, once cool and aloof, poured out superlatives praising her grace, range, control, and musical style. Her performance schedule reached demanding proportions, sometimes as many as seventy-five concerts per year. Even when sidelined with a broken foot, she refused to cancel performances and made entrances and exits behind a closed curtain to conceal the fact that she was incapacitated. She took special pride in personal visits and letters from members of the audience who wrote of their solace from and joy in her singing.

HUMILIATION AND TRIUMPH

One incident stands out as the benchmark of Marian Anderson's career. In 1939, she found herself at the center of an ugly racial controversy after the Daughters of the American Revolution rejected her request for a performance date at Constitution

Hall. To the embarrassment of the prestigious women's club, the press picked up the story.

The DAR quickly concocted a cover-up story about a nonexistent Washington, D.C., law forbidding integrated performances. Club officials claimed that they were challenging the law by making public their inability to accommodate the famed black singer. Later investigation proved that there was no such law and that the DAR was seeking to salvage a sullied reputation by claiming to be noble civil-rights advocates. To members' dismay, the story continues to circulate whenever Marian Anderson's achievements are reviewed.

Anderson was touring California at the time of the fiasco. Her comments were typical of her understated, self-effacing style: "I was saddened and ashamed. I was sorry for the people who had precipitated the affair. I felt that their behavior stemmed from a lack of understanding" (Anderson, 187-188). She also admitted that just as singing soprano did not suit her voice, fighting for the rights of Negro people was not her style. Notable entertainers and public leaders, however, were less reticent and vociferously pressed the issue of racial discrimination.

In protest, Eleanor Roosevelt resigned from the DAR and arranged for Anderson to sing a free outdoor concert on Easter Sunday on the steps of the Lincoln Memorial. The performance drew a crowd of 75,000 and included government dignitaries, representatives from Howard University, and the secretary of the NAACP. Anderson was so overwhelmed with emotion at the sight of the audience that she nearly sobbed when she sang the National Anthem. She mustered professional courage to help her through a varied program of Negro spirituals and classical and patriotic songs, including "America."

That Easter concert was a triumphant moment in Anderson's career. A mural in the Department of the Interior commemorates the precedent of her public concert. Other performers, in a show of support, canceled their own engagements at Constitution Hall. Subsequently, Anderson met Eleanor Roosevelt and was presented to the king and queen of England. Anderson sang at Constitution Hall after the policy was changed to admit Negroes; then she performed at the White House for the inaugural balls of both Dwight Eisenhower and John F. Kennedy. She evolved her own standards and refused to sing in segregated halls.

In the early 1940s, a second significant racial incident marked her career. While touring Poland, Anderson received a return invitation to perform in Berlin. She at first declined but, because of repeated entreaties, agreed to a single performance. To establish that she was acceptable to Hitler's regime, authorities questioned her background. When they learned that she was not Aryan, correspondence on the matter ceased abruptly.

AWARDS AND HONORS

Even though she endured racial slurs and had to enter some buildings through the service elevator, Marian Anderson was no stranger to acclaim. She accepted honorary degrees from fifty universities, including Howard, Temple, Smith, Carlisle,

Moravian, and Dickinson, and awards from the NAACP. In 1939, she received the Spingarn Medal, which honors a U.S. Negro achieving high honors.

In 1941 in a surprise ceremony, the city of Philadelphia presented Anderson the Bok Award of $10,000 to honor the accomplishments of one of its natives. She replied with élan—not with a speech but a song: "I open my mouth to the Lord, and I will never turn back. I shall go to see what the end will be" (Anderson, 275). Then she dedicated the money to establish the Marian Anderson Scholarship, an annual arts scholarship administered by her sister Alyce and open to all races and creeds.

In the later years of her career, Anderson received some of her most memorable honors. In 1950, occupation authorities invited her to sing in Berlin. Five years later, at the invitation of manager Rudolf Bing, she made her debut with the Metropolitan Opera Company in Guiseppe Verdi's *Un ballo in maschera* (*The Masked Ball*), in which she sang the role of the old sorceress, Ulrica. Because she had never studied acting, Anderson practiced her role assiduously and later admitted to some stage fright in her first operatic performance.

After New York, the production toured Philadelphia, where she felt great pride in serving as a role model to black youths of her own hometown. The part of Ulrica became a symbol for Anderson and reminded her of the unfulfilled aspirations of her race. When critics asked why she took so small a role, she responded that Ulrica proved challenging enough. She concluded that any future operatic appearances would be repeats of Ulrica until she had mastered the part.

Anderson produced her autobiography, *My Lord, What a Morning*, in 1956. In her memoirs she related the ironies of her career, such as the time she received the key to Atlantic City but could not get a reservation at a hotel because of the color of her skin. Yet her perseverance helped pave the way for a more cooperative national spirit.

In 1957, she set out on an extensive concert circuit at home and abroad. By 1958, she was serving as alternate U.S. delegate to the United Nations. At sixty-one, Anderson received the Presidential Medal of Freedom. Two years later she retired. In 1978, along with George Balanchine, Arthur Rubinstein, Richard Rodgers, and Fred Astaire, she returned to the limelight to accept one of the first Kennedy Center awards.

A PRIVATE LIFE

Because of her dedication to her singing career, Anderson neglected the more obvious pleasures of private life. She met her husband, architect Orpheus H. "King" Fisher, of Wilmington, Delaware, while they were still in school. He was drawn to her statuesque grace, professionalism, and understated sense of humor. Their friendship passed through many stages before Anderson agreed to marry. In 1943, she settled down in a Danbury, Connecticut, farmhouse. Later, she and King built a new house, the "Mariana Farm," across the street on a 105-acre tract that featured a brook-fed pool.

Their marriage, marked by frequent separations for tours, was satisfying and normal during the summer months, when Marian cooked, sewed, and gardened.

She took particular pride in growing strawberries. For relaxation, she immersed herself in baseball and cheered for the Dodgers. Because she had seen the results of separation in other performers' families, she chose to have no children and sublimated her maternal urge by loving her sisters' children as well as a collection of animals. After King's death in the 1980s, she continued her reclusive suburban life-style.

In 1989, Anderson, white-haired but still majestic at eighty-seven, took center stage for a special concert at the Charles Ives Center in Danbury, which raised funds for the Marian Anderson Scholarship. Honored by prominent performers including Cicely Tyson, Jessye Norman, Phylicia Rashad, and William Warfield, she spoke her love and thanks. She concluded with typical understatement: "I hope that God, who knows my every desire, will do for you what He knows is best" ("A Tribute," 185).

From her autobiography come glimpses of the inner Marian Anderson, who takes pride in making gains for the black race. She believes there is hope that the United States will overcome racism. She declares, "When incidents occur in our land that show a disregard for brotherhood among races our America belittles herself, and her prestige is injured. For he in the highest place can be no greater and no more effective than the least of his followers. He must answer for all" (Anderson, 309).

SOURCES

Anderson, Marian. *My Lord, What a Morning*. New York: Viking Press, 1956.

Cayne, Bernard S., ed. *Encyclopedia Americana,* vol. 1. Danbury, Conn.: Grolier, 1981, 808.

Current Biography. Detroit: Gale Research, 1963, 8-10.

"The Survivors from 1945-1990: The Ebony Years." Forty-fifth Anniversary Edition, *Ebony*, November 1990, 28-33.

Sweeley, Michael. "The First Lady." *National Review*, September 29, 1989, 65-66.

Tedards, Anne. *Marian Anderson*. American Women of Achievement Series. New York: Chelsea House, 1988.

"A Tribute to Marian Anderson. Famed Contralto Is Honored at Gala Concert in Connecticut." *Ebony*, November 1989, 182-184.

Vehanen, Kosti. *Marian Anderson, a Portrait*. Brooklyn, N.Y.: Greenwood Press, 1970.

Corazon Aquino

For any woman, early widowhood is a serious stumbling block, especially if the death of the husband is sudden and violent, as was the public assassination of Corazon Aquino's mate, Benigno Aquino. Her response to loss, sadness, and terror, so thoroughly reported in the international press, left her no privacy and no time for mourning. Rather, she was drafted by Filipinos to take action against Ferdinand Marcos, the greedy autocrat who was laying waste her country's assets.

With her husband's supporters impelling her toward a political career, Aquino astounded critics by advancing from a retiring housewife caring for her five children to president of the Philippines, the only woman and the only chief executive elected by direct draft of the people. Aquino held steady during a turbulent phase of her nation's history. Watched from a modest guest house on the palace grounds, she remained under close guard but managed to travel widely, even journeying to the United States, where she addressed the United Nations and accepted honorary degrees from Fordham and Boston universities. Her crowning achievement was being named *Time* magazine's Woman of the Year.

A MAIDENLY UPBRINGING

Born in Manila on January 25, 1933, of mixed Chinese, Spanish, and Malay ancestry, Maria Corazon Sumulong Cojuangco, the fourth of six children, came from a privileged background. At her home on the island of Luzon in Tarlac Province, fifty miles north of Manila, her father, José Cojuangco, enjoyed power and prestige as a financier and sugar planter on his 15,000-acre plantation and as a representative to the National Assembly. Aquino's grandfather, two uncles, and brother were also successful politicians and officeholders. Her mother, Demetria "Metring" Sumulong, provided the proper model for wife and parent, which for years was Aquino's goal. At Metring's insistence, Aquino avoided the poor-little-rich-girl syndrome and developed character traits such as compassion, respect, morality, thrift, and altruism.

A sweet-natured, good-humored woman, Aquino, delicate and small-framed at five feet two, was never encouraged to demonstrate her wealth in frivolous dress or ostentatious behavior. During the Japanese occupation of the Philippines, she was conservatively educated among upper-crust young ladies at St. Scholastica, a Manila convent school. She excelled in volleyball but preferred studying alone to joining exclusive girls' groups. After graduating as class valedictorian, at age thirteen she journeyed to Raven Hill Academy, a Catholic school in Philadelphia, then to Notre Dame Convent School in Manhattan, and in 1953 she completed a degree in French and mathematics at Mount St. Vincent, a woman's college in Riverdale, New York. Her ambition was to teach school or become a translator. Her command of Spanish, English, Japanese, and Tagalog became important for her political success.

During her college years, Aquino met her future husband, Benigno S. "Ninoy" Aquino, Jr., a garrulous, ambitious journalist whose Filipino background resembled her own. At first, she gave little thought to his love letters, preferring her studies at Far Eastern University Law School in Manila. By 1954, however, she caved in to family pressure and left school after one semester to marry Benigno on October 11 in a formal ceremony at Our Lady of Sorrows Church in Pasay City. The event was socially significant, uniting the Sumulongs, Cojuangcos, and Aquinos.

WIFE AND MOTHER

For twenty years, while her husband, an aggressive, demonstrative personality, furthered his own career as mayor of Concepción and Tarlac, governor of Tarlac, and senator, Aquino was a wife and mother of four daughters, Elena, Victoria, Aurora, and Christina, and a son, Benigno III. As her husband's profession required, she greeted and entertained people from all levels of society and grew accustomed to conversing with the powerful and manipulative. In her free time, she relaxed with movies and handicrafts and by cooking pasta and Peking duck, mixing paté, and gardening. She also enjoyed shopping, reading current fiction, and watching game shows and soap operas on television.

Aquino maintained a home environment suited to her husband's needs. Devoutly religious, she spent much of her time and emotional energy praying the rosary. When Benigno needed a refuge, it was his wife's firm sense of self that replenished his dwindling hopes. As one observer noted, "He was the warrior. She polished his sword and took care of his horse" (Carlson, 39). She knew that he and his Laban party played a tough game of politics but masked her criticism beneath an impeccably upright demeanor.

BEGINNING POLITICIAN

In 1972, Aquino began to take more seriously the political condition of the Philippines, which had fallen under martial law on September 21 when the corrupt regime of Marcos's Nacionalista party placed an illegal hold on power. Filipino society, weakened by terrorism, lawlessness, strikes, and boycotts, tumbled into anarchy. To negate competition and strengthen his unconstitutional grasp of the governmental reins, Marcos suspended the writ of habeas corpus and announced that he was arresting all suspected conspirators. On August 27, 1973, he placed Benigno Aquino, leader of the Liberal party, in Fort Bonifacio prison, headquarters of the national army, and threatened him with execution. The charge was possession of firearms, murder, arson, and subversion.

For the first time in her life, Corazon Aquino took charge. To carry out her commitment to Benigno's politics, she visited him three times a week and endured the humiliation of strip searches by guards, all part of Marcos's intent to discredit and degrade her. Her overnight stays on mattresses on the floor of his cell among mirrors, cameras, and listening devices further demoralized her. Without realizing what she was preparing herself for, she undertook Benigno's responsibilities in the sugar trade and found herself the backbone of his revolutionary movement as she relayed his words and moral support from the jail cell to his waiting followers. A timid, nonassertive housewife, Aquino, in addition to parroting Benigno's communiqués and detailing his hunger strikes, began framing statements for the press and fending for herself in a seamy, hostile political environment that daily threatened her and her children.

Aquino discovered that after her husband's loss of power, recognition passed quickly. As sycophants and hangers-on fell away in search of the next strong man, on her own she continued to press for Benigno's freedom. In March 1980, he suffered acute angina pectoris. With the help of the Carter administration, she acquired permission for him to receive triple-bypass heart surgery at Baylor Medical Center, Dallas, Texas, in May. The procedure was a success, but the Aquinos could not risk his health by sending him home to Manila to serve more time in prison.

An exile in the tony section of Newton, Massachusetts, outside Boston, Aquino, living in a virtual Camelot after seven-and-a-half years of tension, returned to familial duties while Benigno taught as visiting scholar at Massachusetts Institute of Technology and research fellow at Harvard. During this respite in their lives, she oversaw her children's education and developed friendships outside the political community that had dominated her attention in Manila. In the serenity of her pine-shaded yard, she turned to writing, composing a haiku to her stability: "The worst of my life is over, I hope, / And may the best things please come soon" (Chrisostomo, 82).

INTO THE MAELSTROM

By 1983, Aquino's husband felt that he had to return to the Philippines to resume his role as conciliator, peacemaker, and the only viable opposition to Marcos, who was growing more wasteful and less attentive to the disintegrating nation. On the flight to Manila, Benigno telephoned his wife from a stopover in California and revealed his misgivings about the return. Her response was characteristic of her personal strength—she read him Bible verses. On his arrival on August 21, as he advanced down the steps to the tarmac at Manila International Airport amid fluttering yellow ribbons and television news crews, he was shot once in the head, reportedly by Marcos's soldiers. When news of his death reached her in Boston, Aquino, the family's rallying point, calmly led her children in prayer.

Flown from Boston to Manila to arrange his funeral, she insisted on spending moments alone with her husband's remains, which had not been washed or prepared for viewing. She caressed his blood-spattered corpse, allowing her tears to release sorrow, fear, and frustration. She reported, "I pledged to my husband after I kissed him in his coffin that I'd continue his work" (Carlson, 39). The nation was moved by her sincerity and, unwilling to tolerate more ruthlessness and tyranny, forced a showdown between Marcos and the opposition. The spirit of the moment gave them a new leader — Corazon Aquino, whose prim external femininity masked a steely, uncompromising inner core.

Consecrating herself to her husband's task of liberating the Philippines for a free election, Aquino adopted yellow as her symbolic color and the thumb and forefinger extended in an L for the Laban party as she stood before jostling crowds that chanted with increasing intensity, "Cory, Cory, Cory." She hesitated to accept their verbal mandate against so patriarchal a political system as that of the Philippines. A recurrent dream spurred her to reconsider her initial impulse to say no: In the dream, she entered a church and advanced to Benigno's coffin but found it deserted. To her, the dream indicated that his spirit now resided in her. Then two events helped shape her decision: First, petitions containing over a million signatures pressed her to run against Marcos in the February 1986 elections; second, the twenty-five military officials charged with conspiring to murder Benigno Aquino were freed upon their appeal to Marcos's puppet courts.

The next day, Aquino rejected Salvador Doy Laurel's plans to use her as a party symbol and announced her own rather feeble, naive candidacy. For the waiting press, she dropped her customarily demure demeanor and issued an appropriately self-assured comment: "It is I who makes the decisions. It was I who decided finally to accept the draft and it was I who decided by myself to agree to run with Laurel under the Unido banner" (Cooper, 34).

PRESIDENT AQUINO

Abandoning strategy for straightforward truths, Aquino, backed by the Catholic hierarchy, presented her case for change. Harnessing a grass-roots thrust against the Marcos machine, she began to threaten his hold on the Philippines' fifty-five million people with a huge rally at Luneta Park in Manila on February 4, 1986. The band-wagon effect paid off. On February 7, enthusiastic voters flooded polling places. Stubbornly maintaining a majority while refusing to stage a coup, Aquino announced her victory nine days later; her supporters kept Marcos's machine sufficiently off-base with unpredictable public outbursts. Her methods spooked some of his wiliest forces. The results of the election, contested for over two weeks, remained unclear until Marcos's chief of staff, Fidel V. Ramos, and Defense Minister Juan Ponce Enrile deserted him and took refuge in the ministry building, throwing their support to Aquino. When Marcos tried to dislodge them with tanks, Aquino's supporters filled the streets to pray and extend messages of love to startled troopers.

By February 25, U.S. officials, fearing the intrusion of Communists, convinced Marcos to withdraw by helicopter from his opulent palace to nearby Clark Air Force Base. That same day, Aquino delivered her inaugural address, assuring the people that they were no longer exiles in their own land and that "through courage and unity, through power of the people, we are home again" (Chrisostomo, 279). Disarmingly honest, she concluded with a request for prayers during the difficult transitional period. Her first proclamation, issued the same day, called for greater vigilance and patience as she attempted to create a just society.

The news of Marcos's abrupt defection left Aquino somewhat breathless but no less committed to change. Fearlessly, she rallied her supporters with strong, idealistic faith: "We have proven [my husband] correct—that the Filipino is worth dying for.... Twenty years of repression, injustice, corruption, greed, waste, and near despair have finally ended. They were ended by a revolution of peace, prayers, rosaries, radios, and above all, human courage" (Carlson, 37).

Aquino, the first new face in twenty years, bolstered hope for better times in the Philippines, which suffered from a sluggish economy, a 70 percent poverty rate, and graft at most bureaucratic levels. To her early audiences she promised, "I will not tolerate deviation from the path we have pledged to follow" (Carlson, 37). Her first task, accomplished in grueling sixteen-hour days at her makeshift office, was the selection of a cabinet, which she filled with business and professional leaders and a few holdovers from Marcos's regime. To reassure the people that right would prevail under the Aquino administration, she released political detainees and ousted corrupt judges and generals. To recover millions in goods and property siphoned off by Marcos, his family, and his entourage, she pressed suit in U.S. courts. Until a working coalition of political voices could draft a new constitution, she established an interim government and even began talks with the far Left.

FINE TUNING

The task of governing the Philippines proved so demanding in the late 1980s that foreign government placed little confidence in the shrewdness and flexibility of such a lightweight as Aquino. Confident and hopeful of change, she earned respect from business leaders by lessening the foreign debt, boosting foreign investment, and breaking up the cronyism that drained profits from sugar and coconut markets. With the backing of the Reagan administration, she maintained a workable relationship with Enrile and Laurel, both possible rivals, and trounced a coup attempt on July 6, 1986.

Although she often demonstrated ambivalence toward setting a hard line against Communists, Aquino tackled problems of internal corruption in rapid order. Placing former senator Jovito Salongo in charge of her Good Government Commission, she removed herself from the investigation so that an impersonal panel could eradicate the forces who had murdered her husband. Walking a fine line between vengeance and mercy, she demanded only justice, however long it took to secure it.

Other chores required immediate attention. Aquino established a Human Rights Commission, accepted the mantle of military chief of staff, reduced oil prices, and convened a people's meeting for the airing of grievances. At the request of peasants, she disarmed local autocrats and battled criminal syndicates. To calm jitters after her autocratic beginning, she announced local elections as soon as constitutional law could be established. On the international scene, her first priority lay in discussions of the U.S. lease on Philippine military bases, which was to run out in 1991.

A WILL TO SUCCEED

One of the hallmarks of her style of leadership was her dependence on example. In summary of her approach to political life, Aquino once commented: "Faith is not simply a patience which passively suffers until the storm is past. Rather, it is a spirit which bears things—with resignation, yes, but above all with blazing serene hope" (Cooper, 34). Determined to avoid the gilt trappings of the Marcos regime, she opted for simplicity and an openhearted concern for her people's deprivations. She had a nonconfrontational spirit; wreathed in smiles and affability, she was open to all dissident parties that challenged her presidency.

For Corazon Aquino, the abrupt shift from supportive wife to president of her nation uncovered the vein of iron that delineates her character. As Reuters news agency credited her, she had a "great deal more guts and nerve than you might have expected" (Chrisostomo, 36). Like Benigno, she professed a faith in the moment, whatever it brought. Unconcerned about mob violence or assassination attempts, she continued shouldering the tasks that brought the Philippines closer to her ideal.

SOURCES

Carlson, Peter. "A Matter of Family Honor." *People Weekly*, March 17, 1986, 34-40.

Chrisostomo, Isabelo T. *Cory: Profile of a President.* Boston: Braden, 1987.

Cooper, Nancy. "The Remarkable Rise of a Widow in Yellow." *Newsweek*, March 10, 1986, 32-36.

Current Biography. New York: H. W. Wilson, 1986.

Komisar, Lucy. "Cory Aquino: The Story of a Revolution." *New York Review of Books*, June 11, 1987, 10-13.

Paul, Anthony. "Triumph of the Widow in Yellow." *Reader's Digest*, June 1986, 93-98.

Valenzuela, Luisa, and Joe Conason. "Woman of the Year: Corazon Aquino." *Vogue*, May 1986, 288-292.

"The World's Ten Most Important Women." *Ladies Home Journal*, November 1987, 133-140.

Joan Baez

Joan Baez, one of the soulful voices of the 1960s who worked for pacifist, anti-establishment ideals, had to overcome stage fright, racial discrimination, and deep melancholy in order to vent her opposition to violence. A slender madonna-faced woman with dark features, understated wardrobe and makeup, and earthy loveliness, she rejected a Hollywood persona in favor of individualized expression. Singing from an inner impetus, she projected an ease and detachment that disarmed her audiences.

As her stage and recording successes mounted, she found the opportunities implicit in stardom and applied them toward the kind of world she thought humanity should have—one safe for growth and creativity, one in which all types of artistry could be expressed. To make a statement about violence, she arranged a two-week visit to war-torn Hanoi during one of the heaviest periods of U.S. bombing and sang a memorable theme song of love to the suffering populace, "Where Are You Now, My Son?" She performed for the benefit of charities such as Live Aid, CORE, and UNESCO; to support assistance to political prisoners, blind persons, boat people, and migrant workers; and to support education for minorities. In middle age, no longer the "madonna of the sixties," she continued to expend her fame for worthwhile causes while at last relaxing and enjoying the music for itself.

BORN TO SING

The creative, irrepressible grandchild of a Mexican Episcopalian minister and child of Scottish-born Joan Bridge Baez and Mexican physicist Albert V. Baez, a teacher at Harvard, Joan Chandos Baez was born in Staten Island, New York, on January 9, 1941. While Al worked on his Ph.D., the family, also including Joan's older sister, Pauline, and the youngest, Mimi, lived for a time at Peninsula School near Stanford, where they served as houseparents. The Baez girls shared the usual jealousies and collusions, particularly against Mimi, who was the family beauty. The family saved money by moving into a large house, which they shared with Mrs. Baez's sister Pauline and her children. To cut costs, they took in boarders, most of whom were connected with the academic community.

From early childhood, Baez, whom Aunt Pauline referred to as "little songbird," suffered insecurity, which was evidenced by dark moods. As she described them in *And a Voice to Sing With*, "I became weighed down, paralyzed, and frozen; the hairs on my arms and legs rise up and my bones chill to the marrow. Nothing can warm me" (Baez 1987, 22).

Her father, who rejected the rush of other physicists to work on atomic weapons and chose instead to move his family to Cornell University, was also undergoing emotional stress. In her autobiography, she looked back on the significance of this tense time: "We would never have all the fine and useless things little girls want when they are growing up.... Instead we would have a father with a clear conscience. Decency would be his legacy to us" (Green, n.p.).

To provide some spiritual help, Joan's mother began taking her family to Quaker worship services. Even though Joan professed no religious ties, her parents' nonviolent philosophy influenced her and her sisters. She explained, "There are great missionary streaks in my family. Both grandfathers were ministers and my parents are Quakers. Maybe it's in the genes" (Melich, n.p.). She admitted at age fifty that she had evolved a philosophy of nonviolence and a reverence for the sanctity of all life by age five. To offset too much sobriety, she cultivated a cynical wit, which allows her to laugh when the world state triggers her characteristic melancholia.

OUT INTO THE WORLD

In 1951, Al Baez accepted a post at the University of Baghdad, where he worked for UNESCO. Joan contracted hepatitis because she spent so much time in the poverty and unsanitary conditions of the Iraqi people, with whom she began to identify. The family returned to the United States a year later and settled in Redlands, California. Joan, underweight, moody, and perpetually nauseated, began finding excuses to stay out of school, but medical examination failed to turn up the real malady — irrational anxiety complicated by an inability to fit in with either white or Mexican teenagers.

A natural at memorizing lyrics and imitating other singers' styles, Joan developed her voice as a means of breaking out of isolation, and she sang to entertain her peers. She described her early efforts as "a plain, little girl's voice, sweet and true, but stringy as cheap cotton thread, and as thin and straight as the blue line on a piece of binder paper" (Baez 1987, 29). To compensate for the immaturity in her voice, she secretly perfected a vibrato.

At Palo Alto High School, Baez did mediocre schoolwork, preferring music to intellectual pursuits. She encountered a formal statement of her own political beliefs in the words of guest speaker Martin Luther King, Jr., who became her idol. Her pacifism began to take shape through an acquaintance with Ira Sandperl, a mentor who lectured to her Quaker youth group on Gandhi's concepts of organized nonviolence. During a significant incident, when students were evacuated from her school in a mock nuclear-attack drill, Baez stayed seated in protest against the false notion that victims have time to seek shelter. The event strengthened her ties to Ira, who became her constant companion.

DEVELOPING TALENT

At the same time that Baez was formalizing her political outlook, she began asserting her vocal accomplishments. Her unusual voice, which exceeded a three-octave range, required little fine tuning. She learned to play the ukulele and guitar and accepted singing engagements, which helped her overcome earlier diffidence, particularly her discontent with a persistent cowlick, dark complexion, and flat chest. She was afflicted with random bouts of stage fright yet found communicating with audiences rewardingly intimate.

Young, romantic, and nonconformist, Baez longed to locate soulmates who were outlaws like her. After her family moved back east, she associated with folk-singers in the Boston area. She rejected piano lessons, improved her guitar technique, and learned to sing in a variety of styles, from blues, bluegrass, and pop tunes to ballads, spirituals, and work and folk songs.

Baez's father, who recognized his daughter's musical bent, introduced her to Tulla's Coffee Grinder, a haven for beginning singers. For one semester, Joan studied drama at Boston University and collaborated with Debby Green, who increased her repertoire and taught her more about the fundamentals of guitar. From their friendship, Baez developed her own style and began connecting with other coffeehouses, particularly the Golden Vanity, Club 47, the Ballad Room, and Chicago's Gate of Horn. Gradually her fame increased among folk-music aficionados.

Because of her singular concentration on singing and individualism, Baez flunked out of college. She departed with her first lover, Michael, a mystical rebel from Trinidad, and worked for a summer teaching beginners how to drive Vespa motorcycles. By fall she had taken a job as houseparent at the Perkins Institute for the Blind. While in psychoanalysis, she formed deep relationships with other bohemians and molded her singular personality and style.

MAKING HER MARK

At age eighteen, Baez sang before 13,000 folk-music fans at the Newport, Rhode Island, music festival. The appearance benefited her by introducing her to the giants of the folk scene—the Weavers, Pete Seeger, Harry Belafonte, John Jacob Niles, Flatt and Scruggs, and Odetta. Still, she did not feel ready to enter so competitive a market and returned to the safety of Boston. The following year, a second stint at Newport was the impetus to her rise to fame.

Baez remained strongly independent throughout the early days of her professional career. Against her agent's advice, she turned down an offer from Columbia and chose Vanguard, a homier publishing firm, to cut her first album, *Joan Baez*, her unparalleled bestseller. In 1964, she followed it with a book, the *Joan Baez Songbook*. Subsequent albums—*Joan Baez Volume 2, Joan Baez at Newport, Joan Baez in Concert*, and *Speaking of Dreams*—contained works of her friend and idol, Bob Dylan, as well as original tunes. Her most memorable included "House of the Rising Sun," "Wildwood Flower," "All My Trials," "Diamonds and Rust," "Pilgrim of

Sorrow," and "Barbara Allen." These successes earned her eight gold albums and one gold single.

Touring college campuses in 1961, Baez found audiences eager for her pure, stirring soprano and uncomplicated delivery. Critics lauded her control and passion, which was peculiarly unerotic and maternal. She maintained a strong stage presence yet seemed aloof from the audience. Her unadorned style and facility and ease before audiences led to the title Queen of Folk, even though her repertoire advanced quickly beyond the confines of folk music.

Early on, she avoided materialism and chose her own times, places, and styles to perform, often removing her shoes and loosening her hair. She rejected greed by performing only a few months a year, refusing nightclub engagements, and making a single album per year. She abhorred artificial folk and stuck to pure folk tunes. Among her notable performances were concerts at Town Hall, the Hollywood Bowl, Madison Square Garden, Carnegie Hall, Mormon Tabernacle, and Milan's Teatro Lirico and L'Arena.

As a natural outgrowth of her political opinions, controversy followed her. After Pete Seeger was banned from the television show "Hootenanny" because of his outspoken political opinions, Baez joined other performers in boycotting the program. Later, her bias toward the poor and deprived set her apart from singers who placated middle-class followers by avoiding controversial topics. While singing in Salt Lake City, she politely lambasted Mormons for discriminating against blacks. Yet, so straightforward a statement of opinion did not dampen the audience's enthusiasm for her music.

ISSUES AND ANSWERS

Because Baez endured rude comments about her dark skin, she remained painfully insecure and identified with victims of bigotry. In addition to expressing her political views through her music, she allied herself with civil-rights, nonviolence, nuclear-disarmament, and anti-Vietnam War movements. She sang in a hodgepodge of locales—Hanoi bomb shelters, Thai refugee camps, even over the phone to Russian dissident Andrei Sakharov. From her antimilitaristic feelings sprang her support of Amnesty International, Humanitas, and the Resource Center for Nonviolence in Santa Cruz, of which she is founder and vice president. She refused to pay war taxes and went to jail twice in the 1960s for opposing the draft.

Baez met distinguished people of all shades of the political and social spectrum. She sang in black churches and developed close ties with the desegregation movement, which she supported. She influenced world leaders such as François Mitterrand, Lech Walesa, Bishop Tutu, Giscard d'Estaing, and President Jimmy Carter and conferred with other idealists and dissidents including Erich Fromm, Angela Davis, Bertrand Russell, Thomas Merton, Mairead Corrigan, Theodore Bikel, Cesar Chavez, and Elena Bonner.

A PUBLIC FACE

A private person, Baez warred against the intrusion of the media. At the beginning of her career, she and Michael moved to southern California. Surrounded by domestic animals, she made a home in 1961 in a one-bedroom, telephoneless cabin in Big Sur, where she sketched the wild coastline, drove a silver Jaguar, and read extensively. From there the couple moved to Carmel Highlands, where she curtailed access to her private life.

Baez's career continued to soar. On a tour of Mexico, she found devoted audiences who were already familiar with her albums. Pushing herself excessively, she performed nonstop and accepted *Time* magazine's offer of a cover story. Shortly afterward, she was hospitalized for dehydration, malnutrition, and viral infection. After a messy breakup with Michael, she began a tentative lesbian relationship followed by a liaison with Bob Dylan.

The times turned sour for Baez, whose idealism suffered serious buffets because of the assassination of President Kennedy and the escalation of the Vietnam War. She organized an antiwar sit-in at Berkeley in 1964 and wrote a letter to the IRS in which she vowed to retain the portion of her taxes that would support U.S. militarism. Talk-show hosts clamored for her but avoided her outspoken opposition to war.

A VENTURE INTO MATRIMONY

While serving a sentence at the Santa Rita Rehabilitation Center for supporting draft dodgers in 1967, Baez met David Harris, began a serious relationship, and married him the following year. She longed for the normalcy of a stable home and exulted at the news of her pregnancy, during which David was serving a sentence for draft evasion. Baez refused to slow down and even performed at Woodstock. Despite the fact that her husband was in jail, the birth of son Gabriel was a great moment.

The marriage failed in 1974 because Baez needed her freedom and solitude. She regretted that Gabe would never know the ordinary mother-and-father family and was parented by strongwilled social activists. In 1968, she published an autobiography, *Daybreak*, and followed in 1987 with a more perceptive memoir, *And a Voice to Sing With*, which she dedicated to Gabe. Her recordings also branched out with *Baptism*, an anthology of multinational poetry. More albums followed: *Any Day Now, David's Album*, a two-disk set, *The First Ten Years, Blessed Are ...*, and *Where Are You Now, My Son?*

By the late 1970s the Vietnam War was no longer at the forefront of public concern, but Baez continued to champion nonviolence. She pursued her beliefs in performances around the world, particularly the Live Aid spectacular. In 1988, she visited Poland during the jubilation that followed the decline of communism and took pleasure in being on the scene while positive change was taking place.

Baez's unusual blend of singing and politics continued on a true course, memorializing the massacre in Tiananmen Square, denouncing atrocities of El Salvador's inhumane regime, and singing in the Conspiracy of Hope caravan. In true Baez style, she commented, "I can't turn my back on what's going on in the world.... I write about things I hear or see, things that outrage me. I just can't ignore these things" (Romandetta, n.p.). In tribute to her determined stance, Antioch and Rutgers universities awarded her honorary doctorates, and other honors crowned her fight against injustice.

MELLOWED BY TIME

An unforeseen benefit of middle age was Baez's loss of stage fright. By age forty-eight, no longer quailing before each performance or relying on Quaaludes to calm her jitters, she began to look forward to each experience before the footlights. During her two-month thirtieth-anniversary tour, completely at ease with her gray-streaked hair and more contemporary attire, she still communicated her principles through words and through her songs, many of which were originals.

Basically a loner and stolid individualist, she also loosened up on matters of management and collaboration and began traveling with a four-piece band. She characterized the new Baez with a bit of self-denigration: "I'm too thick-headed. I just felt I was supposed to be in this isolated shell. And you know it's not easy coming out of it" (Morrison, n.p.).

Her concerts demonstrated an unforeseen camaraderie with conservatives who ridiculed her during the 1960s. She refused to wallow in nostalgia about her early activism. Instead, she polished new material, such as "A Mi Manera," her flamenco version of "My Way," which she recorded with the Gipsy Kings. When she waded into a crowd of well-wishers, she locked arms with those who used to revile her. With the self-confidence of a mellower, less fearful Joan Baez, she was able to relax, evade the dark moods of her youth, and reacquaint herself with fans.

SOURCES

Baez, Joan. *Daybreak*. New York: Dial Press, 1968.

_____. *Coming Out*. New York: Bantam Books, 1971.

_____. *And a Voice to Sing With*. New York: Summit Books, 1987.

Current Biography. Detroit: Gale Research, 1963, 13-15.

Green, Ann. "Joan Baez: At Ease, at Last." *Durham Morning Herald*, November 17, 1989, n.p.

Hentoff, Nat. "A Passionate Survivor." *Progressive*, February 1983, 52-53.

Holden, Stephen. "The All-American Voice." *High Fidelity*, July 1980, 87.

Melich, Nancy. "Joan Baez Returns." *Salt Lake City Tribune*, October 20, 1989, n.p.

Morrison, Jim. "The Music Is the Message." *Virginian-Pilot*, November 21, 1989, n.p.

Romandetta, Julie. "Baez Continues to Mix Politics and Music in New LP 'Dreams'." *Boston Herald*, November 13, 1989, n.p.

Sager, Mike. "Joan Baez." Twentieth Anniversary Issue. *Rolling Stone*, November 5, 1987, 163-164.

Sanoff, Alvin P. "How the Times They Are A-changin'." *U.S. News and World Report*, June 29, 1987, 60.

Vasquez, Sherri. "Singing of Dreams." *Fort Collins Coloradoan*, October 6, 1989, n.p.

Wilder, Sherri. "Joan Baez Still Sings for Justice." *Capital Times*, November 2, 1989, n.p.

Marvella Bayh

For Marvella Bayh, the wife of Senator Birch Bayh, days were always packed with things to do, challenges to meet, speeches to make, and family to love and care for. Her nonstop drive to support her husband's political ambitions kept her going through difficult days in Washington. For the public, however, she materialized as a true heroine in her last seven years, when she battled cancer while teaching people how to protect themselves from its terrors.

SOONER HERITAGE

Born on February 14, 1933, on a shirttail wheat farm in Lahoma, outside Enid, Oklahoma, Marvella Belle Hern Bayh came from sturdy stock. She profited from the devotion, laughter, and pioneer pluck passed on to her by her diminutive grandmother, Laura Vercilla Murphy Hern. From her mother, Bernett Monson Hern, Marvella discovered that the human spirit is a greater force than the Dust Bowl.

Her father, Delbert, was only nineteen when he dropped out of Phillips University to become a farmer and auctioneer; he, too, passed along some of the grit and character that made his daughter a forceful contender. He volunteered for military service after the attack on Pearl Harbor, was rejected, and, uncomplaining, returned to planting and harvesting for the good of the country. Her early memories place her near her papa, who welcomed her aboard tractor, baler, combine, and wagon. Even while he rode his horse, she trotted alongside him on her pony, Punky.

From her first breath following a torturous forceps delivery, Marvella found life challenging. Her family lived in a small frame house with no conveniences. Depending on outdoor toilet, kerosene lamps, and a wood-burning stove, the Herns were self-sufficient frontier folk who supplied their own meat by hunting and home butchering.

Growing up a tomboy daredevil, Marvella drove tractor and pickup and enjoyed rough play in barn and loft. Her best friends were boys. Her pleasures echoed country life—sweet melons, cold water from the pump, trips to auctions. The family belonged to a country Methodist Church and took an active role in its Sunday School. Their support system gave substance to Marvella's early years. As she characterized them in retrospect: "They gave me lessons in self-sufficiency—and yet they were always there, my great mainstay" (Bayh and Kotz 1979, 25).

GROWING-UP YEARS

In childhood, Marvella developed unusually precocious verbal skills. She took elocution lessons and learned to deliver short memorized pieces before an audience. She put her irrepressible energy and alertness to work early by entering first grade at age five. Her inability to read words prompted her mother to remove her from the Lahoma school and send her to a school that taught phonics, which soon had her reading on her own.

The 1940s brought tough times to the Herns. Bernett, who never recovered from Marvella's difficult birth, was often bedridden with chronic back pain. When hard work and sickness interfered with her motherhood role, Grandma Hern and Aunt Lillian helped out. A trip to the Mayo Clinic in 1943 brought the promise of a surgical cure for Bernett but put a strain on family finances. An additional burden was their move to a modest bungalow at 2024 West Oklahoma in Enid so that she could have an indoor bathroom and quality medical care.

More problems plagued the family. Marvella, deeply affected by her mother's invalidism, gained thirty-five pounds beyond normal weight. She undertook a supervised diet to remove the excess fat and, with a winner's spirit, dropped the pounds. At age eleven she suffered asthmatic bronchitis and took x-ray treatment to cure her lungs.

Because the Herns were determined people, they encouraged Marvella to go to Girls' State. After winning the governorship of Oklahoma, she journeyed by train to Washington, D.C., won the presidency of Girls' Nation, then became the first female to seek a bachelor's degree in her family. She studied home economics at Oklahoma A & M in Stillwater and continued entering speech contests.

BIRCH

One of Marvella's most momentous speaking jaunts was to Chicago, where at eighteen she met the man she would marry. From the first glimpse of his blue eyes, she was attracted to Birch Bayh, an Indiana farmer, Democrat, and Purdue graduate five years her senior. She was impressed by his looks and even more by his drive and innovative chutzpah. She won the national speaking contest and returned home to a long-distance courtship.

Marvella, whom Birch nicknamed Shotsie, accepted his fraternity pin, then married him on August 24, 1952. She moved to Birch's house in Terre Haute and entered classes at Indiana State. She accepted her role as second in command of a 450-acre farm but held her ground on the matter of choosing history teaching as a career. In 1954, a head-on car collision cut short the smooth routine of classes and housewifery. While Birch campaigned for state legislature, she recuperated from a concussion and broken foot and battled bouts of double vision and head pain.

Before Marvella recovered fully, she conceived and bore a child, Evan. While raising a toddler, she convinced Birch to abandon agriculture and take up law as an adjunct to his first choice of careers—politics. While he studied law, she completed her college degree in social studies and secondary education. Undeterred by a bout with hormone deficiency, she thrilled to Birch's election to speaker of the Indiana House in 1959 and a year later took pride in her graduation from college and his from law school.

SETTLING IN

At home in a small blue house in Terre Haute, the Bayhs experienced ups and downs—Birch's failure of the bar exam, Marvella's continued hormonal deficiency. Inspired by the Kennedy groundswell, Birch decided to run for the U.S. Senate. Against great odds, he won. Marvella, who endured four months of campaign hardship, managed as wife, mother, and chief supporter while also helping her father through a severe depression.

The rewards of election to the world's most exclusive political group arrived immediately. President Kennedy called to express congratulations. Lyndon Johnson invited Marvella for lunch and an insider's advice. Ethel Kennedy hosted the Bayhs at Hickory Hill. Settled in a new brick split-level house in the Chesterbrook development of McLean, Virginia, they looked forward to Birch's first six-year term in the Senate.

From the start, Marvella realized that normalcy was never going to be her lot. With no warning, she found a CBS crew at her door to film "The Senator from Shirkieville." More members of the press from television, big-city newspapers, and news and women's magazines demanded instant performances. To add to the tension, Delbert Bayh began losing control of his need for alcohol. The stress unnerved Marvella enough to require more estrogen, thyroid extract, and tranquilizers.

MAKING THE GRADE

As a freshman senator's wife, Marvella had lots to learn. To assure her control of social graces, she studied protocol for ten weeks with Mrs. Gladstone Williams. To clear up puzzling questions and perk up her worn campaign wardrobe with more appropriate Washington wear, she consulted Lady Bird Johnson and Dorothy Stead, both insiders who were happy to lend advice. The demands of travel and politicking kept Birch apart from Marvella. To cope, she relied on her stock of little purple downers.

Whirlwind campaigning blended into frenetic daily life. Marvella journeyed to Paris and London to meet with NATO delegates, then returned to the crisis their home state faced when Studebaker closed its facility. As Birch moved among hotspots, Marvella kept in touch by phone with her father during his alcoholic crises. In the midst of it all came the unthinkable—the assassination of President Kennedy and the inauguration of Lyndon Johnson as his successor. The spirit of the Kennedy years was broken; Washington's leaders floundered for direction.

Marvella had her own trials. Her parents separated. Bernett took over the family finances to save the farm from bankruptcy. On Christmas, worn with worry, aggravation, and illness, she succumbed to a heart attack at age fifty-six. To Marvella's embarrassment, Delbert immediately married a young woman whom he had been seeing.

More difficulties weighed on Marvella. The crash of an ill-fated flight in a seven-seater plane left the Bayhs scrambling to rescue Ted Kennedy, who was more seriously injured than they. The Bayhs required ten days of hospital care. Physical recuperation failed to cure Marvella's emotional upset. To a psychiatrist she finally admitted the pain that unsettled her — she hated Delbert for desecrating her mother's memory.

REGAINING CONTROL

Marvella felt some relief after the psychiatrist named her chief problem — that she had more grieving to do before putting her mother's untimely death out of mind. She continued a dizzying schedule of social and political functions, all part of the demand placed on senators' wives. Wracked by insomnia, she was filled with regret that she had somehow failed her parents.

As the women's movement began to encourage women to make their own choices, Marvella asserted a need to be her own person. It was friend Lyndon Johnson who gave her a chance to shine by offering her the vice-chairship of the Democratic National Committee. But the real test of Marvella Bayh lay in her refusal. The rejection cost her much self-esteem and years of regret that she put her husband before self.

Birch's 1968 reelection campaign quickly filled the void. Marvella, with thoughts of Birch's someday occupying the Oval Office, starred in a half-hour documentary, "The Senator's Lady." Her old battles with Delbert's drinking continued. Adding to conflict on a personal level were her discussions with Birch about the carnage of Vietnam and misunderstandings with his staff, who often made her feel like an outsider. Somehow she found the concentration to script a last-minute appeal to the voters. Partly owing to her astute political savvy, Birch won a second term.

DISCOVERING INNER STRENGTH

The Bayhs' return to Washington challenged Marvella with the city's frenetic pace. She gave in to her body's deficiencies and agreed to a hysterectomy. After her recovery, travel kept her away from home much of the time. She juggled motherhood, speechmaking, and difficult finances. Political indicators pointed more strongly to Birch's candidacy for president. Marvella, steeped in her role as helpmate, continued churning upstream against all odds that she could hold out.

On her thirty-eighth birthday, Marvella felt pain in her right breast. Examination and x-ray failed to locate the trouble. The turmoil of debt and the public's shift to right-wing political opinion caused repeated blowups between Marvella and Birch. In retrospect, Marvella summarized the demands of high office: "When you're in the Senate ... you have bills, goals, tangible things you're trying to accomplish.... How somebody comes out of this with his health intact is beyond me" (Bayh and Kotz 1979, 216). Her statement proved grimly prophetic.

The pain in Marvella's right breast recurred, resulting in more examinations and a mammogram. Her doctor could detect no lump by palpation yet opted to perform a biopsy on a suspicious patch. On October 8, 1971, Marvella lost her breast to cancer. The severity of the mass also necessitated removal of lymph glands and a segment of chest muscle. To contain the malignancy, doctors advised her to undergo radium treatment five times a week for five weeks, followed by a year-and-a-half of chemotherapy. The prospect jeopardized her emotional control.

Marvella's motherhood asserted itself first. What would happen to Evan if his mother died of cancer? Then sleep deserted her each night as she wrestled with the fear of dying. Birch remained firmly devoted to his wife over the demands of his career. He informed his constituents that he no longer considered himself a candidate for the presidency. The Bayhs were at last relieved of the insuperable task of imitating the perfect political couple and were restored to a normal marriage.

MAKING HEADWAY

At first, Marvella's head swirled with regrets—that she had come in contact with DDT on the farm, that she had had extensive x-ray and hormone treatments, that she had dieted, lived on artificial sweetener, taken tranquilizers, and eaten too much red meat. Even more damning were the years of stress when she had pushed human energy into superhuman performance. Without pause, she restored her spirits with good grooming and social involvement. The radiation treatment sapped her energies, but she refused to give in to cancer. Even more, she pledged herself to develop a whole life, one that did not revolve around her husband's political career. It was a vow as sacred as her marriage promises to Birch.

A flurry of public interest in mastectomy followed Marvella's openness to the press. Interviewers for *Today's Health, Medical Tribune,* and the *National Enquirer* reported her tough fight to return to normal life. She appeared on television for the American Cancer Society, then cochaired the 1974 crusade, which involved two million volunteers. The gala kickoff, featuring *The Marvella Bayh Story*, took place in Atlanta.

Marvella's personal campaign resulted in a career offer to serve as consultant for and representative of the society. For the first time in her life, she had something to scribble in the blank beside "occupation." For the first time in Birch's eighteen-year political career, she sought his support for her taking advantage of this chance to grow and contribute. That spring, he, too, had a bout with cancer when a black spot appeared on his lung. Fortunately, he survived the painful surgery. Together, they initiated a healing process.

BEING HERSELF

Marvella Bayh continued plumbing the depths of her ambitions. She reveled in her weekly television reports and, in a most satisfying partnership, worked with Joe Califano, HEW secretary, in the war against tobacco products. By 1977, she could detect progress in their campaign. Appropriately, the American Society of Surgical Oncologists chose her for the James Ewing Memorial Award, given annually to a layperson in the fight against cancer.

Marvella's exuberance over a late-in-life career lasted until 1978, when cancer returned in the form of a swollen node near her clavicle. Careful scrutiny confirmed that a stage-four malignancy had spread to her bones. The report promised her at least a year to live, maybe as many as five or six. Terrorized by thoughts of death, she turned to prayer and begged for a miracle.

After the initial shock, Marvella found strength and pulled in resources from friends and family. An upbeat attitude and faith in estrogen blockers steeled her spirit. Still energetic, she accepted a job on the Cancer Society's public-issues committee to help combat the tobacco lobby. To her dismay, unfavorable reports blotted out her rosy horizons. The metastasis to more nodes indicated that the disease was again on the move.

During 1978, the year that put her to the greatest test, Marvella never stopped campaigning against cancer or seeking peace of mind. Following a productive summer, she confronted the first pain, which eventually spread from a sciatic nerve to the lining of her left lung. Mustering courage and compassion for other cancer victims, in 1979 she published her autobiography. With touching unselfishness, she penned: "If I have been able to survive emotionally this past year, if I am able to help other people, God has all the credit" (Bayh and Kotz, 297-298).

Her last spring was a mix of happiness and family intimacy. She continued crusading for the Cancer Society and received the Hubert H. Humphrey Inspirational Award for Courage on March 28. On April 24, 1979, she died. The *Washington Post*, in a moving memorial, lauded her determination to channel every ebbing ounce into worthwhile effort to make her life count.

SOURCES

Bayh, Marvella, with Mary Lynn Kotz, ed. "My Fight Against Cancer." *Life*, October 1978, 54ff.

Bayh, Marvella, with Mary Lynn Kotz. *Marvella: A Personal Journey*. New York: Harcourt Brace Jovanovich, 1979.

Elizabeth Blackwell

Out of the era that produced Queen Victoria, Florence Nightingale, Lucretia Mott, Harriet Beecher Stowe, George Eliot, Lucy Stone, and Susan B. Anthony came Dr. Elizabeth Blackwell, the first female physician in modern times. She was determined to overcome sex prejudice in order to establish a career that suited her idealism and talents. At the prompting of Mary Donaldson, a young friend dying of cancer, Blackwell poured her energies into medicine. By the end of her career she had made an indelible mark by encouraging preventive procedures, lecturing on prostitution and venereal disease, attacking slavery, and supporting sex education. Ten years after her death, she was remembered not only as a medical pioneer but as a leader of the women's-rights movement.

AN UNASSUMING BEGINNING

Born in Counterslip, three miles from Bristol, England, on February 3, 1821, to an affluent family rife with warriors for women's rights, Elizabeth "Bessy" Blackwell, named for her paternal grandmother, was the third daughter of reformers Hannah Lane, an attractive, cheery woman, and Samuel Blackwell, a well-groomed, good-natured father who was a sugar refiner and lay preacher. A disciple of William Wilberforce, Samuel was a Dissenter who opposed slavery and alcohol and supported school reform and equal rights. A doting parent to his older girls, Anna and Marianne, he nicknamed Elizabeth "Little Shy," although her later show of forthrightness would disprove his early characterization. The family grew to include Samuel Charles, Henry Browne, Emily, Ellen, John Howard, and George "Washy" Washington. Samuel's four spinster sisters and one brother also lived with the Blackwells in a single, close family unit.

Standing out from her brothers and sisters in pride and intellect, Elizabeth, whom they called Elib or just E, was an attractive, self-reliant child with a wide mouth, straight blond hair, delicate facial structure, and blue-gray eyes. Like her parents, she developed a strong religious faith, spartan courage, and spiritual outlook. She enjoyed a comfortable existence and played duets with her sisters on matching pianos. She was scholarly and insisted that her studies be complete to the last detail. In her father's library she read widely from the great writers—Schiller, Coleridge, Carlyle, and Goethe.

THE PRICE OF DISSENT

The Blackwell family occupied an unenviable place in the midst of proslavery forces. After a seething mob erupted into a riot in 1831, the family sugar refinery was mysteriously consumed in a blaze. Even though fellow refiners offered loans, Samuel, after much debate, elected to try his luck in the New World. To provide his children with the best of opportunities, he shepherded his fifteen-member family aboard the *Cosmo* and sailed to New York City in the fall of 1832, when Elizabeth was eleven.

The era was a turmoil of clashing parties, particularly over the subject of slavery. Because the sugar business was founded on slave labor, Samuel found himself in perpetual controversy. He allied himself with local Quakers, who sided with his liberal views and supported his denunciation of the African flesh trade.

To escape the political and physical heat as well as the threat of cholera, Samuel chose a roomy farmhouse in Rockaway, Long Island, where the children could keep horses. There were tutors in music, German, and French as well as private school in Manhattan. During her adolescence, Elizabeth enjoyed great freedom in her social life and attended skating, dancing, and sleighing parties, played spirited games of chess, and went on extensive tramps in the country. To increase her knowledge of the humanities, Samuel introduced her to Shakespearean plays featuring the Kemble family as well as Italian opera, famous orators, and art galleries.

LOSSES AND GAINS

When times grew hard for Samuel's business, the family realized that he was suffering both depression and ill health. To improve family finances, they emigrated to Jersey City and from there by canal barge to Cincinnati in the spring of 1838. Samuel died of bilious fever in August, leaving a house and furniture but little cash. Two weeks later, Elizabeth and her older sisters established a boarding school for girls to help support the family. As Elizabeth described the situation, "We entered upon the sternest realities of life — a struggle for existence without connections, without experience, with cultivated tastes, but burdened by debts which, though comparatively small, seemed formidable to us, in a strange country" (Ross, 65).

Elizabeth Blackwell was twenty-three when she decided to open a girl's school in Henderson, Kentucky. The drab, insular life of backwoods Kentuckians eventually drove her back home to Cincinnati, where she joined Harriet Beecher Stowe's Semi-Colon Club. None of Elizabeth's stopgap pastimes met her intellectual needs. Then Mary Donaldson summed up her quandary with succinct grace: "You have health, leisure, and a cultivated intelligence. Why don't you devote these qualities to the service of suffering women? Why don't you study medicine?" (Ross, 83).

CHOOSING A CAREER

Blackwell agreed that she would rather be a physician than a teacher. Indeed, the suggestion answered her inner muddle over courtship, which never seemed to match her with young men of suitable breadth of thought and ambition. By studying medicine, she could stifle her passions, circumvent the unpleasant prospect of an unsuitable marriage, and, at the same time, improve women's lives, particularly in halting the back-street abortion trade. In her writings she observed: "The idea of winning a doctor's degree gradually assumed the aspect of a great moral struggle, and the moral fight possessed an immense attraction for me" (Ross, 87).

To gain these ends, Blackwell immediately consulted the doctors she trusted concerning where and how she might seek medical training. Their lack of enthusiasm failed to daunt her ardor. Instead, she took charge of her own education by landing a job in Asheville, North Carolina, as music teacher for Rev. John Dickson, in whose library she found a fine selection of medical texts. A year later, she moved to Charleston to the home of Dr. Samuel H. Dickson, Dickson's brother, who encouraged her to study Greek and helped her finance her studies by getting her a job teaching music at Madame Du Pré's boarding house.

By the spring of 1847, Elizabeth was ready to seek formal training. At first, she received rejections from twenty-nine medical colleges in New York and Philadelphia. Condescending males urged her to use her skills in the nursing profession, which welcomed women. One sympathetic Quaker suggested that she disguise herself in men's clothes and attend free lectures in French medical colleges. She arranged for private instruction in anatomy, then was accepted by unanimous vote at the Geneva Medical School in Geneva, New York, which later became Hobart College, a part of Syracuse University.

BATTLING DISCRIMINATION

The triumph of admittance was not the end of Blackwell's battle against sex discrimination. Immediately she perceived ostracism and discourtesy in the boarding house where she roomed and even on public streets. Threats and crank mail arrived at her door. People sniffed at the "doctress," whom they labeled a fallen woman and a lunatic. Gawkers hindered lectures by pressing in to see the freak female studying an all-male profession. Even her staunchest supporter, Dr. James Webster, barred her from dissections of reproductive organs.

Dressed in plain Quaker frock and bonnet, Blackwell went about her studies with determination and dignity. She abstained from social contact with fellow students; her only recreation was exchanging letters with family members. She deliberately ignored public harassment and bridled against exclusion from any aspect of medical training. Her decorum and professionalism impressed the other members of her class, who cheered her on with wholehearted admiration.

During the summer, Blackwell increased her experience by working on the syphilis ward at the Philadelphia Almshouse. Resident doctors expressed their prejudice by shunning her and refusing to cooperate in diagnoses and other professional courtesies. While becoming adept at the treatment of typhus, she also developed a strong distaste for rampant sexual license, a chief cause of social ills. At the end of the second year, she passed each course with honors, graduated first in her class, and in January 1849 received a degree entitling her to practice medicine.

LATER BATTLES

Dr. Blackwell found European medical men as stodgy and bigoted as U.S. doctors. Some relegated her to the role of midwife. Still, she persevered in her search for practical experience. She studied first at the Collège de France in Paris, then worked at La Maternité. While treating a diseased infant, she sprayed an infected solution in her eyes. The malady disfigured her face and limited her vision. After many miserable months, she accepted her fate and had the eye removed and replaced with a glass eye.

Her vigor restored, Dr. Blackwell returned to London to study at St. Bartholomew's Hospital. Petite and unobtrusive, she joined the medical staff without fanfare and quietly accepted the prejudice of certain "moss backs" who rejected any notion of women practicing medicine. During these important months she came in contact with stirring new scientific concepts: ions from Michael Faraday, astronomy from John Herschel, and sanitation from Florence Nightingale, who became a colleague and close friend. In addition, Dr. Blackwell steeped herself in contemporary culture; she especially enjoyed the vocal skill of Jenny Lind and the wonders of the World's Fair and the Crystal Palace.

Upon her return to Cincinnati, Dr. Blackwell announced her decision to practice medicine in the United States, where "women will first be recognized as the equal half of humanity" (Ross, 169). In 1852, she delivered a series of lectures on conditions that debilitate young urban females and on the need for fresh air, exercise, cleanliness, and a simple diet. Later that year her lectures were compiled into a popular book entitled *The Laws of Life with Special Reference to the Physical Education of Girls*. Despite her successes, however, she was still shunned as an unnatural woman who talked of unmentionable subjects from a public platform.

FINDING A NICHE

Dr. Blackwell had need of strong friends during her early years of practice. She relied on her sisters as well as on Horace Greeley, William Lloyd Garrison, Lady Byron, and many Quaker patients, who discovered that a doctor's gender made little difference in the quality of care. In 1853, acceding to the fact that no hospital would extend her professional privileges, she opened a dispensary near Tompkins Square in New York, a region marred by squalid slums in which wretched immigrants lived in substandard, unsanitary quarters. While she subsisted on meager rations and labored far into the night to save penniless patients, she considered her work a pioneer effort for women.

Family and friends failed to fill the emptiness that Dr. Blackwell experienced from constant personal and professional attacks on her dignity. In 1854, she made a giant step toward healing the gap by adopting Katharine "Kitty" Barry, a seven-year-old orphan who became her constant companion. Another encouragement came that same year in the graduation of her sister, Emily, with a medical degree and a special interest in anesthesia to aid women in childbirth. Also, Marie Zakrzewska, a German midwife, joined Elizabeth as an assistant.

As Elizabeth's practice slowly succeeded, her plans for a women's treatment center took shape. She encouraged Emily to learn all she could before taking her place as part of their trio. Together, they turned an old Dutch house on Bleeker Street into a dispensary with three wards, a maternity department, and an operating room. Within seven months, the three specialists treated 926 patients from a mix of countries and speaking a hodgepodge of languages and dialects.

Would-be physicians petitioned Dr. Blackwell for admission for study. Exactly ten years after receiving her diploma, she began her own medical college. She held entrants to rigid standards and rejected the dissolute type of females that often sought the position of nurse. On a subsequent lecture tour in Europe, she found her friend Florence Nightingale opening a similar training school, a real beginning for the women's medical movement in Europe. Dr. Marie, who accepted a new post in Boston, also founded an institution based on Dr. Blackwell's concepts.

Moving the flourishing infirmary to new quarters, Drs. Elizabeth and Emily Blackwell continued to thrive. Possibly because of her limited eyesight, Elizabeth abandoned practice in favor of hygiene, education, and preventive medicine. The Civil War increased the need for medical care, which many women, including Dorothea Dix, Clara Barton, and Drs. Rebecca Cole and Mary E. Walker, were able to provide. To heed the call for more battlefield assistance, Blackwell trained nurses to aid the Union Army.

The idea of women in medicine had come into its own. Three years after the Civil War, to help women like herself who were rejected by a "men only" mind-set, Dr. Blackwell opened the Women's Medical College—which was later absorbed into Cornell University, one of the schools that had previously rejected her for study. By the next year, ten schools were issuing diplomas to women. And the public was beginning to respect females as healers.

NEW DIRECTIONS

Shortly after her own school's opening, Elizabeth Blackwell accepted the leadership of its hygiene department. Because she had caused the death of a baby by vaccination, she never fostered inoculation as a viable defense against sickness, yet she championed the move against infant mortality and fought for cleaner homes, sewage control, recreation, and pure water. Then, to replenish her resources after the war's exhausting pace, she journeyed to England to visit relatives and rest in the Lake District.

Newly revitalized by the controversy over the double standard regarding venereal disease, Dr. Blackwell set up the National Health Society and founded the London School of Medicine for Women, where she served as professor of gynecology until the age of eighty-six. She also dedicated herself to Christian socialism, a concept that foresaw future interest in the role of attitude in overall well-being. In the mid-1870s, Dr. Blackwell's health declined from repeated attacks of bronchitis and liver disease. She traveled to Switzerland with Kitty and took up sketching, an avocation she had enjoyed in childhood. She attempted to tour Italy, but sickness forced her back to England.

To quell her restlessness, Dr. Blackwell wrote *Counsel to Parents on the Moral Education of Their Children*, a treatise on sex education culled from her numerous lectures. Publishing houses, fearful of a public outcry, rejected the work. Undaunted, she retitled the work *The Moral Education of the Young, Considered Under Medical and Social Aspects*. The book found a ready audience and was regularly reissued.

A PATHFINDER

Dr. Blackwell, by now a slightly stooped, white-haired elderly lady, recovered her health in the late 1870s and set forth for more battles against society's ills. She and her daughter Kitty moved into Rock House, a handsome residence facing the English Channel at Hastings, Sussex, which drew a variety of progressive, intellectual visitors. Surrounded by photographic portraits of friends and sketches of the English coastline, Dr. Blackwell moved calmly but deliberately into a new era of activism by forcing politicians to take action against brothels. In 1885 she issued a scathing monograph, *The Decay of Municipal Representative Government*, followed annually by more writings on vice and its role in disease.

By 1902, Dr. Blackwell's lectures had been collected in a single volume, *Essays on Medical Sociology*. Much of her logical argument was prophetic of twentieth-century movements to improve society by uplifting women and children, who suffered most from its excesses. She took good care of her own health, honed her diet to vegetables and fish, and rested on the Riviera in winter and in Scotland in summer. She suffered a serious fall in 1907, which decreased her powers of concentration. By 1909, she was bedfast and, with Kitty at her side, died on May 31, 1910, at Hastings. In its obituary notice, the *London Times* proclaimed her a true pioneer.

SOURCES

Baker, Rachel. *The First Woman Doctor*. Scholastic Biography Series. New York: Scholastic, 1987.

Brown, Jordan. *Elizabeth Blackwell*. American Women of Achievement Series. New York: Chelsea House, 1989.

Latham, Jean L. *Elizabeth Blackwell: Pioneer Woman Doctor*. Garrard Discovery Series. Champaign, Ill.: Garrard, 1975.

Ross, Ishbel. *Child of Destiny: The Life Story of the First Woman Doctor.* New York: Harper, 1949.

Sabin, Francene. *Elizabeth Blackwell: The First Woman Doctor.* Mahwah, N.J.: Troll Associates, 1982.

Smith, Dean. "A Persistent Rebel." *American History Illustrated*, January 1981, 28-36.

Malcolm Boyd

As gadfly, advocate of gay rights, and savvy confessor to the generation that brought Blacks into the U.S. mainstream, Father Malcolm Boyd became not only a spokesperson but also a symbol of open-mindedness and tolerance. He claimed not to have sought causes; instead, he faced the controversies inherent in his milieu. To the public, he was cool, vital—a cleric with understanding. The Episcopal hierarchy often characterized him as an anathema, or at the very least, as an embarrassment.

Whatever the assessment, Malcolm Boyd, dubbed the "secular priest," is a difficult man to overlook (*Contemporary Authors* 1988, 60). The sobriquet indicates more than a pose, for Boyd lives his principles. His activism involves taking part in a freedom ride, witnessing the Los Angeles Watts riots in 1965, supporting voter registration in Black communities, initiating Vietnam-War protests, walking Detroit picket lines, and being arrested for participation in a Chicago civil-rights demonstration. As a writer, he has contributed extensively to major religious journals and critiques films for *Christian Century*. His intense, tightly wound nervous energy catapults him into the right places at crucial moments. For Malcolm Boyd, being an Episcopal priest means getting involved.

A WRITER'S BEGINNING

From boyhood, Malcolm "Mal" Boyd seemed destined for a career in writing. Born on June 8, 1923, in Buffalo, New York, he was the only child of Melville and Beatrice Lowrie Boyd. His alcoholic father, an investment counselor and financier, left his mother, moved to East Orange, New Jersey, and remarried. Beatrice took Malcolm to Denver, where she moved into an old apartment and found work as a legal secretary. In Colorado, he continued to think of himself as a New Yorker and as such enjoyed broadcasts of the Metropolitan Opera, editions of the *New York Times*, and fresh-baked rye bread. Such fragmentary contacts with home, however, failed to save him from casting himself mentally as "a young prince who has gone into exile as a pauper" (Boyd 1969, 8).

Growing up in the 1930s, Boyd had the usual experiences of his generation. He liked visiting his maternal grandmother, who ran a boarding house. He owned a collie named Laddie, listened to "Amos 'n' Andy" and "Fibber McGee and Molly" on the radio, read Dick Tracy comics, and kept up with current events. He possessed talent for in-depth reading, analysis, and creative writing. As a student at North Junior High School in Colorado Springs, he won a prize for writing an essay about his love of history and displayed a knack for interviewing celebrities such as Mischa Elman, Carl Van Doren, John Gunther, H. V. Kaltenborn, Lotte Lehmann, and Wanda Landowska.

While attending East High School, Boyd was a member of the National Honor Society and wrote for the school literary magazine and newspaper, the *Spotlight*, yet remained on the periphery of the school's privileged clique. Exclusion caused an ache that rationalization could not cure: "I raged against it, but was helpless to do anything. I continued to write my interviews but my heart wasn't in it" (Boyd 1969, 10). In 1940, he entered the University of Arizona in Tucson as a journalism-economics major and continued writing for campus publications and editing a frivolous newsletter, the *Bar Nuthin'*. To earn tuition, he waited tables in the dining hall, washed dishes at a sorority house, and mowed lawns for the park system.

An insider among the campus elite, Boyd found himself extremely powerful as a purveyor of printed gossip. He rose to president of his fraternity and chaired important committees. The pressure to succeed socially inspired him to cheat. The resulting scandal led him to see that inclusion among pseudosophisticates was not worth expulsion or damage to his character. Abandoning the superficial friends he had been cultivating to seek higher goals for himself, he began announcing for radio station KVOA and used a thousand-dollar bequest from his grandmother's will to pay the tuition for an NBC radio workshop.

THE REAL WORLD

Graduated in 1944 and out on his own, Boyd, who lived briefly in a minuscule butler's pantry in a sleazy boarding house, at first despaired of achieving his dreams. A victim of bronchial impairment, he received a 4-F military rating and, while other young men prepared for war, journeyed to Hollywood to take a job with advertisers Foote, Cone & Belding, Inc., located near Pershing Square. As low man in the firm, he observed the machinations and reshufflings of the power structure and learned how to pace himself in a competitive setting.

Quickly, Boyd began to achieve results. From producing a live five-days-per-week program he advanced to contact man for a newscast and soap opera. As a junior executive, he bore the outward marks of accomplishment—shiny shoes, neat suit, and coordinated ties. Remembering his youthful zeal for the Hollywood stereotype, he recalled: "I was seething inside with macabre visions of success, while outwardly learning how to cultivate cool, and was in the process of becoming a bright, shiny, pushing, well-groomed snot" (Boyd 1969, 15).

Within two years Boyd's show moved to San Francisco. He opted to work as liaison representing literary properties and negotiating radio contracts for Republic Pictures and Samuel Goldwyn Productions. Fired from his post at age twenty-six, he first attempted writing a humanistic mystery novel, then joined Buddy Rogers and Mary Pickford in forming Mal Boyd and Associates, an independent agency that produced radio and television programming. For his hard work he received a major award, presidency of the Television Producers' Association.

The growth of Boyd's business brought few personal satisfactions. In 1951, he drove into the Arizona desert to be alone and ponder his needs and capabilities. His thoughts turned inward and illuminated obscure elements of his inner need: "I wanted to come out of the imprisonment of the fantasy of full autonomy which was represented by the shell of defenses behind which I lived.... It seemed that I should first have to respond ... to the will of God for me. How could I find it?" (Boyd 1969, 52).

The answer lay in a dramatic change of direction. Only three years into his career as vice president of the firm, Boyd surprised his colleagues by abandoning advertising and show business and entering a three-year program at the Church Divinity School of the Pacific in preparation for the Episcopal ministry. Two hundred friends treated him to a farewell luncheon at Ciro's. Some wept and made their formalized eulogies as if he were entering a stockade or a monastery, never to be heard from again. Boyd, himself uncertain of the days that lay ahead, knew intuitively that choosing to follow God was right for him. Part of the draw of religious service was his belief that worship should not be cloistered within a rarefied, separated world. Rather, in his view, oneness with God should accompany all aspects of a well-rounded life.

ANOTHER WAY

Following ordination, then a year of study in Oxford, England, in 1955 Boyd participated in an interchurch institute in Geneva, Switzerland, and enrolled at Union Theological Seminary in New York City under Reinhold Niebuhr, the evangelical theologian who originated a philosophy based on political realism. These strong ecumenical teachings and experiences dramatically affected Boyd's concept of church. From observations of the oneness of human experiences with all forms of spirituality, he evolved a loving, personal mission.

In the summer of 1957, Boyd expanded his understanding of the role of the worker-priest at Taizé, a Protestant communal society outside Cluny, France, where he labored in the fields. During this period, he published *Crisis in Communication* and *Christ and the Celebrity Gods: The Church in Mass Culture*. Following an internship at an English industrial mission among slum-dwellers in Sheffield, Boyd accepted a lower-middle-class white parish, St. George's Episcopal Church, in Indianapolis. The setting, rife with street violence, family dysfunction, hatred, malnutrition, and sickness, forced him to set in motion his idealized plan for the ministry.

Boyd challenged his parishioners to accept local Blacks as human beings. His push toward exchange of pastorates with a Black minister set off unforeseen racist reactions. Some white communicants refused to approach an altar at which Black hands administered the sacraments. The experience spurred him to fight such blatant bigotry, which lay closer to the surface of human relations than he had surmised.

In 1959, Boyd served as chaplain at Colorado State University, Fort Collins, where he evolved his trademark ministerial stance as informal confessor and adviser.

While overseeing campus religious life, he published *Focus: Rethinking the Meaning of Our Evangelism*, an iconoclastic restatement of the minister's role in human affairs. Local journalists, responding to his informality and popularity, dubbed him the "espresso priest" (*Current Biography*, 61). The church hierarchy, less enthusiastic over his breezy approach to theological concerns, chastised him for meeting parishioners at the Golden Grape Coffee House and local bars. By spring of 1961, he felt pushed to resign his chaplaincy.

Within a few months, Boyd was performing a similar task in Detroit at Wayne State University, where he joined a freedom pilgrimage from New Orleans through Mississippi and Tennessee to Michigan. The event climaxed in Detroit at the Episcopal Church's sixtieth convention. For his dedication to bringing the warring races together, *Life* magazine named him one of the United States' 100 most important young people.

The remainder of the 1960s were productive years for Boyd, who put his writing skills to work for the civil-rights effort. In two years' time, he published *If I Go Down to Hell, The Hunger, The Thirst*, and *On the Battle Lines*, then wrote a series of one-act humanistic dialogues—*Boy, The Job, The Community, Study in Color*, and *They Aren't Real to Me*. Boyd pursued the staging of his works and, as tangible evidence of his ministry, also acted in them. In an interview for the *New York Times*, he declared: "I believe that the most powerful sermons of our time and culture are to be found in the theater, the novel and occasionally in the medium of films. I have something to say about race—or, as I prefer to call it, human—relations" (*Current Biography*, 62).

SUPPORTERS AND CRITICS

Criticism of Boyd's involvement in controversial issues and his use of profanity and jolting, sometimes vulgar street slang led to his resignation. Following a stint as lecturer for the World Council of Churches in Geneva, he migrated to Washington, D.C., and, as assistant pastor at the Church of the Atonement, served U.S. college campuses as itinerant chaplain. In 1965, he produced his most controversial work, *Are You Running with Me, Jesus?*, an upbeat, contemporary prayer book that sold fifteen times more copies than the publishers had anticipated. The book, which removes the artificial distance between God and current problems and concerns, speaks bluntly of human needs.

Critics, repeating earlier charges against Boyd's style, upbraided him for demystifying God and reducing divinity to base, worldly terms. His answer to them leaves no doubt about his commitment to human need: "There's no 'them.' ... The religious issues of today are the racial problem, the population explosion, war and peace—not the silly little things we call religion" (Boyd 1969, 50). Separating himself from the social institution he saw masquerading as a church, in a speech to Jewish women in Detroit, he challenged religious leaders to forget social weddings and political infighting and to embrace and relieve suffering.

Boyd's answer to his detractors was a sequel to his prayer book, a collection of equally hip, idiomatic meditations entitled *Free to Live, Free to Die*. He followed with two editions of readings, *Malcolm Boyd's Book of Days* and *The Underground Church*. On January 30, 1966, to an improvised jazz accompaniment played by Charlie Byrd, Boyd read from his work. The duo repeated their presentation at New York's Broadway United Church of Christ and on an album for Columbia Records.

After replacing Charlie Byrd with stand-up comedian Dick Gregory, Boyd redirected his performance at an unprecedented month-long engagement at the hungry i, a San Francisco nightclub, where he turned his readings into capsule sermons and answered questions from the audience. He donated his earnings of $1,000 per week to the civil-rights cause. More publicity brought a record contract for *Happening, Prayer for Now*, appearances on the "Tonight" show and at New York City's Village Theatre, and a part in the 1968 film *You Are What You Eat*.

When a position opened at Calhoun College on the Yale campus, Boyd moved into the slot as unofficial visiting chaplain. At a time when the university moved toward a coed campus, he engaged students in informal give and take, encouraging them to express their misgivings and hopes for the future. His candor, which moved swiftly and inexorably to the heart of controversy, made them think about ethics, both as ideal and as reality. In short order, students were flocking to Father Boyd to confide their troubles and absorb his wisdom.

In 1969, Boyd published his first autobiography, *As I Live and Breathe*. In the preface, he commented that he did not intend to explain his theology or politics but rather to delineate how he had spent his first forty-five years. He described the project as therapeutic: "It has made me introspective, and therefore outgoing. I am grateful that I could do it for the purpose of better understanding my life; perspective leaps out of new paragraphs" (Boyd 1969, vi).

MINISTERING TO GAYS

Soul-searching in the 1970s led Boyd to divulge his gay orientation. As public testimonial of how he pretended to be straight, then confessed a monogamous homosexual relationship with writer and editor Mark Thompson, he wrote a second autobiography, *Take Off the Masks*, lambasting the rigidity of conservative Episcopalians, who demanded his defrocking. Supporters wrote him of similar experiences with intolerance and applauded his courage and honesty. In 1978, he received an Integrity Award for contributions to the gay movement, particularly to those gays who retain membership in Christian churches in spite of persecution from intolerant heterosexual members.

For long months, Boyd distanced himself from organized religion and pondered giving up his ministry and returning to entertainment production. Determined to work for change, he chose to remain a priest and do his part from inside the Episcopal Church. Returned to California in 1979, Boyd accepted a post as writer in residence at St. Augustine By-the-Sea Episcopal Church in Santa Monica. In 1985, one of his most rewarding temporary jobs was membership in the Los Angeles AIDS Task Force. Also, he published *Look Back in Joy: Celebration of Gay Lovers* and *Gay Priest: An Inner Journey* and began writing a column for *Modern Maturity*.

Perhaps the most challenging obstacle that Boyd's ministry has confronted is firmly entrenched prejudice among church leaders against gays. In 1987, he was appointed director of the Institute of Gay Spirituality and Theology in Riverside, California. The fledgling program, designed to open lines of communication between students and writers and the church, aimed at the distant goal of creating a gay theology and strengthening the link between Christian theology and the feminist outlook. His positive attitude suggested that he had already begun surveying the field and was finding the work promising.

THE REAL MAL

Mal Boyd the man makes a habit of being positive and gives the appearance of symmetry and regularity. He is medium in height and build, with balding head and riveting blue eyes. The disconcerting fact about him is that his thinking exceeds the limits most people set for their minds. Because he deliberately challenges people to think beyond the status quo, he creates a tension that is both helpful and harmful. To people who allow themselves to face controversy, acquaintance with Father Boyd often leads to a rejuvenation of the spirit. To cynics and skeptics, the intensity of his theology immediately becomes suspect. To this latter group, Boyd appears phony and self-seeking rather than illuminating or devout.

Whatever his effect on others, Boyd, a follower of the secular humanist philosophy, remains attuned to all types of people, whether open or closed in their thinking. In an interview, he explained his view of doubters: "The way I try to reach them is not to be dogmatic, not to debate, not to be didactic, but to try ... to realize that *this* is a person. And the person is human and there are links between us" (*Contemporary Authors* 1988, 69).

SOURCES

Boyd, Malcolm. *As I Live and Breathe: Stages of an Autobiography*. New York: Random House, 1969.

_____. *Human Like Me, Jesus*. New York: Simon & Schuster, 1971.

Contemporary Authors. New Revision Series, Volume 26. Detroit: Gale Research, 1988.

Contemporary Authors Autobiography Series, Volume 11. Detroit: Gale Research, 1990.

Current Biography. New York: H. W. Wilson, 1968.

"Gay Theology Institute." *The Christian Century*, July 29, 1987, 650.

Louis Braille

A single slip of the hand and the quick, murderous stab of a sharp leather-crafter's tool ended Louis Braille's vision for the remaining forty years of his life. Yet his alert, adaptive mind managed to overcome the problems of reading by creating a sequential coding system by which texts of all kinds could be accessed by visually handicapped readers. Ironically, the finely honed pointed instrument that blinded him became his prototype stylus—the tool by which he created his special alphabet.

Like other blind people before him, Braille understood that the fingers could be made to do the work of eyes. In his teen years, twelve years after losing his sight, he initiated a discovery that would open the world of reading, science, math, and music to all who learned the Braille system. In time, many blind scholars, including Helen Keller, conquered reading using this simplified code.

A FEW YEARS TO SEE

Born in Coupvray, a small village twenty miles southeast of Paris, France, on January 4, 1809, Louis Braille, son of Monique Baron-Braille and Simon-René Braille, was small and unpromising at birth but developed into a normal farm child. Fourth after Catherine, Simon, and Marie Céline, Louis was part of a close-knit family that continued the trade of his grandfather, a master harness maker and saddle crafter. On Touarte Street, the Braille family occupied an austere five-room stone house with few windows and no conveniences. The residence, on seven-and-a-half acres of land, stood among vegetable patches, hay fields, pasture land, and vineyards.

At age three and a half, Louis, the youngest child, was a handsome lad with blue eyes and light curly hair. His skin was bronzed by the sun as he played near the brook where the women washed clothes. He chased after the mare that pulled his father's plow. On Thursdays, he followed his family to the town square for market day and enjoyed brisk horse trades. He helped his mother unload baskets of artichokes and cauliflowers to sell to townspeople. When business was finally under way, Louis and his brother and sisters were free to watch *Guignol*, a puppet show.

Simon Braille was especially proud of the boy's intelligence and dreamed of providing the education to help him enter his choice of professions. Louis adored his father and toyed with leather scraps while watching him make saddles and cut strips for reins. While investigating the workbench in his father's saddle shop, he leaned too close to his project and accidentally plunged an awl into his eye.

The illiterate family, suspicious of formalized medical treatment, called in a herbalist, who applied lily water to halt the bleeding. She pressed against the damaged eye with cool calomel compresses and held the pad in place with a bandage. Forty-eight hours later, infection set in. Within two years, sympathetic ophthalmia had spread the damage to the other eye, leaving him totally blind.

Clopping along in his wooden sabots, the boy learned by trial and error how to navigate cobbled streets with the cane that his father whittled for him. To expedite movement, he hummed as he walked and followed the echo of sound waves to guide him. During the period he was adapting to his handicap, Braille depended on his sister Monique for stories and entertainment. After she married and left home, the boy suffered from loneliness. During the Napoleonic Wars, the arrival of Russian occupation troops in 1814 brought hard times to the whole village, but especially to a blind boy whom the crude soldiers ridiculed and teased. His family, unable to cope with Louis's special needs, feared that his once-bright future would shrink to a life of mockery and begging on the streets.

SCHOOL YEARS

For a time, Braille studied with Father Jacques Palluy, a kindly cleric who told stories to entertain his blind parishioner. Then, along with sighted children, Louis entered Antoine Becheret's classroom in the town schoolhouse and wept that there were no books for blind children. He had to depend on memory of lecture material and oral review with his brother and sister as his primary means of staying at the top of his class in most subjects.

Braille was adept at literature and enjoyed Bible stories most of all. With the help of Abbé Palluy, on February 15, 1819, he received a scholarship to the Institut National des Jeunes Aveugles (French National Institute for Blind Youth), which had been founded by Valentin Haüy in 1791. Braille's father escorted him to his first venture beyond the little village in which he had spent his life. The departure from Coupvray was painful at first. Braille had to accustom himself to a large, uncomfortable building, dormitory living, and a stiff military uniform. Members of the all-male student body were each issued a single set of clothes and limited to one bath per month. Discipline required frequent beatings to assure good performance.

Braille accepted the rigors of school life and found a lifelong friend in Gabriel Gauthier, who bunked nearby. Later, he made friends with Hippolyte Coltat. The two young men became Braille's school family. His biographer, Etta DeGering, praised his devotion to these alliances: "With him ... friendship was a conscientious duty.... He cultivated it like a rare orchid" (DeGering, 95).

At the Institute, Braille enjoyed field trips to botanical gardens, sack races, checkers, and chess; however, he never adapted well to the dampness and mold of the ancient school building, which caused him breathing problems. Still, the academic stimulus gave him much pleasure. Because of his intelligence and curiosity, he did well in his subjects, particularly knitting, shop, music, math, Latin, grammar and composition, and science.

Music was a particular pleasure to Braille. He sang in the school choir, which performed for noble guests. Playing by ear, he soon mastered piano, pipe organ, and cello. Soon he was playing for church services at St. Nicholas des Champs and two other local churches. Among local people, he was lauded as a talented and versatile pianist who willingly entertained any gathering. With renewed confidence, he turned to greater challenges.

FILLING A NEED

Braille realized that blind students could never learn to the best of their ability without books. He was twelve when he learned about a secret system of phonetic coded dots and dashes. In 1819, Captain Charles Barbier, a French military officer in Napoleon's army, had invented sonography, or l'Ecriture Nocturne, commonly called nightwriting—a series of embossed symbols enabling soldiers to communicate silently on a battlefield in the dark of night. Three years later, Barbier came to the Institute to demonstrate his communication system.

The school utilized Haüy's system of embossed Roman type to teach the blind to read. These books were oversized and bulky, altogether too difficult to manage efficiently and too cumbersome for rapid reading. Braille was certain that another way could be found to record letters for fingers to read. Impressed with the fourteen-character code but convinced of its inconvenience, he began formulating an adaptation of this form of coded writing for blind readers.

With the encouragement of Abbé Palluy, Louis tinkered with possible substitutes for embossing. He tried a geometric system employing circles, triangles, and squares cut from leather. He hammered small nails and tacks into boards and fingered the nail heads as a means of reading. He also experimented with music transcribed from symbols. Historians surmise that he intended to create a music code.

At first onlookers patronized him for his concentration on rows of dots. After considerable work, he achieved a less cumbersome, fingertip-sized six-dot code based on the twenty-five letters of the French alphabet. The arrangement resembled musical notation and could be recognized with a single contact of one digit. Not only was it easy to read, it was just as simple to write. At last, he had solved the problem of books for the blind.

THE BRAILLE SYSTEM

Braille's idea was for the blind reader to slide fingertips over the series of dots and decode the text. The method was simple. Each of sixty-three distinctive clusters of dots represented a single cell and resembled the configuration of a domino, only small enough to fit the pad of a finger. The cell was divided into six locations—one, two, and three arranged in the left-hand vertical row and four, five, and six arranged in the right-hand vertical row. By varying the placement of dots, Braille created a readable code. A single dot at position one represented the letter *a*; two dots in positions one and two, one over the other, represented *b*; two dots side by side in positions one and four represented *c*; and so forth.

The system included all twenty-five letters of the French alphabet (which at that time omitted the *w*) plus punctuation, numbers (which are the letters *a* through *j* plus a dash representing numerals), diphthongs, familiar words, scientific symbols, mathematical and musical notation, and a symbol for capitalization. It required two-handed reading. With the right hand, the reader felt the individual dots; with the left, the reader moved on toward the next line. In this way, blind students acquired a smoothness and speed similar to that of sighted readers as they comprehended words while moving on through the pattern of thought by decoding successive patterns of symbols.

TEACHING OTHERS

By age seventeen, the young inventor was eager to help pay his own way. He worked in his father's leather shop in summer and earned fifteen francs per month as an apprentice teacher of math, geography, history, grammar, and music at the Institute, even though a chronic cough impeded his lecturing. Dr. Pignier, who was named his guardian after his father's death, helped him become a full professor and earn an annual salary of 300 francs. Braille regretted that Simon had not lived to see him attain full professional status.

An excellent teacher, Braille got along well with students, often helping them accept their fate so that they could better blend into sighted society. The writing system that he perfected worked so well in his classes that students were able to take class notes and to write themes. By placing a metal ruler on paper and using openings as individual cells, they simply punched dots with a pointed stylus. At the age of twenty Braille published a monograph describing the use of his coded system. In 1837, he issued a second publication featuring an expanded system of coding text.

REJECTION

The response to Braille's system was unfortunate — rejection of a brilliant invention. Students were eager to employ Braille writing so that they could function as normally as blindness would allow. They anticipated each installment of his *Précis d'Histoire*, which he published for classroom use. Sighted instructors and school-board members, however, were unenthusiastic, feared for their jobs against an increasing number of well-educated blind teachers, and eventually ousted Dr. Pignier, the principal of the Institute, for producing textbooks using the six-dot system. They replaced him with Dr. Dafau, an educator who openly scorned the Braille method because it conferred too much independence on blind persons.

Louis, wearied by the politics that hampered his progress, grew despondent, realizing that his health and strength were at a permanent ebb and that time was running out for the establishment of his system. In 1835, seriously ill with incurable tuberculosis and unsteadying bouts of vertigo, he was forced to resign and return to Coupvray to allow his mother to care for him.

Braille took a second leave of absence from teaching in April 1843 so that he could return to the family farm to recuperate. Because disease imperiled his life, friends and well-wishers petitioned the French government to acknowledge his achievement and to honor him with the Legion of Honor, yet officials made no effort to laud his ingenious system. The crowning blow came when he returned to the Institute and learned that the six-dot system was officially banned.

REWARD TOO LATE

Even though the Braille writing system had been demonstrated at the Paris Exposition of Industry in 1834 and was lauded by King Louis-Philippe, it was not accepted until 1854, two years after the inventor's death, when the Institute endorsed the work of its gifted alumnus. A major reason for the twenty-five-year delay was Haüy's preference for a system that both blind and sighted persons could read. Eventually, educators of handicapped students reasoned that convenience for blind readers far outweighed the importance of Haüy's system.

For many years, other tinkerers altered the system, causing confusion until a standardized Braille system was accepted for all English-speaking readers. It first entered the United States in 1860 at the Missouri School for the Blind, where it competed with other line and point systems such as English Braille, American Braille, and New York point writing. Many theories of embossing competed for prominence with the major theorists of education for the handicapped. For a time, publishers produced books embossed in all major codes to assure maximum readership. By 1868, the Boston Public Library was offering these coded works to blind readers.

The controversy over Louis Braille's contribution, dubbed the "war of the dots," continued until July 1932, when a committee voted on the system that would set the standard. A major deciding factor was the ability of blind persons to write the point system with stylus, ruler, and slate, whereas the more cumbersome embossed letter system could be produced only by machine. During World War I, the Red Cross extended services to blind persons by transcribing textbooks, novels, and magazines into Braille. The demand proved so great that a government agency began subsidizing library services for blind readers through a division of the Library of Congress. A World Braille Council spread the services to all nations.

PERFECTING THE SYSTEM

Crucial to the standardization of Louis Braille's code was the Braille typewriter and printing press. Today, many other items, such as watches, compasses, board games, measuring devices, and carpentry and kitchen tools, are marked with raised dots. Through the aid of the American Foundation for the Blind and the national Braille Press, elevators, water fountains, vending machines, and public-transit signs are available in Braille. Thus, Braille's system became so widespread that it is now the standard method of teaching visually handicapped readers to become literate.

A SHORT, PRODUCTIVE LIFE

Although the Braille system later flourished, Louis Braille, its progenitor, was unable to withstand the buffeting of the final years of his short life. He caught cold and suffered repeated hemorrhages. His brother hurried to his bedside. On Epiphany, January 6, 1852, foreseeing his end, Louis received communion, bid farewell to his family, then let go his tenuous hold on life. His students, overcome by the loss, made a death mask of his face and commissioned a bronze of their beloved teacher, but journalists, unaware of his potential greatness, made no mention of his passing in Paris newspapers.

Braille was buried in the churchyard of his hometown beside his father and sister Marie. There a commemorative plaque honored his contributions to blind readers: "He opened the doors of knowledge to all those who cannot see." The reading of his will confirmed his generosity to servants and students, whose indebtedness he nullified with gifts from his savings.

On June 20, 1952, a century after his death, his body was exhumed and buried among France's great heroes in the Pantheon, a massive national monument near the Seine River in Paris. The doorway immortalized Braille: "To its great men, the country gives honor" (DeGering, 128). But the skeleton of his right hand, with which he created a reading and writing system for blind persons, remains in the soil of the town square of Coupvray.

SOURCES

Ashcroft, S. C. *Programmed Instruction in Braille*. Pittsburgh, Pa.: Stanwix House, 1963.

Davidson, Margaret. *Louis Braille: The Boy Who Invented Books for the Blind*. New York: Scholastic, 1974.

DeGering, Etta. *Seeing Fingers: The Story of Louis Braille*. New York: David McKay, 1962.

Keeler, Stephen. *Louis Braille*. Great Lives Series. New York: Franklin Watts, 1986.

Koestler, Frances A. *The Unseen Minority: A Social History of Blindness in the United States*. New York: David McKay, 1976.

Chang and Eng Bunker

One of the most unlikely of anomalies was the life sentence of Chang and Eng Bunker, which joined them at the navel by a mysterious flexible bridge of living tissue. Known in Europe and the United States as the Siamese twins, they were, more correctly, the world's most famous conjoined twins, affectionately referred to as "the hyphenated brothers." Far from cripples, the boys titillated curiosity seekers with exhibitions of tumbling and badminton and feats of strength. Their oneness raised moot points with journalists, who debated in print whether the law allowed for the incarceration of a single twin, because jailing would wrongfully deprive an innocent man of freedom.

More significant than the quibbles raised by their lifelong tether was Chang and Eng Bunker's example of compromise and consideration in their ability to exist side by side for a normal lifetime. Not only did they exist—they thrived and became successful landowners, marrying sisters and rearing twenty-one children. At the end of their lives, which came within hours of each other, Chang and Eng passed into the history of North Carolina, where they had made their living among fellow farmers and spent their days with as much normalcy as they could manage.

A HUMBLE BACKGROUND

Chang and Eng, who maintained so close a relationship that they signed themselves Chang Eng, were born on May 11, 1811, on a Siamese riverboat in Meklong, sixty miles west of Bangkok. More nearly Chinese than Siamese, their mother, Nok, was one-quarter Siamese, and Ti-eye, their father, was Chinese. The fifth and sixth children in a family of nine, Chang and Eng were small at birth and entered the world one head first and one feet first with their bodies facing each other. Attendants at their birth hesitated to handle the boys, whom they considered a dire omen. Nok, more practical, twisted them into a face-to-face position and washed and fed them.

The twins' face-to-face position changed in time to a side-by-side arrangement. They lived in unique harmony, learned to run and swim in tandem, and helped with the family fishing business. When their father and five siblings died of cholera in 1819, the loss of a breadwinner forced Nok to try several methods of earning a living. At length, the twins, although they never attended school, assumed adult roles, became merchants, and sold ducks and preserved duck eggs at a high profit.

King Rama III sent for the famous twins, who journeyed upriver and briefly studied court convention so that they could make a favorable impression. Rama was so taken with the boys that he awarded them costly gifts, which they sold so that they could better utilize their windfall. Their lives, touched by wanderlust, remained forever changed by their experiences far from home. By their late teens, they were ready to make a permanent break.

INTO THE WORLD

Having made a deal with Robert Hunter, a Scottish trader, the twins requested their mother's blessing, then migrated to Boston from the familiar, comfortable world of their riverboat. In 1829, traveling aboard the *Sachem*, they weathered a four-month voyage with remarkable energy and enthusiasm and even climbed the rigging to view the sea from aloft. Newly arrived in the United States, Chang and Eng underwent detailed medical scrutiny, which determined that their restraining ligature was a primitive umbilicus that passed neurological messages from one body to another. Because of their rare closeness, the boys had little need of speech to relay thought and response. They lived like a single organism.

U.S. medical practitioners concluded that Chang and Eng were healthy and content with their daily compromises. Termed a *lusus naturae*, or freak, in scientific parlance, by age eighteen the conjoined twins weighed 180 pounds and possessed individuality in size, shape, and personality. Chang was more intelligent but less healthy than Eng, who had a more phlegmatic, contemplative nature. Chang stood five feet, three-and-a-half inches; Eng, an inch shorter, wore lifts to compensate for the difference in stature. A few consulting physicians proposed separating them, but the overwhelming vote was to leave them connected to spare them the physical and emotional trauma of so life-threatening a procedure as major surgery, which in those days was considerable.

Managed by Captain Abel Coffin and his wife, Susan, the twins soon moved about Boston as a curiosity. They and the Coffins earned a handsome sum from the showings. After three years, when public interest waned, the twins established their freak show in New York and Philadelphia and in major cities in Great Britain. For fourteen months, they toured Glasgow, Edinburgh, Liverpool, and London before returning to the United States. Along the way, they matured and mastered English as well as business. The upshot of their newfound adulthood was a quest for independence from grasping, chintzy managers.

HOME IN NORTH CAROLINA

When the tightfisted Coffins refused the twins' request for a raise for traveling expenses, Chang and Eng, suspicious that they were being defrauded, rebelled at the arrangement that kept them constantly traveling and performing for oglers and gawkers. In 1832, they hired Charles Harris as their manager and toured Europe. Returning to the United States in the late 1830s, the pair were still homesick for the

Orient. Their contact with Siam was limited to shreds of information from a sailor who reported that Nok had remarried a Chinaman, Sen, but had borne no more children.

While in residence at Peale's Museum, Chang and Eng met Dr. James Calloway, from Wilkesboro, North Carolina. His descriptions of the fine hunting and fishing in his home state lured the twins to a vacation that lasted a lifetime. In this genuine friend, they gained an advocate and adviser who helped them escape life as monstrosities and establish a nearly normal family and home.

With savings above $10,000, the twins retired, settled near Roaring River in the wilds of Wilkes County in 1839, and for a few short months operated a dry goods store. In October, their initial purchase of 150 acres of land at Trap Hill began their career as corn and hog farmers. That same month, they applied for citizenship. Because citizenship required a surname, they adopted the family name of Fred Bunker, a friend who happened to be in the government office at that time.

FINDING WIVES

While attending a wedding, the twins, who had long been the object of perverse sexual propositions and proposals of marriage, met sisters Sarah "Sallie" Ann and Adelaide Yates. Chang and Eng, heartened by the girls' sympathy for their aberration, discussed the unlikely possibility of marriage. Chang summarized the situation: "We are not responsible for our physical condition, and we should not have to die childless on that account" (Wallace and Wallace, 171). Their double courtship produced an engagement between Chang and Adelaide. Sallie, however, remained cool about Eng's proposal.

In time, Sallie acceded, opening the way for an announcement to the neighborhood of the four-way arrangement. Shock and consternation marked the faces of many who doubted that modesty would permit such a bizarre marriage. The Yates family forbade their daughters from carrying out their wedding plans, not because they objected to conjoined twins as sons-in-law, but because of distaste for miscegenation. At length, money and a sizable landholding enticed the Yates girls to buck family pressures and marry the Bunkers.

The betrothed men, having been joined for thirty-two years, decided that the best way to spend their remaining years was apart. Mindful that surgery might kill one or both, they returned to Philadelphia and conferred with doctors. Sallie and Adelaide, who learned secondhand that their fiancés were about to undergo a dangerous procedure, rushed in at the last minute and halted the operation. On April 13, 1843, with their parents' grudging okay, the girls married the Bunker brothers.

THE BUNKER DYNASTY

The unheard-of arrangement of four in a single honeymoon farmhouse raised no eyebrows among neighbors who had come to think of Chang and Eng as friends, not freaks. Well-wishers sent gifts and joined in a wedding celebration and dance. Within nine months, both wives bore daughters, Katherine and Josephine. By 1845, the two cousins were joined by two more, Julia and Christopher Wren. If intimacy presented a problem to the two Bunker couples, they obviously managed enough of a compromise to keep up a productive sex life, as demonstrated by the births of Stephen, James, Patrick, Rosalyn, William, Frederick, Rosella, Georgianna, and Robert to Eng and Sallie and Nancy, Susan, Victoria, Louise, Albert, Jesse, Margaret, and Hattie to Chang and Adelaide.

By the summer of 1845, the Bunker dynasty had outgrown its quarters. The Bunkers moved to Mount Airy, cleared undergrowth and boulders, and began farming by scientific method. Using slave labor, they planted tobacco, traded horses, and raised domestic animals and vegetables as well as gathered honey for their own table. By their mastery of carpentry, the Bunkers built a bigger farmhouse, built some of their furniture, and helped to fashion White Plains Baptist Church.

The lives of the Bunkers remained full. They took an interest in Southern politics, played checkers and chess, performed on the flute, read poetry, and gambled. They managed to ally a Buddhist upbringing with Southern fundamentalism yet remained handy with their fists and were on occasion hailed into court to settle a fracas. To the detriment of their relationship, Chang and Eng developed opposite penchants, Eng for late-night poker and Chang for alcohol. The brouhahas resulting from Chang's drunkenness created discontent in an otherwise harmonious existence.

INTO MIDDLE AGE

Chang and Eng improved their mutual fortunes with practical husbandry and attention to family life. They continued to chat with visitors and reporters while tending the farm. Scurrilous yellow journalism smeared their good names, particularly with accusations of slave beating, and they were forced into litigation in order to defend their reputations. In a letter to the Greensboro *Patriot* in 1852, they summarized their outrage: "Finally, in conclusion, we would like to say to your correspondent, that hereafter when he wishes to parade the character of private citizens before the public in newspaper columns, that his communication should at least have some semblance of truth" (Wallace and Wallace, 204).

Phrenologists examined the skulls of Chang and Eng and reported that the two men were well endowed with belligerence, violence, and secretiveness. The balance was a tendency toward charity and religiosity. Other findings included strong will, caution, closeness, appetite, and parental love. Less evident were conjugal love, language, acquisitiveness, hope, and spirituality.

The cost of supporting two large families eventually returned Chang and Eng to the sideshow circuit. Covering 4,700 miles of New England, the twins each brought along one child and remained in communication with the remainder of their families by letter. At the end of the tour, the men returned home to an armed camp, with Sallie and Adelaide squared off for a showdown over domestic control. The era of four to a bed had come to an end. The only solution was separate quarters and a shared conjugal relationship of three days at each location. Under the new system of tenancy, each twin functioned as host and silent partner, depending on which house he was in. This inflexible rule of head of the house remained in force for the remainder of the men's lives.

THE DEMANDS OF AGE

In 1860, the twins again faced monetary troubles and contemplated a journey to California, where they had never toured. From there they hoped to cross the Pacific to reunite with their mother and meet their stepfather. Then word reached them that Nok had died. Before finalizing plans to take a sternwheeler to Panama, cross the isthmus by train, then continue aboard the *Uncle Sam* to California, Chang and Eng signed on for a brief stint with P. T. Barnum at the American Museum in New York. While appearing on stage, they met Prince Edward, son of Queen Victoria.

Following a successful tour to San Francisco and Sacramento, on February 11, 1861, Chang and Eng set sail for home—just as the Civil War was taking shape. Chang's son Chris, who volunteered for duty in the Confederate Army, was taken prisoner and feared dead. Other calamities stripped the Bunkers of their accumulated wealth. They lost a total of thirty-three slaves and cash from loans to neighbors. The cataclysmic blow to their farm assets put Chang and Eng near bankruptcy. Slaves departed for freedom, then because of lack of employment, returned to their former masters, who hired them for wages. Added to these worrisome burdens were the deaths of two of Eng's daughters.

The twins' only resource lay in further tours, this time by railroad. Ups and downs of fortune continued to plague them. Their manager died. Midwestern turnouts were poor. Chang became ill. Both he and his brother worried about their families back home on the farm. To add to their woes, in 1867 Chang's favorite daughter died of a heart attack.

In time, receipts grew stronger, leaving Chang and Eng in a better financial situation than they had experienced during the war years. For several reasons, particularly the sickness of Kate, Eng's twenty-four-year-old daughter, and the increase in Chang's binges, the twins considered returning to Great Britain to tour and to seek medical help. They wanted not only to find a cure for Kate but, most important, to submit to surgery and end their fifty-three years of linkage.

LAST YEARS

The London doctors' reports failed to aid either Kate or her father and uncle. Compassionately, they urged Kate to accept the fact that she would die of consumption. The twins found no surgeon willing to guarantee the outcome of an operation stressing the peritoneal linings of either twin. The stoic troupe returned to the farm, laden with gifts for all, even the servants.

Chang and Eng, still intent on touring to support their families, ventured into the Midwest, then opted for an ambitious circuit through Germany, Spain, Italy, and Russia. Traveling with sons James and Albert, they cut short the itinerary after war broke out between France and Prussia. In 1870, aboard a transatlantic steamer bound from Hamburg, Germany, to New York, Chang suffered a stroke, which immobilized his right arm and leg. Chang's confinement forced Eng into inescapable invalidism.

The lifelong tether between the Siamese twins became doubly onerous with one failing and one vigorous twin. Their woes increased as Chang drank more heavily to compensate for his loss of health. The men, desperate for the first time in their aberrant yoking, came to blows. They made up before doing irreparable harm to their half-century of togetherness. The onset of bronchitis reduced Chang's last months to misery. Eng, still vigorous and wanting to be fully active, awakened on January 17, 1874, to find his twin dead beside him. He broke into a cold sweat from terror and died before a physician could arrive.

Even in death, the struggle continued. The wives rejected their doctor's suggestion of autopsy and feared that graverobbers would steal the conjoined corpses to exhibit in sideshows. They compromised on the issue of selling the bodies by leaving the final decision to the oldest sons. The boys chose a normal burial for their fathers. Fifteen days after the internment, the family changed their mind. They allowed the bodies to be exhumed, examined, and photographed. They were then repacked and shipped to the College of Physicians in Philadelphia, where an autopsy proved that because of a shared liver, the twins could never have survived separation.

SOURCES

Fowler, Gene, and Bess Meredyth. *The Mighty Barnum*. New York: Garland Publications, 1978.

Harris, Neal. *Humbug: The Art of P. T. Barnum*. Chicago: University of Chicago Press, 1981.

Tompert, Ann. *The Greatest Show on Earth: A Biography of P. T. Barnum*. Minneapolis: Dillon, 1987.

Wallace, Irving, and Amy Wallace. *The Two*. New York: Simon & Schuster, 1978.

Johnny Cash

The act of overcoming obstacles can carry with it a mystique, an aura of legend. Johnny Cash, a country-blues-rockabilly enigma dubbed the "man in black," wears that aura with diffident pride. Having overcome drug and alcohol addiction, he is obviously pleased with his musical success yet not completely at home with the frivolity of fame or adulation. In concert, he tends to rove the stage—tall, restless, raw-boned frame, hands nestling the microphone, head tilted down, and dark, haunted eyes peering up at his listeners. He makes no studied gestures, possesses no polished mannerisms. With his lined face and hard-pressed attitude, he gives the impression of a sincere backwoodsman uttering a painful truth.

Cash's craggy, stormy profile convinces most hearers that his words emerge from genuine torment, even when the song may bear no resemblance to his own circumstances. Many false tales circulate about lurid crimes he's committed or stretches he's served in Folsom Prison or San Quentin, both places he has performed. Obsessed with the dark side of life, his thousand-plus original works center on bums, saddle tramps, traveling men, ex-cons, addicts, dispossessed Native Americans, and other down-and-outers, many of whom abuse or cheat on their wives and girlfriends. To critics he denies a didactic purpose and professes to be no more than a country-music composer and singer. He once declared, "I'm no message bringer. Mostly I just tell stories" (*Current Biography*, 74).

ARKANSAS FARM BOY

Born on February 26, 1932, in a three-room frame house along the railroad tracks of Kingsland in Cleveland County, Arkansas, John Cash, son of Ray and Carrie Rivers Cash, descends from Scottish and Cherokee ancestors and two grandfathers who were fundamentalist ministers. The third son and fourth of seven children, including Roy, Louise, Jack, Reba, Joann, and Tommy, he enjoyed a loving relationship with his parents and Jack, the brother two years older than he who died of gangrene following a sawmill accident when Johnny was twelve. Throughout his adult life, he has made frequent reference to how much he misses his brother, the one member of the family who seemed destined for the ministry.

The Cash family's depression-era financial burden deepened at a time when Ray Cash had to supplement his failing income as a farmer with pick-up jobs in cotton fields, wood yards, and railroad camps. The family moved to a new white five-room house in the rich delta land near Dyess, Arkansas, in 1935. Because of the economic rehabilitation program for farmers during the period of Franklin D. Roosevelt's New Deal, they eked out their livelihood planting cotton and raising vegetables and livestock for home use.

Cash's early life was meager and humble, but adequate. In his memoirs, he rejects romanticized media fiction that depicts his rise to success as a rags-to-riches story. His share of farm chores, including watering and feeding the mules, cow, and pigs and hoeing and harvesting vegetables and cotton left him no time for after-school sports. At age fourteen, he found a job carrying water to railroad workers along the Tyronza River.

The Cash family had few luxuries such as electricity and got along without a car until 1947. To buy a ticket to a movie, John roasted peanuts and sold them to people outside the theater. His social life centered on the Road Fifteen Church of God, where a zealous minister and moaning sinners caused him to associate religion with fear. His only positive memory from these lengthy, emotional sessions of prayer, revival, and repentance were gospel hymns sung to the accompaniment of mandolin, guitar, and banjo.

A LIFE OF MUSIC

Like other impoverished hillbillies, Cash whistled gospel tunes and popular numbers sung by his favorite country stars, the Chuck Wagon Gang, Hank Williams, Eddy Arnold, Red Foley, Roy Acuff, and Ernest Tubb. He tuned in country music on the family's battery radio late at night after the rest of the family had gone to bed. Even though he understood nothing about musical notation, he composed melodies and lyrics to original songs. In his teen years, his tenor voice deepened to a steady, fervid baritone and began to show promise. Persistence and plenty of practice netted him a spot on a local radio broadcast and first place in an amateur contest.

After graduating from high school in June 1950, Cash joined the U.S. Air Force the next month, trained at San Antonio, Texas, and rose to the rank of staff sergeant as radio intercept operator in the security service at a German base. While in Europe, he relaxed by mastering the guitar he bought for five dollars and by fishing local streams, particularly the one flowing through Oberammergau. Newly introduced to youthful indulgences, he and his buddies, uninfluenced by the mores of their homeland, looked forward to three-day leaves, which they spent carousing. He gave up church attendance and learned to swear and drink German beer and cognac. Other wild carouses produced a crooked nose from brawling, a scarred face, and diminished hearing on the left side because a German girl poked a pencil into his ear.

On his return to the United States in 1954, Cash courted Vivian Liberto, whom he had met in San Antonio. Before their marriage, his future in-laws doubted that Cash's religious upbringing would fit in with their Catholic beliefs. He proved them wrong by receiving counseling from a priest and rearing his four daughters, Rosanne,

Kathleen, Cindy, and Tara, in the Catholic Church. Also, he made a sincere effort to give up the dissolute habits he had begun in Germany and to dedicate himself to family life.

While working as a traveling appliance and home-improvement salesman in a seedy section of Memphis, Tennessee, Cash longed to break into radio announcing, which he listened to in his '54 Plymouth. On the advice of a station manager, he used the GI bill to pay tuition at Keegan's School of Broadcasting in Memphis, which he attended part time. Eager to land a job as disk jockey, he studied news broadcasting and announcing.

In his mid-twenties, Cash joined with his brother Roy's friends, bass player Marshall Grant and guitarist Luther Perkins, in a country and gospel trio called Johnny Cash and the Tennessee Two. Because the group lacked a variety of coordinated outfits, they chose black as their trademark color. Their engagements ran to local gatherings and church appearances until they gained the ear of Sun Records' talent promoter Sam Phillips, who liked their sound.

MAKING A START

With Phillips's support, in June 1955 Cash and his musicians wrote and recorded a 78 record that became a modest hit — the railroad ballad "Hey, Porter" and a tearjerker, "Cry, Cry, Cry." Teamed with Elvis Presley, who was already a star, Cash began touring clubs and auditoriums in the southeastern United States, gradually working his way north as far as Canada. He perfected a singular opening: Appearing in swallowtail black coat, striped pants, and leather boots, he greeted his audience with "Hello, I'm Johnny Cash" (*Current Biography*, 74).

A spurt in Cash's career, augmented by regular television appearances on "The Grand Ole Opry," "American Bandstand," "Ozark Jubilee," and "Louisiana Hayride" and by the release of "Folsom Prison Blues" and his 1956 classic, "I Walk the Line," brought him to the nation's attention. Critics admired his direct, gutsy delivery; fans liked his brutal honesty. By age twenty-four, just as he had predicted in his boyhood, he had been labeled a leading composer and recording artist. He produced original songs for other singers and pushed his annual income to a quarter-million dollars.

The late 1950s solidified Cash's position among the great performers of country music. In 1959, he made a home for his family on a ranch in Casitas Springs near Ventura, California, that was a few miles from his parents' home in Ojai. He formed friendships with some of the big names in the business, particularly Waylon Jennings, Bob Dylan, Roger Miller, the Statler Brothers, Jimmy Dean, Roy Orbison, and Charlie Pride. His albums, *Bitter Tears, Songs of Our Soil, I Walk the Line, Johnny Cash at Folsom Prison, Ride This Train, Hymns,* and *Fabulous Johnny Cash,* an appearance at the Newport Folk Festival, and his single recording of "Don't Take Your Guns to Town" kept his name before the public, not only in the United States but also in Europe, Australia, and Japan. In addition to personal and televised appearances, he undertook roles in minor movies, including *The Night Rider, Hootenanny Hoot,* and *Five Minutes to Live,* none of which displayed much promise.

THE END OF GOOD TIMES

At the age of forty, Cash began to show evidence of too many performances, too much stress, too many drugs. In 1957 while touring with Ferlin Husky and Feron Young, he was introduced to bennies. A ready supply was available at any truck stop; they helped him feel more vibrant, less prone to stage jitters. By late 1959, he was hooked. He experienced twitches in his neck, back, and face. His wracked body responded with numerous symptoms: "My eyes dilated. I couldn't stand still. I twisted, turned, contorted, and popped my neck bones. It often felt like someone had a fist between my shoulder blades, twisting the muscle and bone, stretching my nerves, torturing them to the breaking point" (Cash, 93).

At home, the Cash family feared the change in him, especially when he mixed vodka or wine with amphetamines. By Christmas, he was too strung out to open gifts with the girls. After midnight, they could hear him pacing away the dark hours. Often he drove the streets at night to burn off excess energy, frequently endangering himself, pedestrians, and other drivers. Only exhaustion quieted him, leaving him depressed, guilty, and praying for strength.

The drug treadmill influenced Cash's artistry as well as his personal life, robbing him of a full voice and the will to perform. After each show he would rage out of control in his dressing area and smash guitars or furniture to vent unexpressed hostilities. Colleagues avoided mentioning his abuse of pills lest they provoke his anger. A fit of temper on the Grand Ole Opry stage, in which he broke footlights with one sweep of a microphone stand, cost him his job and humiliated him publicly. To combat his frustration at being banned from the mecca of country music, he drove away, wrecked his car, and woke up with a broken nose and splintered jaw. His immersion into dependence caused him to lose weight and to miss more show dates and recording sessions. In his words, he was alone with beer and drugs, pacing the floor, "trying to outwalk and outlast whatever demon was snapping at my heels" (Cash, 18).

Paranoid, Cash deviated further from his normal life-style. He lied and deceived, took daredevil rides in the California desert, and carried a gun as protection against the police and unknown people he mistakenly believed were plotting his ruin. He depended heavily on diet pills and tranquilizers to get him through his demanding tour schedule, even defrauding doctors to get prescriptions and attempting to burglarize pharmacies to assure his supply. In 1959 he was jailed for public drunkenness; on five other occasions he served sentences for cursing, fighting, trespassing, and disorderly conduct.

Cash was pulled further into the undertow of addiction. In 1965, on a drug-buying trip to Mexico, he was followed by a plainclothesman, then detained before his plane could taxi. On the ground, he was arrested for possession of an illegal supply of Dexedrine hidden in his guitar, suitcase lining, and a sock. He was handcuffed and jailed for one night in El Paso, Texas. This time, news of his degradation reached the media and embarrassed him before his colleagues, parents, and children. Two years later, Vivian, alienated and disgusted, divorced him.

FINDING JUNE

After Cash returned to Tennessee, the seven-year drug cycle ended with a renewed relationship with Ezra and Maybelle Carter, who gave him the use of a room, then moved into his house during the month it took him to recover from addiction. Onstage in London, Ontario, he proposed to their daughter, old friend and fellow performer June Carter, who was a child member of the Carter Family singers from 1939 to 1943, the years when Cash was most influenced by radio broadcasts of country music. In his autobiography he mused, "June was always an inspiration, and I just felt like I did a better job knowing she was in the wings" (Cash, 191). They married on March 1, 1968, in Franklin, Kentucky.

Life with June proved to be the stabilizer Cash needed. The couple made their home in the rugged hills of Hendersonville and toured Hamburg, Munich, Frankfurt, Glasgow, Dublin, and London before taking a private vacation in Israel, from which came his album *Johnny Cash in the Holy Land*. In fall 1968, he had achieved a signal honor—an invitation to sing at Carnegie Hall, where he packed the house. In January 1969, while on tour of military bases in Subic Bay and Saigon, he briefly returned to drugs and alcohol. The terrible resurgence of negative influences forced him once more to swear off substance abuse. By 1970, he had even kicked the cigarette habit, which he had started in boyhood.

Again a happy man, Cash began to reacquaint himself with his former pleasure in entertaining. With June's assistance, he strengthened his failing career, raising his annual income to $2 million. He toured the country, fortified by a documentary film, *Cash!*, which aired on public television on March 16, 1969. Six weeks later, he introduced his own television show on ABC-TV, which ended in 1971 because of too much network interference in his choice of material and guests. During this period, he was surprised to see "A Boy Named Sue" become one of his biggest and least-anticipated hits. Because of this upsurge in his popularity, his picture appeared on the covers of several national magazines. Following the birth of John Carter Cash on March 3, 1970, Cash, still high with the joy of the birth of his first son, received another honor—an invitation from President Nixon to sing at the White House.

In 1975, in nine months' time, Cash penned his autobiography, *Man in Black*. The book describes him as a changed man, dedicated to Christian principles, particularly the belief that drugs subvert God's path for human life. The opening chapter explains how his journeys to Israel and correspondence courses in the Gospels moved him toward the composition of religious music, closer relationships with his daughters, and the formation of more productive friendships. He crowned this era of mature reflection with *Gospel Road*, a filmed statement of his religious beliefs about the life of Jesus.

AWARDS AND HONORS

Cash's career as a recording artist, television personality, and composer has turned him into a country-and-western idol. In 1971, he received an honorary doctorate from Gardner-Webb College, followed in the mid-1970s by two honoraria from the National University in San Diego. For his best work he earned a Golden Plate Award, a Number One Hit Song Award, and, in 1980, inclusion in the Country Music Hall of Fame. He has also been named one of Columbia Records' five top recording stars.

As president of House of Cash, Inc., and vice president of Family of Man Music, Inc., he remains active in the music industry. His volunteer work involves him in worthwhile projects, especially the Peace Corps, the John Edwards Memorial Foundation, and the Country Music Association. His charitable works include a benefit for the South Dakota Sioux and the establishment of a burn center at Vanderbilt University in memory of his deceased colleague, Luther Perkins.

Kicking drug addiction has not been easy for Cash. Staying straight has required two-week relapse-prevention treatments following a stomach operation in 1983 and coronary bypass surgery in 1988. But he remains in control of self and career, which has taken a new turn toward the simple songs and delivery of his early days. With the publication of his album *Boom Chicka Boom* and the paring down of his entourage, he is as eager as ever to entertain with some of his early hits, such as "Ring of Fire" and "Jackson." With the simplicity that has become his trademark, he declared, "It really feels good to get back to basics" (Eck, n.p.).

SOURCES

Cash, Johnny. *Man in Black*. Grand Rapids, Mich.: Zondervan, 1975.

Current Biography. New York: H. W. Wilson, 1969.

Eck, Michael. "Cash Returns to Early Sound." *Times Union* (Albany, New York), November 18, 1989, n.p.

Griffin, William. "Johnny Cash." *Publishers Weekly*, October 3, 1986, 94-96.

Hefley, James C. "The 'Man in Black' at Fifty." *Christian Herald*, May 1982, 28-31.

Tomson, Ellen. "Johnny Cash Coming to Regal, Population 45." *Pioneer Press-Dispatch* (St. Paul, Minnesota), August 14, 1989, n.p.

Wyatt, Gene. "Didn't Want 'a Hell Like That Again.'" *Tennessean* (Nashville), December 10, 1989, n.p.

Max Cleland

Max Cleland's vita appears at first to be like the record of any hard-driving, ambitious politician. The list of his accomplishments speaks well for his youth and intelligence. He earned a bachelor's degree from Stetson University in 1964, fought in Vietnam with the Signal Corps for three years, and completed an M.A. at Emory four years later. He served in the Georgia senate from 1971 to 1975, then as Commissioner of Veterans Affairs in Washington, D.C., which led to a political appointment. While working as administrator of the VA from 1977 to 1981, he earned a doctorate.

What this list does not include is a description of Cleland's handicap—the loss of both legs and his right forearm from a grenade explosion. Through tours of the country and television interviews Cleland has attested to his Christian faith. He has championed the need for better hospitals and education benefits, pensions, death benefits, alcohol treatment centers, loans, and disability payments for other veterans from his post at the VA. He once explained his purpose to an interviewer as a public reminder of the price of war, or as Abraham Lincoln phrased it, "To care for him who shall have borne the battle" ("60 Minutes," 17).

THINKING POSITIVE

A native of Lithonia, Georgia, a few miles east of Atlanta in Dekalb County, Joseph Maxwell Cleland, born August 24, 1942, is the son of Juanita Kesler, a secretary, and Joseph Hugh Cleland, an auto-parts salesman. A handsome, ebullient six-footer with blue eyes and blond hair, he was blessed with a winning attitude from high-school days, when he excelled in academics and took part in band. A serious, intense athlete, he learned to shoot hoops with both his right and left hands.

After leading his basketball team in scoring and snagging a state junior tennis championship, Cleland lettered in basketball, baseball, swimming, and tennis. When he graduated in 1960, he received the *Atlanta Journal's* trophy for outstanding senior. After college studies in DeLand, Florida, he pursued a master's degree in U.S. history and political science, then interned in Congress before entering the army as a second lieutenant in the Signal Corps.

Cleland's military training was rigorous and thorough. He received basic training at Fort Benning, Georgia, then joined the paratroopers. His most significant training came at radio school at Fort Monmouth, New Jersey. Of his zest for this branch of the service, he proclaimed, "Air mobility is the wave of the future.... It is the way to fight a war of national liberation in the underdeveloped world" (Cleland 1986, 21). The thrill of partaking in this innovation in U.S. warfare filled him with pride.

At first, Cleland was passed over for service in Vietnam and was instead assigned as aide to Brigadier General Thomas M. Rienzi. Then the war escalated, testing U.S. loyalties. The seeming triviality of the stateside post weighed heavily on Cleland as he considered the sacrifice other U.S. soldiers were making on the front lines in a lengthening, dispiriting conflict. As he worded his frustration to a reporter, "It got to me, sitting behind my walnut desk and walking on two-inch carpets knowing less-trained guys were being drafted to fight in my place" (Denny, n.p.).

INTO THE ACTION

Cleland's second attempt to volunteer for battlefield assignment placed him in the 1st Air Cavalry, which was based at Fort Benning. He mobilized immediately after completion of work on his master's degree but before the degree was conferred. Literally whisked away with cap and gown in hand, he was eager for opportunities to apply military training in the field.

Going from classroom to battleground, Cleland found himself ready to fight in the central highlands of An Khe, where he volunteered for rescue missions to troops locked in a dicey extenuated ground offensive at Khe Sanh, thirty miles west of Hue on the border of Laos. For seven months, nothing special happened with his outfit. During the Tet offensive, Gleland was promoted to captain and moved to Hue as signal officer. After his men forged through thick rocket fire to aid wounded marines on April 1, 1968, he received the Silver Star.

Seven days later, only five weeks before he was slated to return home, Cleland, ranking signal corps officer, arrived by helicopter atop a mountain ridge east of Khe Sanh to set up a radio relay station. The chopper had just pulled away, leaving Cleland behind, when he noticed an unsecured grenade lying on the ground and thought it had fallen off his own gear. Reaching for the live grenade cost him full mobility for the rest of his life.

The Tet offensive, spurred by Communist hopes that a mass attack would lead to peasant revolt, dragged on for five horrendous weeks, killing 32,000 North Vietnamese, 2,000 South Vietnamese, and 1,000 Americans. Cleland, an accidental victim during that offensive, remained conscious and assessed the loss of his right hand, right leg, and left foot. Attempts to cry out were stifled by a shrapnel wound to his windpipe. Fortunately, flash burns stanched the loss of blood. Four medics leaped to his aid and applied tourniquets to the bloody shreds of his limbs. Morphine relieved him temporarily of sensation.

RECOVERY

The intense medical treatment that saved Cleland's life required five hours of surgery and forty-three pints of blood over a two-day period. By the time surgeons at the Quang Tri medical center, forty miles away on the coast northwest of Hue, completed their treatment, he had lost both legs above the knee. He was airlifted to the village of Thuy Hoa, where he suffered fever, intense thirst, and convulsing chills. The changing of bandages brought cruel waves of agony. At that point, he doubted that he would recover, but he managed to talk with his parents by shortwave, reassuring them that he intended to come home.

Cleland transferred to Yokohama, Japan, then flew the Arctic route through Anchorage to Washington's Walter Reed Hospital, where flashbacks and bouts of depression overwhelmed him. He had feared facing his family and friends and had sobbed on his way back to the United States. He was repulsed by the smell of his body, which could not be thoroughly cleaned until the stumps began to heal. Apprehensions about artificial limbs and addiction to painkillers floated through his mind. His doctor gave him little hope that he could manage without knees.

Cleland questioned himself relentlessly about the incident and heaped himself with blame for the loose grenade. In his autobiographical account of the healing phase, he admitted the gritty side of accepting life as a cripple: "Once it became apparent that I was going to live, the question became, 'Is life going to be worth living?' Yes, I thought about suicide" (Denny, n.p.).

Friends and family reintroduced Cleland to a full life. His parents took him out to dinner, where he was repulsed by the curious and pitying but accustomed himself to them. Joy, an old friend, visited him at the hospital, then extended their visits to short dates at hamburger joints. His first wheelchair brought mobility. A celebration at a nurse's quarters reintroduced him to feelings of worth. With real buoyancy, he commented, "I didn't think I had anything to offer. But apparently I did" (Cleland 1986, 75).

NEW LIMBS

Buoyed by a strong will to live and the comfort of Christian faith, Cleland insisted on being fitted with prostheses. Doctors at first urged him to accept life in a wheelchair, then granted him a try at "stubbies," or truncated artificial limbs, which are the only hope of amputees so severely impaired. In an article for the *Christian Herald*, Cleland described his sinking heart at the sight of the limbs: "They stood on the floor—grotesque, squat things. I couldn't believe they were to become a part of my body. They looked more like something from a medieval torture chamber" (Cleland 1981, 15).

Jim Cloud, the technician who assisted Max with the prostheses, himself an amputee, made Max's first experience with cold, manufactured replacement limbs as easy as possible. Max first applied wool socks to pad his stumps to protect them from injury. Then he swung monkey fashion from the helper's neck and aimed his legs into the gaping sockets below like six-guns into holsters. His first response was intense misery from the itch caused by vessels and nerve endings familiarizing themselves with the contact.

The brace that enabled Max to stand upright once more was an awkward affair crafted of balsa wood, metal braces, and a leather girdle. By leaning forward, resting on his buttocks, and exerting back muscles, he was mobile, but unstable. Part of his difficulty lay in a new center of gravity and the realization that he was kneeless and only four feet tall. The resulting gait lacked grace, but at least he was making headway on his first trek across the rehabilitation room.

From guarded first steps, Cleland moved to the parallel bars, which gave him the claustrophobic sense of bumping into the sides of a stall. He forged ahead, ignoring the bulkiness and inconvenience, and concentrated on the return to upright mobility. Covered with sweat, he relinquished his new limbs to the staff for needed adjustments and congratulated himself on the initial success.

Max later abandoned his replacement legs as too cumbrous and returned to his wheelchair, in which he became proficient owing to powerful manipulation from his beefy, muscular shoulders. During this period, he learned to adapt to apartment life in his furnished studio near the hospital and developed a sense of independence by swimming in the pool. The boost to his spirits moved him to greater challenges—an artificial arm, driving, then dancing.

Following a year and a half's worth of hospitals and rehabilitation clinics, Cleland became frustrated with the Veterans Administration's mechanical treatment, which he thought reduced him to a faceless number in a computer. In December 1969, he fought back against the dehumanizing bureaucratic process by testifying before an investigatory Senate committee chaired by Senator Alan Cranston. The thrust of Cleland's testimony aimed at the Vietnam veteran, who, in his words, "is more likely to have doubts about the validity of his sacrifice" (Cleland 1986, 121).

BACK TO NORMAL

Two years after the nightmare of learning to walk and to function with only one hand, Cleland won a seat in the Georgia senate, where he boosted interest in the struggles of the handicapped. With his help, public facilities were made more available to disabled citizens. But he was no single-issue senator. He also pushed for state education funds to supplement federal aid to veterans. His conscientious efforts brought him reelection in 1972.

Cleland's next political venture resulted in defeat. He ran for the post of lieutenant governor but lost in the 1974 Democratic primaries. In search of meaningful work, he opted for the Senate Committee on Veterans Affairs. As a watchdog over medical care, he toured VA hospitals around the country in his specially equipped Toronado and attempted to humanize services, which often bypassed the individual.

A major aim of Cleland's service to veterans was his insistence on counseling for returning soldiers. He rejected the melodramatic views of Vietnam vets and pursued better, more accurate media coverage of the issue of compassionate care. His one-man crusade for Vietnam veterans came to the attention of President Jimmy Carter, a fellow Georgian and old campaign buddy. In 1977, Carter named him Administrator of Veterans Affairs.

GETTING THERE

Suddenly, at the age of thirty-four, Cleland was catapulted to a major governmental post. In terms of people served, it was the second largest in the country, affecting 220,000 employees and 171 hospitals. He headed not only medical care but also pension, education, and insurance programs for five-and-a-half-million ex-soldiers. While making his troubleshooting rounds in the first six weeks in office, he had to ward off a bureaucratic push to dissolve the VA and reshuffle its duties to other governmental agencies. To substantiate his belief that the VA was by nature a unique contribution to U.S. health care, he supported his claims with reams of documentation. His enthusiasm for this public-service role nourished a plan for better care for alcoholics and innovative research into spinal-cord injury.

Cleland's administration met with its share of adversaries. Critics claimed that he lacked managerial background and that the $20 million budget overtaxed his experience. Still, he turned the country's attention to a situation that called for immediate action — the plight of returning Vietnam vets as well as the rising number of retiring World War II vets, who would soon swamp VA hospitals with their needs.

After the change of command in Washington that ousted Jimmy Carter and brought Republicans to power, Cleland left his administrative position and returned to Georgia. In 1982, he successfully ran against incumbent David Poythress for secretary of state and was reelected the following term. With this accomplishment, he became the youngest elected state official in the United States.

A USEFUL LIFE

A genuine wartime hero, Cleland, who lives alone in Washington, D.C., devotes his energies to his profession. He remains optimistic about his work and bolsters his health through regular water sports, wheelchair basketball, and physical-fitness training. Fiercely independent, he spurns a government limousine, drives a car, cleans and manages a one-room apartment, and can be found challenging neighborhood hoop shooters in afternoon games of basketball.

As might be expected, the nation has responded with warmth and pride to Cleland's accomplishments. He bears the Bronze Star and Soldier's Medal. He received the Distinguished Alumnus Award from Stetson in 1972. Other honors include the Greater Georgian Award from WSB Radio, Jefferson Award, U.S. Army Inspiration Award, AMP of the Year Award, Life Inspiration Award, Golden Key Award, Gold Medallion, American Patriot's Medal from the Valley Forge Freedom's Foundation, J. O. Wright Award, Neal Pike Award, Citizen of the Year Award, Jaycees Outstanding Young Man Award, and Outstanding Disabled Vet Award.

On September 25, 1977, Mike Wallace interviewed Cleland, the youngest person ever to head the Veterans Administration, on a segment of CBS's "60 Minutes."

Cleland closed his comments on the show with the recitation of a prayer written by an anonymous Confederate soldier:

I asked God for strength that I might achieve;
I was made weak that I might learn humbly to obey.
I asked for help that I might do greater things;
I was given infirmity that I might do better things.
I asked for riches that I might be happy;
I was given poverty that I might be wise.
I asked for power that I might have the praise of men;
I was given weakness that I might feel the need of God.
I asked for all things that I might enjoy life;
I was given life that I might enjoy all things.
I got nothing that I asked for, but everything I had hoped for.
Almost despite myself my unspoken prayers were answered.
I among all men am most richly blessed ("War Heroes' War Hero," 18).

His recitation brought bags of reader responses and over 5,000 requests for copies of the prayer, more than any other episode in the program's ten-year history.

The real test of Cleland's ability to overcome the loss of three limbs is his attitude, which acquaintances and staff describe as unfailingly upbeat. In his autobiography, *Strong at the Broken Places*, he borrowed Hemingway's belief that all people are broken by life and that some grow stronger at the "broken places." Cleland phrases his own version of that philosophy with simple logic: "Life doesn't revolve around an arm and a leg…. People look at you the way you look at yourself" (Rowan, 56).

SEEING THE SELF

In the introduction to his autobiography, Cleland explained that believing that strength can derive from weakness was a new concept for him. He stepped back from his own losses to view the overall tragedy of Vietnam. With nobility and perception, he concluded, "All of us who were part of that war have had to work out our own personal odyssey, our own readjustment back to this world" (Cleland 1986, 9).

Cleland, who maintains a close association with televangelist Robert Schuler, declares that even though some scars, like his three amputations, are obvious, others are invisible, striking victims in the heart. He admits that like any handicapped person, he envisions himself standing on two legs, a whole man, revitalized by sports and the sphere of activities that produce a sense of masculinity. He prides himself on turning pitying stares into full acceptance of himself as a man.

SOURCES

Cleland, Max. "Four Feet Tall." *Christian Herald*, March 1981, 15-18.

_____. *Strong at the Broken Places*. Marietta, Ga.: Cherokee, 1986.

_____. "The South Will Rise Again." *U.S. News and World Report*, January 19, 1987, 5.

Current Biography. New York: H. W. Wilson, 1978.

Denny, Dann. "Max Cleland: 'Strong at the Broken Places.'" *Bloomington Herald-Telephone*, November 2, 1986, n.p.

Rowan, Carl T. "Words That Give Us Strength." *Reader's Digest*, April 1987, 49-54.

"The War Heroes' War Hero." Transcript of an interview with Mike Wallace for CBS's "60 Minutes," September 25, 1977, 12-18.

Christina Crawford

At the age of thirty-nine, Christina Crawford, to rid herself of unbearable memories, wrote a book about her childhood, disclosing extensive personal trauma. In this public fashion, she tried to exorcise the specter of child abuse and adult treachery that burdened her until well into middle age. As the first of Joan Crawford's four well-publicized orphan adoptions, Christina bore a debilitating load of shame and recrimination for the perverse, crippling upbringing that she endured at the hands of an alcoholic and mentally unstable mother.

No matter how Christina reacted—loving or rebellious—she made no inroads against Joan's obsessive organization and crushing, senseless mistreatment. It was not until Christina weathered further adversity in the form of a stroke and divorce that she found a way to live with her memories. With knowledge gained from self-study, she developed a new self, one more capable of quelling the animosities of the past.

JOAN'S CENTERPIECE

The cast-off child of a student and a sailor, Christina was born July 11, 1939, and left Hollywood Presbyterian Hospital with a birth certificate indicating "girl." Still bearing the undefined look of infancy when Joan received her, she would one day develop into an ash blond, green-eyed beauty with rounded limbs and radiant health. Within a few weeks, she arrived at a professional adoption agency on North Bristol Avenue. With the help of underworld mogul Meyer Lansky, a year later, by her first birthday, she became the legal daughter of Joan Crawford, glamorous Hollywood film queen and relentless social climber.

After she was rejected by the Los Angeles County Bureau of Adoption as a suitable parent, Joan divorced her second husband, actor Franchot Tone. To assuage her loneliness and despair at being childless, she installed Christina in her Brentwood, California, home and carried her everywhere she went—to fittings, on the set, and to social events. Joan, pretentious with her love, surrounded her daughter with toys, clothes, and baby jewelry and hired the first of a series of full-time nurses, Aunt Kitty. As the center of Joan's world, Christina grew spoiled and self-centered and learned from infancy to perform for company.

At first, the child was named Joan Crawford, Jr., as her monogrammed towels displayed; then, to avoid confusion, she was renamed Christina and affectionately called Tina. Among Christina's playmates were James MacArthur, son of Helen Hayes, Shirley Temple, and the offspring of other screen stars. Her life with her doting mother was filled with carefully managed photographic moments in which mother and daughter sported matching outfits in velvet, organdy, or taffeta. The storybook quality of their smiles suggested a posed reality intended to impress fans. The frenetic fantasies created for Christina's birthday parties attested to Joan's attempts to give the impression of the perfect parent.

MONSTER MOTHER

Beneath the surface of this "idyllic" home life dwelled a truth that overwhelmed Christina. Lurking under the smiles and affability of Joan's public mask was an insecure, demon-ridden woman who demanded dominance over other people's lives, whether parent, child, husband, lover, agent, secretary, or servant. When Christina disappointed her, Joan whipped her soundly, then humiliated her. Once she forced her to wear a shredded dress for a week; another time, she tried to chasten her by locking her in a dark closet. In every instance of punishment, Joan twisted the child's words against her, making certain that Christina was at fault for every incident, however slight.

In 1942, Joan married actor Phillip Terry, who served actively as the child's stepfather. The next year, Joan and Phillip decided to adopt a boy, Phillip, three years Christina's junior, whom they renamed Chris. Christina grew fond of Chris, a fellow sufferer of Joan's violent temper tantrums. At times, Chris and Christina were dressed in similar outfits and wore white gloves while making public appearances. They shared lavish Christmas mornings heaped with packages and treats, but the reality of their lives with a demanding, insensitive mother belied the niceties displayed for the camera. By Christmas afternoon, most of the gifts were confiscated to be used as presents for other people.

In 1946, after Phillip left Joan, she tried to obliterate him from the children's lives by shredding and dismembering his image in family photos. To Christina and Chris, the message was clear: Mommie dearest was capable of destroying people who displeased or betrayed her. The message encouraged both children to avoid the same obliteration by staying on Joan's good side, whatever the cost. In later episodes, when Joan "developed" the children's sense of humor by ridiculing them, her brutal assaults on their self-worth caused them to feel vulnerable and helpless. Equally distasteful, her force-feedings made them gag on unappetizing foods. Christina, mournful and rebellious, longed to run away, but had nowhere to go and no one to turn to except an occasionally compassionate cook, gardener, or nurse.

MISERY

In 1947, Joan adopted Cathy and Cindy, whom she identified as twins but who bore little resemblance to one another. Christina realized the adoption broker's sham, but, cognizant of Joan's ability to turn a harmless statement against her, wisely kept her observations to herself. The arrival of two more children failed to relieve the prison camp atmosphere of the house, which Joan commanded like a warden. Christina characterized it bitterly: "This was Mommie's house, to be run entirely on her orders, for her personal convenience. No one else had any rights, no one else had any say in what went on or how things were to be done" (*Mommie*, 47). If Christina infringed on her mother's domain, she could expect a painful spanking, which often broke the hairbrushes, yardsticks, and wooden hangers Joan struck her with.

Other wretched memories that haunted Christina's childhood were the nighttime cleaning raids that Joan conducted unannounced. With no warning, she raged into the room that Christina shared with her brother, ripped their clothes from the closets, and hurled garments at the wall, often finding no more damning evidence than wire hangers brought in with the dry cleaning. Muttering vengeful imprecations, she tore bedding from mattresses, then, in an equally inexplicable tirade, stalked out of the room and slammed her door, leaving two sleepy children to cope with the mess. These unforeseen episodes, accompanied by screaming, slapping, and hair pulling, terrified Christina and left her helpless to cope with her crazed mother.

Other perversities set Christina and her brother apart from normal children. Both Chris and Christina were forbidden to get out of bed without permission, even to go to the bathroom. Chris, long past the infant stage, was secured to his bed by a harness held together by an oversize safety pin, which inhibited him from getting up without assistance. Christina grew cunning enough to circumvent Joan and allow Chris a moment's freedom, carefully timed so that she could refasten him in the contraption before Joan returned to discover their disobedience.

In similar fashion, Joan degraded nine-year-old Christina by forcing her to scrub Joan's dressing room, then tearing into Christina's room late at night to complain about the work. When Christina thoughtlessly commented that she saw no fault with the job, Joan beat her over the head with an open can of cleanser and commanded her to clean up the powdery residue. Christina, laboring until daybreak to remove the fine particles without a vacuum cleaner, longed to vanish into the earth as a respite from her misery.

To compound the chaos in the Crawford household, Joan, a reclusive alcoholic, began to drink more heavily. At times, Christina found her passed out and, with the help of the nurse, dragged her mother to bed. Hired help, many of whom were incompetent and apathetic, worked short terms before quitting on the spot in disgust. More and more chores and responsibilities fell to Christina, who even mixed drinks for her mother's string of lovers, each of whom Christina was instructed to call "uncle." Adding to Christina's unrest was Joan's mistreatment of Chris, brought on by her distrust of men. When the boy reached adult size at age fifteen, Joan banished him from the house and scarcely mentioned his name, even while he served as a soldier in Vietnam.

During one episode, Joan, sodden with drink, lost control after lying to a friend that Christina had been expelled from school. When Christina bridled at the blatant falsehood, Joan grabbed her about the throat and pummeled her to the floor. Child abuse had become attempted murder: "Her mouth was twisted with rage and her eyes—her eyes were the eyes of a killer animal, glistening with excitement. I gasped for air and felt myself sinking into unconsciousness as I tried desperately to fight back, to free myself." (*Mommie*, 160).

After a secretary intervened and pulled Joan away so that Christina could breathe, Joan locked Christina into small servants quarters and summoned a juvenile officer. The kindly man, who realized too well the duress Christina faced, questioned her and learned the whole story about the lie and the beating. Unable to combat Joan's studio clout, he urged Christina to bear the mistreatment as best she could to prevent future episodes. The only alternative was a home for incorrigible girls, which she certainly did not deserve.

AWAY FROM JOAN

In some respects, particularly the time she spent away from Joan, Christina's childhood resembled that of other children. During these growth years, she participated in Brownies and Girl Scouts, learned to swim, attended camp, rode horseback, infrequently attended Sunday school at the Christian Science Church, visited her grandmother, and played in piano recitals. Her school experiences were first rate: a West Los Angeles elementary school, where she skipped segments of two grades because of her excellent scholastic performance, followed by Chadwick, a boarding school in Palos Verdes, which she entered in February 1950.

Under the care of Mrs. Chadwick, the headmistress, Christina found some relief from the insufferable regulations and draconian punishments she knew at home. Still, the normalcy of living in the girl's dormitory was disrupted when Joan punished her for a tiny infraction by carrying off all of her clothes, except for two plain dresses. Christina, clad in coat, cotton dress, and wornout shoes, garnered the sympathy of most of her classmates and teachers, who realized the grotesque nature of her life at home.

Because Joan sensed how important the Chadwicks had become to Christina, she transferred her daughter to Flintridge Sacred Heart Academy, a Catholic convent school outside Pasadena. Under the supervision of the sisters, Christina was treated like a prisoner in solitary confinement and served a lengthy purgatory for deception, unruliness, and other crimes she did not commit. Her mother continued to coerce her into servitude and penance by threatening to cancel college tuition payments if Christina demonstrated the slightest bit of independence.

Christina graduated from Flintridge, then developed her acting and communication skills at Carnegie-Mellon University and the Neighborhood Playhouse Professional School. From ages eighteen to thirty-three she modeled and took acting jobs in summer stock, performing in *Barefoot in the Park*, her first film, in 1960, the soap opera "Secret Storm," and guest spots on "Marcus Welby, M.D.," and "Sixth Sense."

On May 20, 1966, she married and reestablished herself in her mother's love. Joan, by then widowed seven years after a four-year marriage to Pepsi Cola magnate Alfred Steele, revealed her inner fears about money, even though she had done well with *Whatever Happened to Baby Jane?*, a 1962 box office hit.

Christina, after divorcing her husband in Mexico, failed to keep her career alive. Still haunted by her mother's cruel manipulations, yet helpless to circumvent the power her mother wielded over her, she returned to school and earned a bachelor's degree from UCLA in 1974 and a master's degree the following year from the Annenberg School of Communications at the University of Southern California.

ESCAPING JOAN

By trial and error Christina made a normal life for herself. She found work in public relations first at a large company producing films and videos, and then for Getty Oil. On February 14, 1976, in Palos Verdes, she married David Koontz, a writer/advertising producer who hired her to do stunt driving for a Chevrolet commercial. They honeymooned in Hawaii, then settled in Tarzana, California. With David's help, she launched her own communications firm.

Joan Crawford died of heart failure on May 10, 1977, in New York. Christina stood alone with her mother's anorexic corpse and wept out of frustration and an unfulfilled desire to be loved by her mother. Across time and space, Joan reached out one more time to upbraid Christina and Chris by cutting them out of her will. The characteristic vindictiveness left Christina wondering how so intense a hatred could survive in the face of the intimacy they had shared in more recent times. In her reflections, Christina wrote, "Throughout all our years together, I was never absolutely sure of the reception I was going to get from her. I never knew whether it would be a big hug of loving affection or a verbal slap in the face" (*Mommie*, 13).

Mommie Dearest, Christina's best-selling 1978 autobiographical exposé of her wretched childhood, brought a stronger reaction than she expected. In her own mind, it was a release from the hell of "unresolved helplessness" (*Survivor*,). The fight against secret sufferings gave her the courage to launch an unsuccessful suit contesting Joan's will. During the lengthy proceedings, a publicity tour to England brought Christina to the brink of exhaustion. By 1981, the Paramount movie version of *Mommie Dearest*, starring Faye Dunaway, preceded an avalanche of interviews with radio and television talk shows and pushed Christina into the capacity of advocate for victims of child abuse.

Following a stroke in 1981, Christina found herself bedfast and dependent on David to compensate for aphasia and paralysis in her right hand. The diagnosis confirmed her suspicions: Her life had been too tightly laced with tension and stress, all of which came flooding back during her reassessment of the past. After dangerous tests and surgery, she returned home in August and began searching for a method of living with her memories. Bound for Europe aboard the cruise ship *Norway*, she realized that David was drifting from her and that divorce was inevitable. Once more alone, she felt defenseless and out of control.

Gradually, Christina reshaped her life, in part through her reliance on homeopathy and encounter groups, as well as baptism into the Episcopal Church. Writing for *TV Guide, Ladies' Home Journal,* and *Redbook* helped her work off some of her inner turmoil. In 1988, she published an updated account of her nightmares of child abuse in *Survivor,* the book she dedicated to "friends and teachers in all realities who have seen me through past years of painful chaos so that we may share together this present time of healing and happiness" (*Survivor,* 5).

Living in Los Angeles, Christina finds contentment at her ranch in San Luis Obispo, where she tends her favorite Appaloosa, Pappy. She has served as county commissioner of Children's Services and Dependency Court and received recognition for her work in child abuse prevention. On the personal side, she has reestablished her link with Phillip Terry, her first adoptive father. Their shared warmth has helped her cope with her distrust of people, a maladjustment dating to age six when her mother first subjected her to mental torture. She concluded *Survivor* with a positive outlook: "Where I had been used to seeing the world as a confrontation, now my course was to learn trust in the quality of the universe itself.... What began to emerge, after the very painful and confusing clearing process, was a new life" (*Survivor,* 263).

SOURCES

Crawford, Christina. *Mommie Dearest.* New York: William Morrow, 1978.

_____. *Survivor.* New York: Donald I. Fine, 1988.

Frederick Douglass

Many impassioned speeches about human life refer metaphorically to the burden of slavery, even though few people know it firsthand. One of the most sensitive witnesses to the ignominy of the slave trade was Frederick Douglass, who left a record of the misery it caused in his autobiographical works. A bright, articulate firebrand, he stirred audiences with his personal remembrances and helped launch the avalanche of abolitionism that fostered the revolt against slavery in the United States. With similar zeal, he advised five presidents and expanded his human-rights efforts to the incipient fight for women's rights. Immortalized by C. W. Chesnutt and Booker T. Washington, he exemplified the rigors of slavery as well as indomitable courage and ambition.

FROM SLAVE BOY TO EDUCATED MAN

Born into slavery in a cabin in a stand of woods in Talbot County near Tuckahoe, Maryland, on the Atlantic shore, Frederick Augustus Washington Bailey could only estimate his birth date as sometime in February 1817, although recent evidence suggests 1818 as the actual year. He resented the lack of information about his past, which his master, Captain Aaron Anthony, did not allow him to question. Douglass's only clue to his age came from an unguarded remark by his master.

Douglass named a very dark slave woman, Harriet Bailey, as his mother. His maternal grandparents were Isaac and Betsey Bailey, both black; his father was probably Captain Anthony, although no data exist to establish the fact. As Douglass explained in his narrative, the social situation allying the master-father with his slave-child was complex and generally unfavorable for the child. To stave off complaints of partiality and sibling rivalry and to spare the feelings of his white wife, the master frequently sold his black offspring to buyers who lived far from his own home.

As was the custom, Douglass was separated in infancy from his mother, who was sent twelve miles away to work for a Mr. Stewart. Her only means of communicating with her son was by walking the whole distance after dark following her day's toil. For six years, Douglass lived in his grandmother's cabin on the periphery of the plantation, then near Easton on Chesapeake Bay; part of the time he spent as houseboy at Wye House. He was often hungry and battled Nep, the dog, for kitchen scraps.

His mother died by the time he was eight; because she was so distant from his life, he suffered no grief at her passing.

Douglass recalled that Captain Anthony's holdings were small, amounting to two or three farms and thirty slaves. The overseer, a vicious drunkard named Plummer, ruled over his charges with lash and cudgel and, like Anthony, was insensitive to slave sufferings. From childhood, Douglass witnessed the savage beatings Anthony and Plummer ordered against male and female slaves alike.

A CHANGE FOR THE BETTER

Douglass later lived in the Fells Point district of Baltimore and worked in the home of Captain Hugh Auld as houseboy. In an urban setting, Douglass discovered that city owners dared not abuse slaves lest they incur the disapproval of sensitive neighbors and stir up antislavery feeling. His life improved with better food and clothing and more opportunities to move about than he had known on the plantation.

At age eight, Douglass experienced an unusual educational opportunity. In a society where educating a slave was against the law, his altruistic mistress, a weaver by trade, taught him his letters and a few simple words. Auld interceded and warned his wife that such knowledge would spoil a good slave: "A nigger should know nothing but to obey his master—to do as he is told to do.... If you teach that nigger how to read, there [will] be no keeping him" (Douglass, 237).

In spite of Auld's interdiction, Douglass continued his studies on his own, for he perceived that a full life required a better preparation than the one offered by his master. He became his own language teacher by snatching bits of learning from conversations with neighboring white schoolchildren, some of whom he bribed with bread. In private, he pored over "The Columbian Orator," a compendium of popular declamation that cost him fifty cents and contained a dramatization of a slave arguing against enslavement with his master. From these readings grew Douglass's consuming interest in human rights, which formed the nucleus of his adult activism.

As Auld had predicted, Douglass's blossoming scholarliness sowed the seeds of discontent. Ambivalent toward his status, he commented, "I would at times feel that learning to read had been a curse rather than a blessing. It had given me a view of my wretched condition, without the remedy" (Douglass, 241). While in this confused state, he studied the meaning of abolition and read a city paper describing the antislavery movement.

While observing carpenters at Durgin and Bailey's shipyard, Douglass set himself to learn to write. His intention was clear—to be ready to snatch freedom when the time came by writing his own pass. By tracing letters on the sides of ships and tricking white boys to outdo his command of letters, he developed his skill. He practiced on fences, walls, and pavement with a lump of chalk, copied from a spelling book, and filled in blank spaces in the master's son's copybook.

FROM SCHOLAR TO FIELD HAND

Douglass passed on to the service of Thomas Auld of St. Michael's, forty miles south of Baltimore. Auld farmed him out to a wily, pitiless overseer, Edward Covey, on January 1, 1833. Douglass was remanded to field labor on the plantation near Chesapeake Bay, where he performed poorly and suffered the lash. Farm drudgery weighed heavily; as he described it: "I was broken in body, soul, and spirit. My natural elasticity was crushed, my intellect languished, the disposition to read departed, the cheerful spark that lingered about my eye died; the dark night of slavery closed in upon me; and behold a man transformed into a brute!" (Douglass, 247).

The crucial confrontation with authority came on a day when Douglass collapsed while fanning wheat. Knocked in the head with a slat for his recalcitrance, he left the farm and complained to his owner. Douglass, failing to win his sympathies, returned to Covey and defied him. The overseer was cognizant of his adversary's height and broad shoulders yet challenged him, then ended their fight after two hours. Their set-to, the turning point in Douglass's internment as a slave, rekindled his waning sense of self.

On Christmas Day, 1834, Douglass was sent to work for William Freeland. In better circumstances, Douglass opened a Sabbath school to teach fellow slaves to read. Even in good times, throughout his teen years, escape had dominated his thinking. On Good Friday, 1833, he had made an abortive plan to paddle a canoe seventy miles across Chesapeake Bay. He and four companions were betrayed and apprehended on the day they were to leave. For his pains, Douglass, the leader of the insurrection, was locked in solitary confinement in the county jail in Easton.

Captain Auld considered Douglass too valuable for common labor and, promising to free him at age twenty-five, sent him to live with Hugh, Auld's brother, in Baltimore, where he undertook shipyard work. Under the tutelage of William Gardner, he served a team of carpenters but received a savage beating that endangered the sight of his left eye. Hugh Auld removed Douglass from Gardner and placed him in the charge of Walter Price, who taught him to caulk a ship.

A skilled worker, Douglass thrived. He was allowed to run his own operation and make his own contracts. His expertise brought him the highest wages, sometimes nine dollars a week. Still, he had to turn his wages over to Auld, a requirement that left him more determined to break out of servitude.

HIS OWN MASTER

On September 2, 1838, Douglass quarreled with Auld over money, then made his move. Carrying seventeen dollars and phony papers identifying him as a freedman sailor, he boarded the northbound train, changed in Wilmington to a boat headed for Philadelphia, then pressed on by night train to New York, where David Ruggles, secretary of the Vigilance Committee, assisted his escape. In New York City, Douglass reunited with his fiancée, Anna Murray. The two were married by a former slave, then moved to New Bedford, where he escaped detection by adopting the surname Douglass from the hero of Sir Walter Scott's *The Lady of the Lake*.

For three years, Douglass sequestered himself and worked as a common laborer. A liberated man at last, he continued to yearn for his Southern homeland, which he called his "own dear native soil" (Wilson and Ferris, 206). A noted humanist and social engineer, he read William Lloyd Garrison's abolitionist journal, the *Liberator*, the impetus for his radicalization. Among the sentiments they shared was their mutual distaste for the "back to Africa" movement.

In 1841, while accustoming himself to freedom, Douglass joined the Massachusetts Anti-Slavery Society and, in Nantucket, despite public harassment and threats of violence, demonstrated before 500 hearers the persuasive extemporaneous speaking talents that distinguished him as one of the great orators of the age. Freed from grueling day labor, he accepted the post of society agent. A handsome, commanding stage presence, he often stood at the Worcester pulpit, where Charles Dickens, Matthew Arnold, Ralph Waldo Emerson, Abraham Lincoln, and Henry David Thoreau had spoken.

By recreating scenes from slave life, over a period of four years Douglass roused audiences to denounce slavery and demand its abolition. Proslavery factions associated him directly with the violation of slave owners' rights. His notoriety brought frequent beatings, one in Pendleton, Ohio, where rowdies crushed the bones in his right hand. Despite these setbacks, within seven years, he delivered over 650 addresses. His evangelistic power swept thousands of converts into abolitionist activism. He polished his syntax so thoroughly that some hearers doubted that he had ever been a slave.

WITNESS TO SLAVERY

Proof of Douglass's past came in his best-selling memoir, *Narrative of the Life of Frederick Douglass, an American Slave* (1845), which sold 30,000 copies in five years and was followed by more reflective views in *My Bondage and My Freedom* (1855) and *Life and Times of Frederick Douglass* (1881), an upgraded version of his original autobiography, which he expanded again in 1892. This admission of names, dates, and facts took courage, for disclosure left him open to reenslavement under the Fugitive Slave Law. On the strength of these superb slave narratives, he established his credentials as the greatest black emancipationist of the nineteenth century.

Douglass toured Great Britain and assured his safety from bounty hunters through the intercession of British supporters willing to put up $700 for his manumission. While enjoying the acceptance of English liberals, he perceived the importance of economic and spiritual equality. Safe at last from bondage, in 1847 he returned to the United States and settled in Rochester, New York.

Remaining firmly entrenched in the antislave movement, Douglass expended much of his personal wealth in helping fugitives escape, many of whom he conducted personally to Canada. Part of his lecture fees underwrote the Rochester branch of the Underground Railroad. During the uproar over the Harpers Ferry raid in Virginia in

October 1859, Douglass was linked to the raid because of monetary dealings with John Brown; Douglass eluded arrest as an accomplice by fleeing to Canada.

As a part of his philanthropy, he considered opening a trade school for Negroes but chose as more practical the founding of an abolitionist newspaper, the *North Star*, which British supporters underwrote with a donation of $2,175. The journal remained in circulation for seventeen years, appearing as *Frederick Douglass' Paper* in 1851, then as the *Douglass Monthly* in 1859. The masthead of his paper blazoned his indomitable stand: "Right is of no Sex — Trust is of no Color — God is the Father of us all, and we are all Brethren" (Miller, 209).

Philosophically, Douglass was sophisticated and multifaceted. In 1848, he demonstrated his dedication to the cause of women by attending the first women's-rights convention. Likewise, he championed temperance and nonviolence. His support for the abolition of slavery moved him out of the Garrison camp toward the Republican party and the Constitutional Abolitionists, who were gaining strength. As repayment for his patronage, postwar candidates rewarded him with federal appointments, which raised him to the highest government rank ever held by a Black.

WITNESS TO CHANGE

When war broke out between North and South, Douglass, who proclaimed the bloodshed a necessary crusade against evil, pushed for Black regiments in the Union Army and helped recruit men for the 54th and 55th Massachusetts Colored Regiments, including some of his own five children. His involvement in the war effort earned so much praise that President Lincoln consulted with him concerning the use of Negro soldiers. His advice to Lincoln was to arm slaves and make a frontal assault on human bondage.

In 1865, Douglass realized that the battle for freedom was only just begun by Lincoln's Emancipation Proclamation. Douglass answered many questions about racial inequality with his famous speech, "What the Black Man Wants," delivered in Boston to the annual meeting of the Massachusetts Anti-Slavery Society. His dramatic oratory poured out in heartfelt cadence: "By depriving us of suffrage," he challenged, "you affirm our incapacity to form an intelligent judgment respecting public men and public measures; you declare before the world that we are unfit to exercise the elective franchise, and by this means lead us to undervalue ourselves" (Miller, 210).

Douglass's rallying cry called not for pity but for justice, as demonstrated by massive reform in education, prisons, sexual equality, labor, temperance, and voting rights. During Reconstruction, he continued to assist his race in fighting the oppressive Jim Crow laws, which supplanted the Civil Rights Act of 1875 and sanctioned discrimination in theaters, hotels, and public conveyances. As a personal defiance, he ignored Whites Only signs and wrote heated antidiscrimination letters to leading newspapers. After his intensity was diminished by greater opportunities for Blacks, he continued to travel and lecture on U.S. ideals, notably the self-made man, one of his prime topics.

In 1871, Douglass established a home in Washington, D.C., edited the *New National Era*, and accepted the presidency of the Freemen's Bank. Over a period of fifteen years he served as Santo Domingo's under secretary, as marshal and recorder of deeds in the District of Columbia, then as U.S. ambassador to Haiti, a post he resigned because of his adverse reaction to Caribbean heat. He moved to Cedar Hill in Washington, D.C., in 1877, where he lived out his remaining years.

A LIFETIME OF COMMITMENT

Douglass pursued his ambition to make a more hospitable world for free Negroes. In 1883, at age sixty-six, he addressed the National Convention of Colored Men in Louisville. His message decried the mockery of emancipation, which only dangled freedom before the eyes of former slaves. Blending Jefferson's and Lincoln's precepts, Douglass concluded: "We hold it to be self-evident that no class or color should be the exclusive rulers of this country. If there is such a ruling class ... this Government of the people, by the people and for the people will have perished from the earth" (Ravitch, 174).

In 1884, two years after Anna's death, Douglass stirred controversy by marrying Helen Pitts, his forty-five-year-old white secretary. They enjoyed a year of happiness on an extensive European tour. Still active in the cause of women's liberation, he fell dead from heart failure following a suffrage rally on February 20, 1895, and was buried in Rochester's Mount Hope Cemetery. His pallbearers included a Supreme Court judge and two U.S. senators. A commemorative statue stands in Highland Park; the Maryland Historical Society raised a second monument on Route 328 at the Tuckahoe Bridge.

In Douglass's honor, Elizabeth Cady Stanton, spokesperson for the women's-rights movement, penned a moving tribute: "Frederick Douglass is not dead! His grand character will long be an object lesson in our national history, his lofty sentiments of liberty, justice, and equality, echoed on every platform over our broad land, must influence and inspire many coming generations" (Miller, 209).

SOURCES

Douglass, Frederick. "Narrative of the Life of Frederick Douglass, an American Slave." *Black Voices*. New York: New American Library, 1968, 231-269.

Miller, James E., Jr., Kerry M. Wood, and Carlota Cárdenas de Dwyer, eds. *The United States in Literature*. America Reads Series. Glenview, Ill.: Scott, Foresman, 1987.

Quarles, Benjamin. *Frederick Douglass.* Great Lives Observed Series. Englewood Cliffs, N.J.: Prentice-Hall, 1968.

Ravitch, Diane, ed. *The American Reader.* New York: HarperCollins, 1990.

Wilson, Charles Reagan, and William Ferris. *Encyclopedia of Southern Culture.* Chapel Hill: University of North Carolina Press, 1989.

Mary Baker Eddy

After many years of excruciating pain, Mary Baker Eddy discovered not only relief for her body but, out of her experience with suffering, created a full-fledged religion of metaphysical healing that promised health to all sufferers. Having run the gamut of orthodox healers, homeopaths, hydropaths, and assorted quacks, she interpreted scripture from the point of view of an invalid and concluded that the spirit was the true healer of those in physical pain. Restored to vigor, she devoted her life to helping others seek health through the Christian doctrine of infinite goodness.

Eddy hoped to revitalize existing Christian denominations with her new philosophy; frustrated in this enterprise, she deduced that she needed a fresh look at religious organization and practice. After a shaky beginning, her church, Christian Science, founded in 1879, thrived in urban, scholastic, and residential centers; its 3,500 branches extended to over fifty-seven countries; its philanthropies aided catastrophe victims. Appealing mostly to middle- and upper-middle-class Americans, the church relied on a trained staff of teachers and practitioners, still adhering to the philosophy of its founder, a pioneer in harnessing the mind to cure the body.

A FOCUSED IDEALISM

Eddy, an intellectual and idealist whose desire to excel was constrained by delicate health, achieved through purity, contemplation, unselfishness, and noble purpose. In reflection, she wrote: "From my very childhood I was impelled, by a hunger and thirst after divine things—a desire for something higher and better than matter, and apart from it—to seek diligently for the knowledge of God as the one great and ever-present relief from human woe" (Powell, 52-53).

A native of Bow, five miles from Concord, New Hampshire, Mary Morse Baker Eddy was the youngest of six children—Martha, Samuel, George, Abigail, and Albert—born to Mark and Abigail Ambrose Baker on July 16, 1821. She was plain but appealing with slender form, reddish-brown curls, and sparkly blue eyes. A chronic spinal ailment early in her life, which was never fully described in her biographies, kept Eddy from completing her education. The family doctor urged her father not to allow her abundant intellect to overtax her physical capabilities. The invalid nine-year-old obeyed her father's exhortation to gain intellectual stimulus by studying and revering the Westminster Catechism. She depended on the tutelage of her older brother, Albert, a Dartmouth student knowledgeable in Greek, Latin, Hebrew, philosophy, and ethics. He became her idol and cohort; his word carried great weight.

With this home training as a foundation, Eddy, an obvious prodigy, read on her own and wrote extensively but never became a strong speller. Her personal tastes in subject matter inclined toward manners, morality, and patriotism, as shown by her comments in the margins. She also enjoyed reading aloud and discussing with her well-read father notable current events such as the abolitionist movement.

Unlike most young New England intellectuals, she disdained the theater and took no interest in the arts. Her pious family supplemented her study with fervent prayer and Bible reading, which became her mainstay during bouts of illness. Completely attuned to a godly calling, like Joan of Arc, she reported hearing heavenly voices.

From childhood, despite a dependency on doctors to treat her delicate body, Eddy demonstrated her ability to think for herself, particularly in matters of conscience. She avoided the gray areas of morality and adhered to simple black and white. She challenged her father's strict Calvinism, particularly the notion that a large portion of humanity was damned because it did not belong to the elect. Choosing to follow her mother's more humane example, she evolved a deep religiosity. At age seventeen, she demonstrated her sophistication by contesting the doctrine of the Congregational church she sought to join.

Married to contractor and builder George Washington Glover in 1843, Eddy sailed south from Boston to her new home in Charleston. Under a pseudonym, she published her abolitionist opinions in the local papers. She protested local slave ownership and urged her husband to manumit his servants. Before Glover could accede, he contracted yellow fever during a business trip to Wilmington, North Carolina, and died in her loving, prayerful care. While settling his estate, she freed the family slaves.

Eddy returned to New England before the birth of her first child, George, Jr., in September 1844. His difficult birth endangered her life; she also suffered from separation from the baby, whom she was too ill to care for. Her father, to lessen his daughter's anguish, spread straw outside the house to muffle the sounds of traffic and rocked his daughter as tenderly as though she were an infant. The loss of her mother in 1849 and the subsequent arrival of a stepmother deepened her emotional trauma.

On her own with no inheritance, Eddy taught school and wrote part time for a local newspaper. She could not afford to keep George, who boarded in Groton with his former nanny, and went to live with her sister Abigail. Because she and Abigail quarreled over the issue of slavery, Eddy sought to end her dependence on relatives. In 1853 she married itinerant dentist Daniel Patterson, who brought her closer to her son and encouraged her experimentation with homeopathy to end bouts of indigestion, depression, and hypersensitivity. The match failed to live up to her expectations after he changed his mind about having the rowdy young George under his roof. A greater grief befell the family after Patterson's capture by Confederate soldiers.

THE SEARCH FOR A CURE

Beset in mind and body, Eddy sought a cure from Phineas P. Quimby, a Portland, Maine, faith healer and disciple of French hypnotist Franz Mesmer, who incorporated the writings of Thomas Carlyle, Emanuel Swedenborg, and John Ruskin into an eclectic whole. Quimby asserted that the cultivation of good thoughts could overpower and supplant bad thoughts. Eddy deduced that his healing method resembled that of Jesus and compared him to John the Baptist. Her delight in improved health led her to claim the Quimby system as her own invention and to lecture and publish periodicals on the subject of spiritual healing.

Critics point out that although Quimby did originate the concept, Eddy refined the technique by studying Hegel, Kant, and Berkeley and by grounding her simplistic, idealistic healing methods wholly on scripture. Late in her life, as her diaries show, she became obsessed with fear of plagiarism. She scrupulously copyrighted her works and sued people who copied her. To protect others from improperly crediting source material, she forbade notetaking in her classes.

After Quimby's death, Eddy's health worsened. A life-threatening fall on the icy streets of Lynn in 1866 produced internal injuries and plunged her anew into despair. She wrote to one of Quimby's assistants and implored his aid. After a three-year period of intense reading of the New Testament, particularly the teachings of Christ and St. Paul, she experienced a recovery over a period of three days. This second rejuvenation, which believers term a miracle, spawned her sect, the Christian Scientists. Ridding herself of Quimby's influence, she organized and launched her vigorous new church, selecting the life of Christ as the model of regeneration.

Personal trials forced Eddy to turn inward for answers. While separated from Patterson, whom she divorced in 1873, Eddy despaired of her son, who had moved west. She spent years in soul-searching, writing, and formulation of her personal philosophy of spiritual healing, which she claimed to be "uncontaminated and unfettered by human hypotheses" ("Mary Baker Eddy," 779). According to her explanation of the relationship between sin and disease, the fallible human mind is responsible for suffering, which can be relieved and ultimately cured through the Holy Spirit, the metaphysical incarnation of Christian Science. She maintained that human beings could spare themselves toil in the afterlife by beginning their conversion on earth through meditation and prayer.

Eddy advertised for pupils and taught disciples Hiram S. Crafts and Richard Kennedy how to heal the sick. The preponderance of her following were people interested in occult practices, some with unstable personalities. Difficult relationships sprang up as a result of her adamance and the vagaries of her pupils. One female practitioner, Josephine Woodbury, claimed to have produced a son by immaculate conception and named him the Prince of Peace. Mary Plunkett, another follower, concocted a Christian Science divorce and remarriage, which violated Eddy's prudishness.

Other scandals were attached to Eddy's name. Some students charged that she bilked them of their money and rejected their interpretations of her teachings. To counter their accusations, she took them to court for libel and malpractice or misapplication of method. To set the appropriate moral tone and to avoid ridicule of her piety in the midst of these controversies, she forbade tea, coffee, alcohol, and tobacco and conducted her life on an elevated plane of austerity and intellectualism. A few of her followers carried their behavior to nunlike extremes of celibacy. All were enjoined to avoid bookstores that carried publications criticizing the Christian Science movement.

A NEW APPROACH TO PAIN

In 1875, Eddy published her major thesis, *Science and Health*, which grew into a later version, *Science and Health with a Key to the Scriptures.* The publication, considered by her followers to be divinely inspired, formed the nucleus of her tenets. According to her optimistic beliefs, the sensations of flesh, or "animal magnetism," are mere illusions and conflict with God, who is the only reality. She claimed to possess the secrets of healing and of raising the dead, both of which could be proven by written testimonials.

A central tenet of Eddy's sect was the rejection of the efficacy of drugs, surgery, and other curative or manipulative methods of healing, although she did not refuse the services of dentists and optometrists. She taught that a changed attitude was the only way that the body could transcend physical pain. By harmonizing with God, Christian Scientists, she claimed, could attain perfection or absence of pain. The only method of reaching this perfected state was through intense prayer, either by the petitioner or by a member of the Christian Scientists.

Eddy organized public symposia in Lynn, Roxbury, and Boston, Massachusetts. Settlement in Boston helped stabilize her movement by distancing her from the most vocal of critics and detractors. In 1877, she married one of her converts, Asa Gilbert Eddy, a plainspoken, undemonstrative man who gave her a stable home. Two years later, her sect, named the First Church of Christ, Scientist, was formally chartered as an ecclesiastical adjunct to the body of therapy practitioners and teachers of healing. That same year, a student, Augusta Stetson, pushed for a sizable New York branch of the Boston church on Riverside Drive at the cost of $2 million.

By 1881, Mary Baker Eddy advanced her theories at Massachusetts Metaphysical College, where she taught for eight years. For $300, a student could study three weeks, then advance to the level of practitioner, complete with conferred degree as Christian Scientist or metaphysical obstetrician. A widow by 1883, she closed the college and devoted herself to the outreach program, which she moved to Boston's mother church in 1895. There it remained until 1906, when there was a need for larger quarters. A home for retired Christian Scientists was constructed in 1927, in Concord, New Hampshire. This building with its imposing Georgian facade was paid for by donations, proceeds from publications, and the annual tax on members. Called Pleasant View Home, it featured 144 rooms—lounges, parlors, reception halls, auditorium, library—barns, and sixty acres of arable land.

THE CHURCH

Mission branches moved into the field and onto university campuses. They were under Eddy's centralized control through a board of directors and her *Church Manual of the Mother Church*, which established acceptable codes of conduct for all practitioners. Although disciples added their own refinements to her theories, she remained in control of the new sect, a democratic organization that spread its beliefs through reading rooms and Sunday schools. She supplanted ordained ministers with impersonal, nonjudgmental readers, who promulgated paired teachings from the Bible and Eddy's canon, for instance, on God, on humanity, on eternal punishment, or on reality.

The choice of Sunday-sermon material remained severely regimented by the mother church, which introduced twenty-six subjects in a twice-yearly rotation. Weekly services included hymn singing but rejected emotionalism. Individual members depended heavily on personal responsibility and witness to maintain the church and its beliefs. Wednesday meetings emphasized individual testimony to successful healing, which was usually given without substantiation. The church celebrated no traditional Christian holidays and was devoid of sacraments. Twice a year devotees knelt in memory of Christ's return from death to partake of breakfast with his followers beside the Sea of Galilee.

Eddy promoted her ideas tirelessly through lectures, committees, and sixteen publications, particularly her *Miscellaneous Writings* (1896), *Retrospection and Introspection* (1892), *Unity of Good* (1887), and *Rudimental Divine Science* (1908). The new sect found voice in three publications: the *Christian Science Journal*, a monthly bulletin founded in 1883; the *Christian Science Sentinel*, begun as a weekly paper in 1898; and the *Christian Science Monitor*, famed national newspaper originated in 1908. Reaching a circulation of 165,000, the *Monitor*, which appeared in tabloid form in 1975, was dedicated to the propagation of wholesome news devoid of sensationalism. The *Christian Science Quarterly* supplied Bible lessons for individual devotionals. In addition, *The Herald of Christian Science*, a newsletter, was issued in twelve languages and Braille.

Eddy's beneficent influence was the cornerstone of her church's stability. After her death on December 3, 1910, at Chestnut Hill, Massachusetts, the church, grown to 100,000 members, entered a difficult period of power shuffling, which ended in schism and protracted litigation. A few fanatics averred that their prophet and founder would return from the dead. Most waited patiently for her replacement, who Eddy has predicted would come to lead the faithful.

Eventually, the body of believers acquired rights over individual directors. In the meantime, two rivals, Mrs. Annie C. Bill in England and Mrs. A. E. Stetson in New York, fought for control, which continued to fluctuate among squabbling would-be inheritors of the faith. To add to the uncertainty, Eddy's poorly organized texts suggested that she left her philosophy in a state of revision, although devout cult members adhered to her every word and even revered her mediocre poetry.

Historical opinion varies on the purpose and method of Eddy's teachings. Some critics labeled her a crank and a fraud. A host of diverse voices, including Conrad

Nagel, Dr. William Mayo, Cecil B. DeMille, and a list of world religious leaders of all faiths, claimed otherwise. In the words of Mark Twain, Eddy's admirer and contemporary: "Mother Eddy deserves a place in the Trinity as much as any member of it. She had organized and made available a healing principle that for two thousand years has never been employed except as the merest kind of guesswork. She is the benefactor of the age" (Powell, 37).

SOURCES

Carpenter, Gilbert C., Sr., and Gilbert C. Carpenter, Jr. *Mary Baker Eddy: Her Spiritual Footsteps*. Santa Clarita, Calif.: Pasadena Press, 1985.

Dakin, Edwin F. *Mrs. Eddy: The Biography of a Virginal Mind*. Magnolia, Mass.: Peter Smith, 1990.

"Mary Baker Eddy." *Man, Myth, and Magic*, Volume 6. New York: Marshall Cavendish, 1970, 779-780.

Powell, Lyman P. *Mary Baker Eddy: A Life Size Portrait*. Boston: Christian Science Publishing Society, 1950.

Smaus, Jewel Spangler. *Mary Baker Eddy: The Golden Days*. Boston: Christian Science Publishing Society, 1966.

Zweig, Stefan. *Mental Healers: Franz Anton Mesmer, Mary Baker Eddy, Sigmund Freud*. New York: Frederick Ungar, 1990.

Betty Ford

The rise of Betty Ford from wife of the House minority leader to the thirty-eighth U.S. First Lady was propitious for her and for the nation. At a trim 108 pounds for her five feet eight inches, she projected poise, style, and sense. She graciously and competently handled the transitions from wife of a congressman to wife of a vice president, then president's wife.

As her husband wrestled with affairs of state, Ford confronted her own dragons—first a pinched nerve and arthritis, then breast cancer, then an addiction to prescription drugs and alcohol, which she whipped in her sixtieth year. In her calm, reflective manner, she put her dependency in perspective: "Drinking was a way we relaxed, a way we celebrated, and it was good until it went bad. If you're not alcoholic, it doesn't have to go bad, but I'm alcoholic. I just didn't know it for thirty years" (Ford and Chase 1987, 30).

BUDDING DANCER

A native of Chicago, Elizabeth Anne Bloomer Ford, the youngest child and only daughter of William Stephenson and Hortense Neahr Bloomer, was born on April 8, 1918. With a winsome smile, auburn hair, and green eyes, she was an understated, somewhat chubby beauty from childhood. Her family moved to Denver, then to Grand Rapids in 1921, where her father, an employee of Royal Rubber, sold conveyor belts. Her mother, connected to an old, established family, was a community activist. The family, including Ford's older brothers, Bill, Jr., and Bob, made annual treks to a getaway cottage at Whitefish Lake until they had to sell it because her father had lost most of his resources during the 1929 stock-market crash. He died accidentally from carbon monoxide poisoning while repairing a car engine in 1934; to support the family, his widow sold real estate.

The Bloomer children were brought up with firmness and love. Betty had to wear a hat and gloves for shopping trips and was admonished for improper behavior. The family could not afford all that she wanted. She played piccolo in the school band and began training in social dance, Spanish dancing, acrobatics, ballet, and tap in 1926 at the Calla Travis Dance Studio and continued through her years at Grand

Rapids High but did not have the money to add piano to her list of accomplishments. She did have her way with religion and changed from the family membership in the Christian Science Church to Episcopalianism.

To supplement the family's straitened income during the 1930s, Ford gave dancing lessons for fifty cents each. For a dollar, she rented space in her aunt Flo Jones's basement recreation area and later at the YWCA. Another dollar paid for Wally Hook to play the piano. These rudiments produced students proficient in waltz, foxtrot, and the Big Apple.

CHOOSING A CAREER

Ford later regretted never earning a regular degree, but she did attend two summer sessions at the School of Dance at Vermont's Bennington College, studying her first love, modern dance. Her teacher, Martha Graham, a disciplined dancer and instructor, became her idol and fed her dreams of a professional career. Ford recalled Martha's starchy attitude toward instruction: "I admired that kind of strictness. You can't be a dancer without it; not only your body but your mind must be disciplined" (Ford and Chase 1979, 24).

With her mother's grudging concurrence, Ford begged her way into Martha Graham's New York school, performed with the second-best troupe, the Martha Graham Concert Group, from 1939 to 1941, appeared at Carnegie Hall, and modeled furs, dresses, and hats for the John Powers Agency. During this respite from her mother's control, Ford roomed with another dancer near the Chelsea section of New York and walked to the Graham studio on Fifth Avenue. After three years of dancing and modeling for fashion shows, at the urging of her mother, she returned to Michigan and worked as fashion director of Herpolscheimer's Department Store in Grand Rapids from 1943 to 1948. As a sideline, she taught local couples the conga and formed her own troupe.

She was surprised that opportunities in Michigan satisfied her career urge and that she no longer pined for New York. These years utilized specific talents, particularly window dressing and grooming models for fashion shows. They also refined her social skills. In 1942, Ford, an ardent Junior Leager who had flirted her way through a long list of likely males, wed insurance salesman William C. Warren in a garden ceremony. They moved to Maumee, Ohio; Betty commuted to Ohio University in Toledo to teach dance and worked in a department store.

The marriage brought unforeseen compromises to both parties. Bill's employment changed to sales, taking him on the road and away from his bride much of the time. Unprepared for domestic duties, Ford failed most obviously in cooking. The couple's home life foundered after Bill became ill with diabetes; they had to move in with his parents. She remained loyal and learned to administer his insulin injections. After they faced the truth about their bankrupt relationship, the five-year marriage ended in amicable divorce.

MRS. GERALD FORD

Ford abandoned the single life once she met Yale graduate Gerald Rudolph Ford, a thirty-five-year-old war veteran, attorney, and candidate for Congress. She enjoyed his companionship and loyalty. Another plus for Gerry was the wholehearted approval of Betty's stepfather, Arthur Godwin, and her mother, who had advised against her first marriage. Gradually, she encouraged Gerry to edge out other suitors and assume first place in her affections.

With second thoughts about cold-weather sports, Ford let Gerry teach her to ski and followed him to football games at Ann Arbor. After their engagement, she devoted evenings to his campaign, which she doubted would amount to anything. They married October 15, 1948, at the Grace Episcopal Church and settled temporarily in her apartment. She envisioned a safe, Midwestern life with Gerry conducting his law practice and coming home for pot roast.

The reality of their union set in when she perceived his political potential. After the November election, the Fords moved to Q Street in Georgetown, where, over a period of seven years, she acclimated herself to the Washington scene. She joined the Congressional Club and formed friendships with Bess Truman, Muriel Humphrey, and Lady Bird Johnson, all of whom helped the wife of a freshman congressman feel at ease with protocol. Over a period of eight years, Ford bore four children, Michael, John, Steven, and Susan, and fulfilled a community role in the Episcopal Church, scouts, PTA, Little League, and volunteer work, particularly as drive chair for the Cancer Fund, Heart Fund, and Red Cross.

An aura of rightness permeated the Ford household. No dividing line separated her casual drinking from escapism and the beginnings of alcoholism. As she looked back on those years, she called them "very middle American ordinary. From the outside, our life looked like a Norman Rockwell illustration" (Ford and Chase 1987, 33).

During this era of genteel parenthood, Ford accustomed herself to continual pain from a pinched nerve in her neck, a problem that lasted throughout her lifetime. At George Washington Hospital, she tried acupuncture, heat therapy, traction, massage, and eventually drugs. Her abuse of prescription medicine seemed a normal outgrowth of doctors' orders. A serious adjunct to her dependence on painkillers was her self-pity after her husband's success as House minority leader and her emptiness because of his frequent travels and late hours. As her awareness of his rise in politics grew, her self-esteem deflated. In her self-demeaning view, she had had a mediocre dance career and had fallen into the boring role of typical mom.

PRESSURE AND PAIN

At one point, the damage done by heavy drinking showed up in pancreatitis. Ford's doctor suggested that she give up alcohol, so for two years she remained voluntarily dry. In 1965, domestic stresses complicated by politics, Gerry's frequent absences, plus pain from the damaged cervical nerve, forced her to admit her dilemma and seek psychiatric help. Gerry, cognizant of the part he played in his wife's suffering, promised to withdraw from public service. Instead of retiring, however, he found himself shoved into the public limelight as a replacement first for Spiro Agnew in October 1973 and then for President Richard Nixon, who resigned in August 1974.

Ford at first doubted that her husband could be spared from Congress to accept the vice presidency. In her first autobiography, she explained how the choice of an experienced leader with Gerry's record was necessary to hoist the failing Republican party from the political mire: "[Nixon] needed a Mister Clean. Especially since the 25th Amendment to the Constitution said that Congress had to confirm his choice" (Ford and Chase 1979, 145). In short order, the cover of *Time* magazine heralded the Fords' arrival at the White House.

Ford made the transition from her Crown View address to 1600 Pennsylvania Avenue with public grace but with private agony. The president acknowledged at his swearing-in that he owed a singular debt of thanks to his wife, who had supported him through the transition. Ford opened chapter 1 of her autobiography with a description of the "saddest day of her life" (Ford and Chase 1979, 1). Weighing the responsibilities that were now hers, she commented, "I really felt like I was taking that oath too" (*Current Biography*, 134).

Interviewers found Ford approachable and forthright in her attitude toward women's issues, including abortion, child abuse, and the Equal Rights Amendment. Her openness to the media continued unabated in September of that year after she lost her right breast, muscle tissue, and lymph nodes to cancer. She took comfort in being in a position to influence other women to seek diagnostic tests to lessen the chances of dying from an undetected malignancy. In exchange for candor she received a deluge of letters and accolades.

FIGHTING ADDICTION

In time, political interest turned away from President Ford. His loss of the next election brought more freedom for Ford to drink away her anguish over the nation's rejection of her husband. A new doctor examined her neck problem, then confided to the Fords' next-door neighbor that he could not help her until she was weaned from pills and alcohol. That fall, she narrated a performance of Tchaikovsky's *Nutcracker*. Critics picked about the edges of her addiction by lambasting her somnolence and lack of alertness. Unable to face her drunken performance, she viewed the damning tape only once.

More evidence piled up. Ford's view of the world grew oversensitive, sometimes maudlin. To combat weakness and loss of weight, she took weekly B12 injections. Her inability to attend social functions, to eat a meal, to dress herself within a reasonable time became a family embarrassment. Her secretary requested that she not take medication before interviews. Even her Secret Service agents became annoyed at her erratic behavior.

In the spring of 1978, shortly after the move to their new home, Ford's family confronted her with her dependence on bourbon, vodka, sleeping pills, relaxants, pain pills, and a host of uppers to offset the downers. In short, she was hooked and needed a push to face her addiction. At the instigation of daughter Susan, an intervention team presented the facts. Her response was the classic pattern for alcoholics—anger, humiliation, and denial.

To Gerry's comments about her falls and the number of times she had been incapable of completing an obligation because of drunkenness, she responded by feeling betrayed. Leaning on family and the assembled medical staff, she assessed her predicament and concluded that with dependency, "your self-esteem gets so low you're sure nobody would want to bother with you. I think intervention works because suddenly you realize somebody *is* willing to bother, somebody cares" (Ford and Chase 1987, 23). Pressure from the group changed her mind about seeking treatment.

Her week of detoxification, which was supervised at home, left Ford nauseated, weak, and shaky. The chronic neck pain nagged at her. Her mainstays were exercise and long walks, soaks in the Jacuzzi, and repetition of the Serenity Prayer. Admission to the Long Beach naval hospital brought her to the edge of patience. She rebelled at the four-person room and at the press release that divulged her private troubles to the world.

For treatment, she studied Alcoholics Anonymous's twelve steps and entered group therapy. She listened politely to other people's descriptions of their alcoholic miasma yet distanced herself from their experiences. While trying to write a short exercise in autobiography, Ford found herself incapable of admitting her addiction. She saw herself as the First Lady, dependent on prescription medicine but certainly not a drunk.

During her first year of sobriety, Ford experienced the ups and downs common to most newly sober alcoholics. Her nerves stayed on edge; her relationships with family and staff strayed from their usual equanimity to unpleasant scenes and bursts of temper. Demands on her time took her away from the Fords' new home, which had become a refuge. First came an extensive tour of the Middle East, then Susan's wedding to Chuck Vance, whom Ford did not prefer as a future son-in-law.

THE CHALLENGE

Near the end of that first year, she changed direction. She began to use her fame and influence in a mission to help other people fighting to control their lives. She and Leonard Firestone started a drive to build a rehabilitation center. Within three years, they had collected $3 million. Her push to complete the project got a boost from Gerry, who announced in March 1980 that he was withdrawing from the presidential race.

Having defeated addiction, she headed the Betty Ford Center, nicknamed Betty Camp, at Rancho Mirage, California, which she founded with the help of Joe Cruse and Leonard. Situated within sight of serene mountains on parched desert soil, the facility opened in the fall of 1982 and was toasted by the Ford family, George and Barbara Bush, Bob and Dolores Hope, and the staff of "Good Morning America." At the dedication ceremony, Betty commented, "This was a pile of sand, and we've made it come alive. And it's going to be even more alive, because people will come here for help; there is going to be a way for them, a new life" (Ford and Chase 1987, 6).

Ford attested to the hard road facing congressional wives and recovering alcoholics in her autobiographical works, *The Times of My Life* (1979) and *Betty: A Glad Awakening* (1987), both written with journalist Chris Chase. Gerry, proud of his wife's resilience and perseverance, claimed that she had become more popular than he, a former president. People from all walks of life, celebrity and ne'er-do-well, seek her out for advice and emulate her example.

Betty Ford continues to reach out to people through volunteer work for the National Arthritis Foundation and as trustee of the Martha Graham Dance Center, Bob Hope Cultural Center, Eisenhower Medical Center, Palm Springs Desert Museum, National Symphony Orchestra, Nursing Home Council, Golden Circle Patrons Center, and the Lambs. Among her achievements are an honorary doctorate from the University of Michigan and the Silver Humanitarian Award for work with retarded citizens. Perhaps even with these involvements and her role as former First Lady to her credit, Ford is proudest of her courageous stand for sobriety.

SOURCES

Angel, Sherry. "This Ford Has a Future." *50 Plus*, September 1986, 24-27.

Current Biography. New York: H. W. Wilson, 1975, 133-135.

Ford, Betty, and Chris Chase. *The Times of My Life*. New York: Ballantine, 1979.

_____. *Betty: A Glad Awakening*. New York: Doubleday, 1987.

Fortino, Denise. "No One Wants to Think of Herself as an Alcoholic." *Harper's Bazaar*, September 1981, 313-316.

Simpson, Kathleen. "Betty Ford: A Lesson in Caring." *Good Housekeeping*, May 1981, 108-112.

Steinem, Gloria. "Betty Ford Today: Still Speaking Out." *Ms.*, April 1984, 41-45.

Indira Gandhi

Growing up amid civil strife and political discord, Indira Nehru Gandhi, child of India's most prominent nationalists, learned early that activism bears the price of loneliness, deprivation, and insecurity. In response to her parents' frequent jailings, she once said, "I have lived in crisis since earliest childhood. Perhaps that's why problems don't overwhelm me" (*Current Biography*, 116). Facing difficulties with a pragmatic rationality, she earned the world's respect for her open-mindedness and sensitivity to multiple points of view. A pleasant gray-haired matriarch known to followers as Indiraji, Gandhi, ruler of the world's most populous democracy until her assassination in 1984, came to symbolize the Westerner's concept of Indian sagacity and perseverance.

BORN TO THE BEST

Named Priyadarshini, or Beautiful to Behold, at her birth in Allahabad, a sacred city on the Ganges River in the northeast quadrant of India on November 19, 1917, Gandhi, at four pounds, was the only child of a distinguished family of Kashmiri ancestry. Her legendary grandfather, Motilal Nehru, who crusaded for India's westernization, and her father, Jawaharlal Nehru, a scholarly, cosmopolitan attorney, established significant places in the fight for independence from British colonialism. Her bold and self-assured aunt, Vijaya Lakshmi Pandit, was the first woman to preside over the United Nations General Assembly. Eager to keep up the family's high standards, Gandhi's grandmother sniffed that the tiny newborn female should have been a boy; her husband retorted optimistically, "This daughter of Jawahar, for all you know, may prove better than a thousand sons" (Masani, 2).

Growing up among adults in the splendor and luxury of Anand Bhavan, her family's estate, Gandhi knew material wealth, including libraries, spacious gardens and orchards, a swimming pool, bridle paths, and tennis courts. She enjoyed the constant personal care of her mother, Kamala, a shy, unsophisticated ascetic and devout Hindu who prayed, meditated, and indulged in psychic phenomena. Although pampered and treated to a deluge of sweetmeats, delicacies, and expensive toys, Gandhi suffered emotional traumas from early childhood, especially the snobbery of her father's family, which forced Kamala to withdraw into depressed silence.

Throughout her life, Gandhi remained close to her mother and defended her from criticism.

Controversy was a way of life for the Nehru clan. While Gandhi was still a toddler, her family burned their Western attire and followed family friend and inspirational leader Mohandas K. Gandhi's example of simple native garments. Keeping in the spirit of their sacrifice, little Indira set fire to her foreign doll. Years later she recalled the brave symbolic act, which forced a painful schism between her family and westernized Indians: "The tears came as if they would never stop and for some days I was ill with a temperature. To this day I hate to strike a match!" (Masani, 15). At age three, Gandhi, nicknamed Indu, or Little Moon, was attending party meetings; at four, she sat on her grandfather's lap during his trial for sedition at Naini Prison; at five, she interrupted her father's trial for criminal intimidation by asking, "Mummie, are they going to have a bioscope show?" (Masani, 15). She played political games with her dolls and fantasized that she was Joan of Arc, martyred at the stake.

Forced to adjust to her parents' devotion to nationalistic ideals, Gandhi spent much of her childhood in the care of her nanny while Kamala and Jawaharlal served prison sentences for conspiring to overthrow the British raj. Her father, to relieve her tedium at being kept home from school, wrote her letters from 1930 to 1933— collected in *Letters from a Father to His Daughter* and *Glimpses of World History*—a home-study course intended to detail for her the underpinnings of international affairs. He also asked about her devotions and urged her to learn to spin yarn on her new spinning wheel. Her mother, weakened by two stillbirths and pulmonary tuberculosis, suffered his absence without complaint but relieved her frustrations by championing feminism.

While Kamala served a sentence for picketing and demonstrations, Mohandas Gandhi inspired the twelve-year-old Indira to show compassion to India's poor and to join the pacifist movement for independence so that she, too, could take part in her family's crusade. She launched the Allahabad branch of the Monkey Brigade, a 6,000-member youth group that supported adult nationalists. She exhibited a strong streak of defiance in saying, "I wanted to be a member of the Congress Party—but they turned me down. They said I would have to be [older]. I was exceedingly angry and I said 'I'll have an organization of my own!'" (Masani, 29). She became adept at smuggling messages, spying on police surveillance, and performing mundane office chores. That same year, after Jawaharlal donated his home to be used as party head-quarters and a hospital, she joined adult women who served as aides.

EDUCATING A LEADER

Gandhi's education began in a private Indian school in Poona and continued at L'École Nouvelle in Bex, Switzerland, in 1926 while Kamala was hospitalized in Geneva. Already too mature for her peers, Gandhi became a loner but learned enough French to acquaint herself with local happenings. On her mother's recovery, the family returned to Allahabad in December 1927; Gandhi enrolled at St. Mary's Convent school, then at Vishwa Bharati University, poet Rabindranath Tagore's austere, peaceful ashram in Bengal, until Kamala's illness forced her to accompany her mother to a German sanitarium. Kamala, who had fought respiratory illness through many prison terms, died in Lausanne on February 28, 1936.

Although she lacked her usual chipper outlook toward school, Jawaharlal decided that his nineteen-year-old daughter should study history at Somerville College in Oxford, England. She floundered socially and intellectually; her health declined as her emotions churned from the loss of her mother. Homesick for India, she halted her education in 1941 when the blitz threatened her safety in London.

LIBERAL LEADERSHIP

Already a member of the British Labor party, Gandhi allied with India's left-leaning Congress party in 1938. On March 26, 1942, overlooking her father's disapproval of a Parsi-Hindu union, she married old family friend and party member Feroze Gandhi, an attorney and political activist who had courted her in England and Switzerland. In August, the couple were accused of subversion and served thirteen months in prison. Gandhi, proud to emulate her family's tradition of serving sentences for their beliefs, used her time to plant a garden and initiate literacy classes for fellow inmates. Upon their release, the Gandhis established a home in Allahabad and within two years produced two sons, Rajiv and Sanjay.

By 1947, as her marriage foundered because of her lack of interest in Feroze's career, the civil turmoil wrought by the creation of the free states of India and Pakistan brought new opportunities for Gandhi in public service. She forged a peaceful link between squabbling religious groups and spread the message of peace into isolated villages. After her father was named India's first prime minister, Gandhi left her husband and moved into the official residence in New Delhi to fill a place as the widower's hostess.

Serving as "India's first lady" and "daughter of the nation," Gandhi managed various responsibilities, from housekeeping and menu-planning to overseeing protocol and acting as a confidante (*Current Biography*, 15). When her father traveled on state business she accompanied him and established friendships with world leaders in the Soviet Union, China, and the United States. In 1955, her interest in India's culture, education, and welfare encouraged her to seek membership on the Congress party's executive committee, where she specialized in helping women and children.

A POLITICAL LEADER

Within four years, Gandhi, who gained a reputation for fairness, determination, and candor, rose to the presidency of her party despite her father's concern that people might accuse her of relying on kinship as a means of garnering political power. She conducted meetings with efficiency, cutting through tedious speeches and pointless minutiae. Shrewd and patient, she learned to control ennui while listening to the proposals of others, partly as a means of assessing character. She developed successful strategies for coping with internal problems, such as the promotion of young party members. One of her wisest moves was the trouncing of a Communist threat to the Kerala branch.

Recuperating from an acute kidney disorder late in 1960, Gandhi remained in touch with India's political affairs. In 1962, following a border clash between India and China, she proved herself ready to resume political activities by forming a civil-defense network to protect soldiers and their families. Within two years, she was teaching mothers how to care for children through a UNICEF initiative in the Indian countryside and was serving on the executive board of UNESCO.

MAKING DECISIONS

When her father lay terminally ill from a stroke during the first five months of 1964, Gandhi superintended his care and performed official duties while suffering her own miseries from a slipped disk. Upon his death on May 24, his successor urged her to fill the vacant post of foreign minister, an opportunity she declined during her period of mourning. Upon being pressed about her answer, she snapped, "If you don't believe me, I will write it down on paper!" (Masani, 130). On June 6, she accepted the role of minister of information and broadcasting. She excelled at finding the best-qualified people for the job, freed facilities of partisan control, and doubled broadcast hours from nine to eighteen.

After filling a seat in the upper house of India's parliament, Gandhi distinguished herself by the skillful settlement of an uprising in Madras of speakers of Tamil, who opposed recognition of Hindi as the national language. Her short stint as councilwoman ended after the unforeseen death of Prime Minister Lal Bahadur Shastri on January 11, 1966. The Congress party proposed Gandhi as his replacement, ostensibly because party members assumed that she could be easily manipulated. After a vote of 355 to 169 in her favor on January 19, she became India's third prime minister. To complaints that a woman could never handle the burdensome position, she replied, "I don't regard myself as a woman. I regard myself as a person with a job.... I feel neither excited nor nervous. This is just another job I have to do" (Mohan, 263).

HEAD OF STATE

As India's head of state, Gandhi handled predictable jobs—managing the Atomic Energy Commission, assessing the depressed state of agriculture, battling the phenomenal birthrate, and keeping her predecessor's commitments with neighboring nations. The unpredictable demands of her high estate, however, immediately vied for attention. Within weeks of her swearing-in, she reinstated Kerala's rice-distribution centers, thus quelling food riots brought on by one of India's recurrent famines. More pressing, perhaps, than these civil disruptions was the separatist movement of the 7 million Sikhs of Punjab. To placate the rebels, she had to counterbalance an upsurge in Hindu unrest.

Relations with industrialized nations brought their own set of problems. In 1966, Gandhi conferred with Hubert Humphrey, visiting U.S. vice president, who sought India's backing of the Vietnam War. Her answer, tempered with characteristic logic, was that India, as head of the International Control Commission on Vietnam, refused to be drawn into the confrontation.

While studying the crises that plagued nations, Gandhi, focused on common human suffering, continued to aid peasants in rural areas and served on hospital, arts, and education boards. As vice-chair of the International Union of Child Welfare and head of a children's home and a children's museum, she pushed for governmental intervention in problems of Indian youth. Among her improvements were a Delhi training center for poor children, the nationalization of fourteen major financial institutions, and the demotion of maharajas through cancellation of state allowances.

Governmental control moved in and out of Gandhi's hands during the height of her career. In 1969, dismayed with the nepotism of the Congress party, she organized a divergent branch. As a means of keeping in touch with Communist party leaders, she conferred with Premier Kosygin yet preserved a cool detachment in assessing Indian-Soviet relations. In March 1971, immediately following India's trouncing blow against Pakistani aggression, constituents acknowledged her success with astounding results at the polls. To assure peace, she extended border surveillance by supervising outposts overlooking Kashmir. During this tense period, to ally more strongly with the United States, she visited the White House for a banquet in her honor hosted by President Richard Nixon.

Charged by her Socialist opponent with violating election laws in 1975, she faced a high-court inquiry, which found in her accuser's favor. To regain her former stature, she declared martial law during periods of civil lawlessness and famine. For two years, civil liberties were suspended, elections were postponed, and thousands of rebels suffered detainment. To counter growing domestic problems, she instituted strong birth-control initiatives and sought better control of Indian economics and social welfare.

A major crisis erupted after the Janata, or People's, party seized control during the 1977 elections and unseated Gandhi. On March 22, she made her resignation official. To upbraid her for coercive methods during the state of emergency, her successors charged her with constitutional violations and graft and sentenced her to a symbolic week in prison. She returned as head of her party in 1978, recouped her earlier lead, and in 1980 was reelected prime minister.

The final years of Gandhi's rule were less productive than her earlier years. Unwilling to denounce the Soviet Union's assault on Afghanistan, she faced growing unrest and outbreaks of violence. In June 1980, she suffered the loss of her son Sanjay, who was killed in a plane crash. With her son Rajiv's assistance, she remained in office until her assassination in New Delhi on October 31, 1984, when extremist Sikh bodyguards shot her.

A PRIVATE PERSON

To the outside world, Gandhi, slender, diminutive, clad in traditional saris, and casting somber brown eyes on domestic and international problems, was a comforting sight in her maternal stability. To balance sixteen-hour workdays with normalcy, she turned to cooking, folk and classical music, horticulture, and her three golden retrievers. She read widely from a private collection of biographies and anthropological texts. Not ostentatious about religion, she nevertheless often salted her speeches with quotes from the Bhagavad Gita.

While living in the glare of public attention, she maintained a sedate private life that did not always conform to the ideal. Her husband, whose condemnation of government actions cast a shadow on their relationship, separated from her in 1958. He suffered a heart attack in 1959 and a fatal stroke the following year. Her intense reaction surprised those who surmised that she no longer cared for him: "I should have expected that he would die. However, it was not just a mental shock, but it was as though somebody had cut me in two" (Masani, 117).

After Feroze's death, Gandhi devoted herself to raising her sons, whom she groomed for political service. Deeply imbued with maternal love and concern, even though her house staff stood ready to fill in, she was often torn by the pull of state affairs and the overwhelming need to be home to tend a sick or troubled child. She compromised by being available during vacations and by writing intimate letters filled with honesty and warmth.

Gandhi received her share of notoriety for bettering the living conditions for countless people and for helping to ensure India's place among nations. She accepted a Mothers' Award of the USA, Yale University's Howland Memorial Prize, an Italian medal for diplomacy, and numerous honorary degrees. Perhaps a more appropriate honor was her followers' slogan, "Indira is India, India is Indira" (Masani, 320).

SOURCES

Current Biography. New York: H. W. Wilson, 1966.

Masani, Zareer. *Indira Gandhi.* New York: Thomas Y. Crowell, 1976.

Mohan, Anand. *Indira Gandhi: A Personal and Political Biography.* New York: Meredith Press, 1967.

Esther Hautzig

At age ten, Esther Hautzig, a victim of deportation during World War II, faced resentment against Jews and endured internment on the Russian steppes. Not all barriers are crossed in adulthood. Following the forced removal of Polish Jews to Siberia, she and her parents and paternal grandmother lived in Rubtsovsk, where war-threatened industrial facilities were moved from the eastern front. Surrounded by strangers speaking an unknown tongue, she and her family learned to cope with adversity, steeled themselves to survive savage winters, and held out for better times.

Returned in 1946 to Lodz, Poland, which was much changed from the town her family had left five years before, Hautzig made a decisive break with her family in order to emigrate to the United States. As a new citizen, she discovered the joys of living in a free land. She went to college, married, and established a career as a crafts expert. She first wrote about knitting and other crafts and then, as the process of putting her thoughts to paper stirred her memories, about life as a deportee in Russia. Through her clear, straightforward retelling, a generation of young readers has learned of a harrowing era of religious prejudice.

JEWISH CHILD

An only child, Esther Rudomin Hautzig, a native of Vilna, Poland, was born on October 18, 1930, the well-disciplined daughter of a comfortably middle-class family headed by merchant Samuel "Tata" and Raya Zunser Rudomin. At one time, Vilna boasted libraries, schools, and temples and thrived from the cultivation of its Jewish populace. It was the "oldest seat of Jewish culture in eastern Europe, the Jerusalem of Europe" (Hautzig, 24). She was taught to revere local history and recalled the distinguished lives of her ancestors—the rabbis, scholars, and social reformers.

Life in the family compound seemed serene as war raged in Eastern Europe. Hautzig, oblivious to the menace of decreasing civil liberties for Jews, took a ten-year-old's delight in mystery books and her grandfather's garden. The charge of Miss Rachel, a doting governess, she practiced piano, dancing, and gymnastics and attended the Sophia Markovna Guerwitz School. There she learned Yiddish and studied Jewish literature and culture.

Hautzig wept over separation from Samuel, who served a short stint in the military, then returned after his entire battalion was wiped out. In June 1941, the Rudomin family's happiness at his return was disrupted by soldiers. Bearing fixed bayonets, they came to arrest Samuel and Raya, who, along with Esther and Grandmother Anna Rudomin, were labeled capitalists and enemies of the people because of Samuel's commercial success. They were separated from Grandfather Solomon and transported by cattle car to an unknown destination. Hautzig never saw her maternal grandparents or her aunt Sonia again. As Grandfather departed to a labor camp, the Rudomins joined a double line of forty people, boarded a train, then journeyed for six weeks in the dim, fetid compartmentalized car.

In the train, which rattled along affording no privacy or basic comforts, Hautzig felt oppressed. The car stank of animal dung. Four small square holes in the upper corners of the car and slivers between slats in the walls provided limited access to light and air. Makeshift upper and lower bunks served as their living quarters. Her father, a natural leader, helped organize an orderly allotment of these spaces to each family.

Hautzig, bewildered by the unceremonious uprooting from their comfortable home, got a last glimpse of Vilna from one of the holes high in the car. She communicated her distress to the family in hoarse whispers and envied in silence the passengers who had brought food. At a tiny rural station, the train's first stop, a soldier supplied the inmates with a pail of drinking water and a ladle. He indicated the train's only toilet, a V-shaped slot opposite the door, which her father concealed with a sheet.

Hautzig's queasy stomach rejected the communal meals served from a rusty pail of soup containing orange liquid afloat with bits of tomato, carrot, and cabbage. Her wretched experience was eased by the cooperative spirit of other exiles, who shared what they had. When opportunity permitted, her parents bought goat cheese, milk, and black bread from vendors at rural stations.

Because the train traveled no faster than twelve miles per hour, the journey dragged on. She became feverish from the heat, stench, and lice. Before their arrival at Rubtsovsk, a frontier village in the Altai Territory of the USSR, her father entertained her by identifying the Ural Mountains and explaining that the family was passing from Europe into Asia. From that point on, they traveled another thousand miles before coming to a stopping place.

ADJUSTING TO DEPORTATION

Hautzig quickly summed up the qualities of their temporary home. Steeped in world literature, she scrutinized Rubtsovsk and noticed that the ticktacktoe arrangement of streets reminded her of the market in Harriet Beecher Stowe's *Uncle Tom's Cabin*. Lodged in barracks twelve kilometers from a gypsum mine, the family came under the superintendency of Popravka, a good-natured man who assigned them tasks—she in the potato fields, Raya as a dynamiter, Grandmother to shovel gypsum, and Samuel to drive a horse cart. As she yanked at offending clumps of weeds, Hautzig looked fearfully into the distance to the steppes, the great Ukrainian grasslands that extended along the Black and Azov seas to the Altai Mountains in western Siberia.

Hautzig inured herself to extremes of weather and general privation. In September, she learned that Siberian storms were swift and deadly and that warm clothes were a must. That winter, frost killed crops, and many internees died from the cold. The next summer was hot and dry; strong winds swept in because no mountains impeded. Harvests were disappointing as a result of summer drought.

Rations of cheese and bread were scant, but after an amnesty declaration between England and the Soviet Union on July 30, 1941, assured freedom for Polish prisoners, the Rudomin family and other deportees were allowed to move closer to the village. They were paid a minimum wage for their work and on Sundays, their day off, could shop at the *baracholka*, or village market, a three-hour walk from home. There, Hautzig and her grandmother absorbed the colorful activity of free Kozhak peasants and bartered for food, trading scarce luxury items—Raya's elegant silk slip, Samuel's silk shirt, and Grandmother's black silk umbrella—for meat, flour, and sunflower seeds.

The family chose to move to the village and shared bleak quarters with other Polish families. Raya was assigned a bakery job; Samuel worked as a bookkeeper on a construction project. Gradually, life improved after the family located warmer housing. Hautzig, like her grandmother, was free of work detail and could continue her education.

MAKING HER WAY

She attended a bare, no-frills school containing only blackboards and portraits of Marx and Engels, the founders of communism, and Lenin and Stalin. The school provided a communal outdoor stove where students could boil meat, mix dough from flour and water, and bake thin cakes of bread. There was little variety in her diet because the family had no opportunity to grow potatoes, carrots, or other root crops in the implacable gypsum soil. Only her infrequent trips to town with Grandmother provided the meager treat of roasted sunflower seeds.

Hautzig was placed in the fifth grade but was slow to progress. Lonely for a friend among Russian-speaking children, she contended with Svetlana, an envious, unfriendly rival with whom she shared textbooks, and Raisa Nikitovna, a formidable and unsympathetic teacher. Even in shabby refugee clothing, Hautzig stood out as a poor little rich girl among scruffy, ill-fed Russian peasants. The steely eyed teacher, resenting Hautzig's inability to speak fluent Russian, did little to assist the child in adapting.

Hautzig's lessons challenged her. She tackled the works of Krylov and garnered the unused pages of a notebook. Facing the challenge of the Cyrillic alphabet, she became adept at the Russian language and literature; mastery of math, however, proved more difficult. To compound her problems, a months-long bout with bronchitis kept her at home in bed for most of the winter, but she took some comfort in trips to the town library.

The war dragged on. News reached the Rudomins that Grandfather Solomon had died in a labor camp. Samuel was questioned by the secret police because Jews had come to the house to observe funeral rites for Solomon. He circumvented trouble by explaining that such gatherings were part of Jewish worship.

Because their landlady became pregnant, the family was forced to move; they located an alternate shelter, a bare dirt-floored hut. After patching the walls with manure and digging a root cellar, they took up residence in the humble makeshift dwelling and, to augment their diet, established a vegetable garden. Local authorities forced them to shelter an unfortunate Ukrainian shoemaker who had lost a leg in a Siberian prison camp.

More hardships made internment especially bitter for Hautzig. During the hot summer, Samuel received orders to join a labor force on the front lines. The family feared for his welfare, but Samuel, ever the optimist, reassured the three women. Hautzig, his pet, grieved openly at his going. The second winter was even more difficult than the first because of the summer crop failure. To lighten the grimness of their lives, Raya organized a party for Esther's twelfth birthday and served the guests the only food she had—potato goulash. When cold threatened their lives, Hautzig joined a band of children who stole coal and wood shavings along the railroad tracks.

DEVELOPING HER TALENTS

To ease tight family finances, Hautzig began knitting custom-made sweaters. Finding wool was even more difficult than finding customers. For one woman, Esther washed and unraveled a discarded red skirt and knitted a sweater in exchange for potatoes and milk. She developed a friendship with a local couple who were connected with the new tractor factory and lived in a comfortable two-room residence, a luxury in comparison to the Rudomins' rough quarters. The new friends provided a few extras, such as a cake of soap, but Raya insisted that Hautzig not expect their friends to support them.

Often cold and poorly dressed, Hautzig found warmth while reading books at the local library. She worked hard to win the August declamation contest by memorizing Tatyana's dream from Alexander Pushkin's *Eugene Onegin*. Her teacher embarrassed her for arriving at the contest dusty and barefooted and pretended that she could not find her name listed among the other contestants' names. Hautzig returned home for a pair of Raya's felt slippers and ran back to recite her piece. Wearied by her exertions, she lost the contest, yet she was determined to avoid humiliation and acquire a pair of shoes to replace her outgrown oxfords.

Other challenges demonstrated Hautzig's courage and persistence. She traded goods at the market and ran successfully for the elected office of editor of the school newspaper. In order to gain the attention of Yuri, a fellow student, she tried unsuccessfully to borrow a ball gown from a theatrical company. Undaunted, she managed to put together a borrowed costume. Gradually, she surrounded herself with friends among the open-faced Russian peasants, whom she grew to love.

AN END TO THE WAR

The final spring in Siberia brought her greater evidence of war's devastation. Cattle cars arrived loaded with German prisoners of war, who overtaxed village housing. More barracks were thrown together. Villagers who were once compassionate toward Polish deportees showed their resentment of German atrocities by vilifying and spitting on the prisoners. Hautzig, less willing to victimize others, spit defiantly on the road.

In May 1945, the news was both good and bad—the war was over, but President Roosevelt, hero to Hautzig and other deportees awaiting rescue, died. By May, Germany had surrendered to the Western Allies at Rheims. News of Samuel's release brought her joy, yet the realization that most of the family had been slaughtered by Germans filled her with deep sorrow. They learned that their home in Poland had been ransacked and taken over by a member of the secret police.

In August, the Rudomins began planning their return to Poland. In December, her teacher, Anna Semyonovna, announced another declamation contest and urged Hautzig to enter it. She longed to polish her speech for a second try, then rejoin her family in Barnaul, but Raya vetoed the separation. On March 15, 1946, three days before the second contest, the family boarded a cattle car once more and traveled to Lodz to join Samuel.

Hautzig's only comforts to flagging spirits were her new vest and boots, the traditional garb of the steppes. Along the way to Poland, she joined in the singing of joyful Polish folk songs and looked forward to the end of both the journey and exile. By accident, she became separated from the passengers during a brief stop and was nearly left behind. A friend jumped off, threw her back on the train, and ran to catch up. Arriving in Moscow for a day, she looked forward to sightseeing at Red Square, the Kremlin, and the Bolshoi Theater when a sudden lurch threw her against the stove in the middle of the railcar. A severe burn on her hand forced cancellation of her plans.

As Hautzig neared Poland, she sobered to jeering catcalls from anti-Semitic Poles. Her first view of Lodz proved that life in war-torn Poland had been difficult. Streets were filled with rubble, but she took heart at first sight of Samuel, whom she rushed to embrace. By April, her family, whittled down to four members, were reunited for a year in their old home.

THE AFTERMATH

Hoping for a better life, Hautzig separated from her parents in Stockholm and sailed alone to the United States to live with her uncle. Repatriated in a new land, she attended Hunter College from 1948 to 1950 and married concert pianist Walter Hautzig, whom she met on the boat to the United States. Making their home in New York City, the couple had two children.

Hautzig created a satisfying career in young-adult literature. She served as secretary at G. P. Putnam's Sons, as publicity assistant for the Children's Book Council, as director of children's book promotion at Thomas Y. Crowell, and has worked as a consultant and free-lance writer since the 1960s. Among her other published works are books on cooking, making presents, and redecorating. In addition, she wrote *In the Park: An Excursion in Four Languages* (1968), *At Home: A Visit in Four Languages* (1969), *In School: Learning in Four Languages* (1969), *The Case Against the Wind and Other Stories* (1975), *The Seven Good Years and Other Stories* (1984), and *Make It Special* (1986).

In contrast to these, her autobiography, *The Endless Steppe*, stands out as a tribute to the pluck and perseverance of Hautzig and her family. In her comments to *Horn Book* (August 1981), she noted that the book was not originally intended for children, although it quickly found a place in young-adult nonfiction. Beginning work in 1959, she heeded the urging of Adlai E. Stevenson, who had visited Rubtsovsk and urged her to write a memoir of frontier life in the Soviet Union during the war. In 1966 she sold the autobiography to a publisher of children's literature and did not have to alter the text to meet the needs of young readers.

The book earned immediate acclaim: The Shirley Kravitz Award, the Jane Addams Children's Book Award, the Lewis Carroll Shelf Award, Best Jewish Novel, ALA Notable Book, and honor book of the *Boston Globe* and *Book World* Spring Book Festival; she was a National Book Award finalist. Critics noted that because her words filled a gap in young readers' knowledge of World War II, Hautzig has not only survived anti-Semitism but helped to prevent it in younger generations. By maintaining normalcy in her life through friends, work, study, and worship, she demonstrated that barriers like war and bigotry need not be devastating.

SOURCES

Contemporary Authors, Volume 2R. Detroit: Gale Research, 1980.

De Montreville, Doris, and Donna Hill, eds. *Third Book of Junior Authors*. New York: H. W. Wilson, 1972.

Hautzig, Esther. *The Endless Steppe*. New York: Harper & Row, 1968.

Something About the Author, Volume 4. Detroit: Gale Research, 1973.

Ishi

Of the many catastrophes that can befall a human being, perhaps the worst is the fate of Ishi, a Native American of the Yana nation who outlived his people, their culture, language, and gods. Born in the natural wealth of California's mountain country, he grew up loved and educated by his small family. Then one by one, they departed from his life, leaving him alone in a world gradually giving way to the white settlers' encroachment, fed by their lust for gold.

Ishi wandered about without hope or direction until he was captured, then rescued by a white man who could speak his language. Grasping at this slim tether, he formed a strong bond to sustain him against the loneliness that overwhelmed him. In his existence as a living museum exhibit, he demonstrated to the white world that the last of the Yahi tribe was capable of dignity and purpose. At his death, he left a coterie of friends who vowed to keep alive the skills and beliefs that formed the basis of his extinct life-style.

BOYHOOD IN CALIFORNIA

For a white child, the state of California, which was admitted to the Union as the thirty-first state in 1850, was a promising area in which to be born. The decades that followed the gold rush of 1849 brought three newspapers to Sacramento, a surge in population from 15,000 to a quarter-million, and stagecoach service via the Butterfield Overland Mail. The Pony Express, the expansion of telegraph service, and the convergence of the Union Pacific and Central Pacific railways at Promontory, Utah, joined California's settlers, oblivious to local Indian culture, to the rest of the white world.

For Native Americans, progress did not imply hope. Rather, it threatened annihilation. Around 1875, the Yahi tribe of the 4,000-year-old Yana nation, who were members of the Hokan-language family, lived along Deer and Mill creeks near Mount Lassen in the Sacramento Valley in northern California. By this time their population had dwindled from 1,500 to only 7 members. Tehna-Ishi, or Bear Cub Boy, who was born about 1861 or 1862, was living with his widowed mother, parental grandparents and uncle, a female cousin on his mother's side, and an unrelated adult male, Timawi. Ishi's uncle served as *majapa*, or headman, of their commune, which followed traditional ways. The remainder of the Yahi tribe had been killed or driven out of the mountain area by a variety of savage acts perpetrated by white invaders, against whom Ishi whispered curses.

Relatively at peace in his Native American world, Ishi had no memory of a disaster that had taken place early in his life in August 1964, when miners massacred Gahma, a Yahi village, leaving his small cousin Tushi an orphan among the fifty survivors. Only from stories did he learn of the sound of gunfire and horses' hooves that marked the turmoil across the ridge. As his great uncle described the scene, the River Banya ran with Yahi blood.

Adult males from the village of Tuliyani tried to negotiate the release of Yahi prisoners. Laying their hunting bows before the whites, they gestured their wish to exchange weapons for three bound captives. The white men confiscated the bows but refused to barter. An old woman whom they held captive urged the Yahi to leave before they too were captured. Later, Ishi's great uncle tried to track the captors but stopped at the edge of the valley, where natural cover grew too thin to protect him.

SECRET DREAMS

In his growing years, Ishi followed Yahi tribal customs in his everyday behavior. He received love, instruction in religion and woods lore, and wholesome nourishment in the daily meals of acorn mush, fresh salmon and game, herbs, berries, and tender bulbs. He frolicked with his cousin Tushi and anticipated the ritual of manhood, which required him to fashion his own bow and arrows of stout juniper wood and obsidian using primitive rasps and knives made from stone.

Hunting in the safety of darkness, he and his companions hid in caves and made caches of venison for the tribe to share. They named themselves the Fire People because they alone kept alive the Yahi hearth. Three years later, he followed the trail of the Yahi, recalling early memories of his father, a brave man who died fighting twenty white invaders.

To avoid contact with encroaching white settlers, he had learned to move quietly in the territory's forests, ridges, streams, canyons, and meadows. Setting out alone, he regularly crept up the ladder through the smokehole and exited the men's lodge while the tribe slept. Outside, he crawled through wet bushes, scaled a vertical bluff, followed a familiar trail, and arrived at Black Rock, his private spot for observing the world below.

From his secret hiding place, Ishi waited until the light grew stronger, then looked out on the Great Valley and the River Daha. He observed the peculiarities of gold prospectors and other whites as he waited for the whistle of the train, a rumbling beast that made its appearance twice a day. Lying still as he strained his eyes far into the distance, he avoided mounted white men who clattered past without seeing him. Undetected, he made his way back to Tuliyani.

Safely returned to his family, Ishi divulged the dreams that he had experienced in his secret praying place. He saw himself journeying to the Great Valley through the snow. He swam Yuna Creek out of the Yahi world and continued into the River

Daha all the way to the ocean. A companion of the sacred salmon, he remained for many months in the ocean and returned home when the salmon swam upstream toward the village.

THE FIRST LOSS

Ishi prospered, but the other members of his tribe met tragedy. First Timawi took him on a journey to locate new lodging for the tribe. Along the way, after burning a white man's storehouse while Ishi slept, Timawi was attacked by dogs and fatally shot at the foot of an oak tree. Ishi, shouldering a man's responsibility and abstaining from food and sleep for six days, performed ceremonial rites for his companion in Ancestor Cave.

Significant to Ishi's view of the order of things was a proper burial. In the dark and quiet of the cave, he sensed the presence of spirits. He cleansed the stone slab and laid out Timawi's body for purification. Protecting himself from animal intrusion by rolling rocks over the mouth of the cave, Ishi built a fire of tobacco and pine resin and allowed it to burn itself into ash. After six days of ritual burning, he deposited Timawi's remains among his ancestors, placed bow and arrows, pouch, treasure bundle, and acorn meal alongside the body, and rolled the stone slab over the cave opening until future burials.

Journeying wearily homeward to Tuliyani, Ishi arrived bearing signs of mourning. His hair was burned off close to his head; his face was painted with black stripes. His uncle, who understood the meaning of the paint, blew a pinch of sacred tobacco on Ishi and repeated protective prayers to guard him from any danger he might have encountered in the spirit world. Then he blew five more pinches of tobacco to the west to mark the way for Timawi's spirit as it journeyed to the Land of the Dead. After more prayers, he listened to Ishi's account of Timawi's death.

Ishi's uncle praised the boy for following tribal ritual. The others refrained from speaking of Timawi by name and used instead Our Friend or The Restless One. In order to protect themselves, the remaining six tribal members moved mortars, stores, tools, blankets, and food north and west from the pleasant streamside camp at Tuliyani to a rock ledge and abandoned bear's den in Banya Canyon on Wowunupo Mountain. The secrecy of their going obscured their presence from white men in the area.

THE LAST HOME

At the new site, Ishi and the two other male members of the tribe built a soil-covered addition to the cave. Outside they added a storage house, smoking shelter, and lodge. The three women constructed their own lodge. Shaded over by pines, the clearing served well as a new village center. Hunting was easy, but carrying water up the canyon was a daily chore, except in winter, when snow was available at higher elevations.

In the peace of their new home, Ishi's family began its inevitable atrophy. His aged grandparents succumbed to unnamed diseases. First his grandfather died; within three years' time, his grandmother suffered respiratory difficulty, then joined her husband in the Land of the Dead. Their deaths stood out as significant omens to the remaining four people—Ishi, his mother, cousin, and uncle. In Ishi's mind, they became the "Ending, the Last People" (Kroeber, 115).

Even though the tribe's new location seemed well hidden from interlopers, in 1908, when Ishi was forty-seven, a work crew of eight men from the power company swung axes and dug with shovels as it inched its way up a hidden passage in the undergrowth. Ishi's uncle escaped with Tushi, leaving Ishi to guard his disabled mother. The white invaders did Ishi's mother no harm but carried off the tribe's remaining stores, tools, and weapons, leaving only the drying frames behind. After their departure, Ishi took his mother to the lookout point for shelter and searched in vain for the rest of his family, endangering himself by divulging his location to the white workers. In his frenzy, he located only Tushi's shell necklace. All other traces of his uncle and cousin were gone.

Initially, Ishi did not verbalize his fears, but his mother interpreted his grief from his facial expression. The two survived on roots, bulbs, and seeds and made the best of their isolation and sorrow. She bolstered his pride by calling him *wanasi*, or good hunter. A month later, they clung together and wept for their departed family. Stricken with swelling in her legs, Ishi's mother died, leaving him as the only surviving tribal member. During a hunt, a bear wounded him on the shoulder; he bound the wound with herbal poultices. In a daze from trauma, pain, and loss of blood, he wandered the valley where he and Tushi once played, unable to focus on a purpose for living.

Finally, as his old dream predicted, in 1911 Ishi found himself alongside the corral of a slaughtering pen where the Oroville sheriff discovered him, the last surviving Yahi, docile and manageable. As white men surrounded him, spitting tobacco juice and ridiculing his words, the foul smell of the bloodstained slaughterer's apron they had given him to wear overwhelmed him. Scattering the hangers-on, the sheriff took him into custody, handcuffed him, and locked him alone in a jail cell.

COPING WITH THE WHITE WORLD

Ishi had difficulty adapting to the malodorous whites and their peculiar ways. His mind turned to disquieting tales he had heard of hangings, scalpings, and other forms of violence. Each day his sleep was interrupted by the screech and rumble of the passing train, which he envisioned as a smoking monster. The sheriff showed kindness and patience, providing him with a towel, clean clothing, food, a cigar, and protection from less-hospitable whites. He also brought a simple meal as well as people who tried to communicate with Ishi. Before leaving for the night, the sheriff looked in on the sleeping Yahi.

An unarmed stranger came to Ishi's rescue the next day. Surprisingly, he knew a few simple terms in the Yahi language, such as pine, fire, tobacco, star, baby, and home, which he patiently intoned. Ishi, released from isolation, talked out his harrowing experiences until he was too weary to continue. At noon, the stranger returned and continued the conversation. By the end of the day, they had become friends.

The stranger offered to take him back to the Yahi world or to a reservation, both of which Ishi rejected. The third offer—a museum—was more to Ishi's liking. Transported by train to the junction of two rivers, Ishi and his white companion boarded a ferry and crossed the bay. Arriving in the city, they journeyed by trolley to the massive flight of stone steps that led up to the Museum of Anthropology of the University of California in the Parnassus Heights section of San Francisco. As Ishi grew accustomed to his quarters, he accepted the newness of a private room with bath and clothes closet.

He reestablished his life among curators and technicians, including Alfred Kroeber, who chaired the anthropology department. Ishi grew accustomed to sleeping on a bed and wearing white man's clothing, even though he rejected shoes as an encumbrance to his communion with the earth. As his boyhood dream had predicted, he learned to swim in the Pacific Ocean.

In the museum's collection, he found two baskets made by Tushi. Contact with these items flooded him with nostalgia for her soft voice. Later, an anonymous donor returned his personal belongings—his bow and arrows, quiver, and knife. To subdue the anguish he felt from so complete a separation from the Yahi life-style, he wandered Sutro Forest, where an encounter with a small girl reminded him of his love for Tushi. By sharing woods lore with the girl, he turned sad thoughts into useful teaching. He also took seriously his role as mentor to Maliwal, or Young Wolf, son of a white doctor, whom he trained in the same style as he had been trained.

With Kroeber, the museum curator, Dr. Pope, and the doctor's son, Ishi agreed to traverse the land that had once sheltered his tribe. During these two months he relished plain food, a sweatbath in the lodge, old stories told by firelight, a meadow game, a shared smoke, and a private journey to Ancestor Cave. On his way back to San Francisco, he predicted that he would grow old and die there.

In 1912, he demonstrated how the Yahi craft their weapons. After flaking an arrowhead from glass, he indicated that he could make other arrowheads, a harpoon, and a bow to occupy the museum shelves. He drew a map of Yahi territory, marking mountains, creeks, rivers, and the trail his tribe had followed while hiding themselves from whites.

The curator, eager to preserve as much of Native American culture as possible, noted Ishi's words and tribal customs and received his approval to publish a book about the Yahis. Because Ishi was eager to help preserve tribal memories, he was pleased that the curator would immortalize the tribe by writing about it. He lived out his days at the museum, content among white men yet fearful that his spirit would never find eternal rest or food and weapons with no one to perform the ritual funeral.

Ishi suffered an onset of tuberculosis in 1915 and died in March 1916 at age fifty-five. His friends, knowing of his concerns about the afterlife, released his spirit in the traditional manner. As accompaniment for his journey to the afterlife, they buried him with bow, arrows, acorn meal, pipe and tobacco, and treasure bundle. Every sundown over a period of five days, the mourners scattered acorn meal on the ocean waves and called his name. They recalled his parting words: "It is a five day's journey down the Spirit Trail and at its end is the Yahi Land of the Dead, where the Old Ones, the Ancestors, live.... I will never again be separated from Tushi and my father" (Kroeber, 208-209).

A LASTING ACCOUNT

Among Ishi's contributions to the world's knowledge of Native American culture are his descriptions of gods and heroes, a compendium of words, stories, and songs, and an overview of the Yahi's mannerisms and philosophy. In 1925, Alfred Kroeber, using material culled from Ishi's lectures and demonstrations, published *Handbook of the Indians of California*. Drawing on her husband's experiences as background, in 1964 author Theodora Kracaw Kroeber published *Ishi: Last of His Tribe*. The story of Ishi, which won a silver medal from the Commonwealth Club of San Francisco, has been well received by both social scientists and leisure readers.

The lesson that Ishi taught was worthwhile. As a model for white society, Ishi set an example of cleanliness and harmony in the natural environment. A reverence for life was inherent in the Yahi's beliefs. While white settlers destroyed the valley in search of gold and other personal enrichment, Ishi and the Yahi people lived in spartan simplicity, taking only what they needed and respecting life of all kinds. This message, imparted to all who knew Ishi, made his San Francisco sojourn a learning experience not only for staff and children but for patrons who observed Ishi's ways.

SOURCES

Kroeber, Theodora. *Ishi: Last of His Tribe*. New York: Bantam Books, 1964.

Something About the Author, Volume 1. Detroit: Gale Research, 1971.

Jack London

Taming a gnawing inner demon sometimes leads tormented people to desperate attempts to escape as well as significant acts of creativity. Reality, however, impedes them from running away from self, or, as Aesop describes the peculiarly human phenomenon, they change place but cannot alter their nature. Such is the case with Jack London, one of America's finest naturalist writers of fiction, who traveled some of the least civilized parts of the globe, searched for new experiences, and identified with humanistic causes in his attempt to rid himself of insecurity. The offshoot of his unrest was a serious writing career devoted to fresh, virile, action-packed fiction and nonfiction books, stories, and essays about survival, the subject that compelled him to characterize the quest for adventure.

ILLEGITIMACY AND POVERTY

On January 13, 1876, John "Jack" Griffith, who received no surname, was born in San Francisco, California, the unacknowledged son of Professor William Henry Chaney, an itinerant astrologer, and his mistress, Flora Wellman, a palm reader. Flora, whom Chaney deserted during her pregnancy, begged him to legitimize their child, but he rejected her and suggested that she seek an abortion. She went through the motions of attempting suicide, yet failed to convince him of her despair. Chaney moved to Oregon, leaving Flora to fend for herself. She appealed to friends who offered her a room in which to give birth to her son.

In 1881, she married John London, a farmer and widower with eleven children, who gave her five-year-old boy his name. John London developed a father-son relationship with the boy by sharing with him his love of the seashore. The family moved from San Francisco Bay to other locales on the West Coast in search of a piece of land that they could farm. On their twenty-acre spread in Alameda, California, London, an undersized, lonely, and introspective child, attended grade school for a year before his parents moved to a seventy-five-acre ranch near Colma, south of San Francisco.

London was a beautiful child with soft, wavy brown hair, long, curly eyelashes, appealing brown eyes, and a delicate complexion. From early childhood, he loved reading, particularly the adventure stories of Rudyard Kipling. Ambivalent about how to escape the poverty that plagued his family, he longed to become an electrical engineer so that he could attain a secure income and a modicum of prestige.

Throughout London's adolescence and adulthood, a nagging curiosity spurred him to learn more about his father, whom he sought in the seamier parts of the California coast. London's youth, which he spent in the waterfront slums of Oakland, was a time of discontent, delinquency, and unemployment. He quit school at fourteen · but educated himself through extensive reading at the Oakland Public Library, where the director introduced him to classic authors.

A YEN FOR ADVENTURE

Quick to learn the trade of oyster piracy, London joined other bay trollers in pilfering commercial beds, which earned him the name "Prince of the Oyster Pirates" (*Encyclopedia Americana*, 700). When intuition warned him that he would end up jailed or shot by an irate fisherman, he switched sides and used his navigational skills as a successful bay patroller, a job he described in his books *The Cruise of the Dazzler* and *Tales of the Fish Patrol*. Bored so close to home, by seventeen he was sailing for Japan and Alaska aboard the schooner *Sophie Sutherland* on an adventure that formed the nucleus of his novel *The Sea Wolf*, featuring his most dashing hero, Wolf Larsen.

A year later, grieved by the sufferings of poor working-class people like his parents, London allied with members of Coxey's Army, a group that, led by Jacob S. Coxey, marched from Massillon, Ohio, to Washington, D.C., to support legislation to create jobs following the panic of 1893. On the way, his idealism wavered. Again a loner, he wandered north to Canada in the summer of 1894. In Niagara Falls, New York, where he slept outdoors and enjoyed his freedom, London was mesmerized by the power and majesty of the falls' tumbling waters. The idyll ended with his arrest for vagrancy and a month's sentence in the Erie County jail, a misadventure that cured his urge to drift.

Back in Oakland in 1895, London completed high school in one year. By the age of twenty-three, he had held a variety of jobs—newsboy, longshoreman, coal shoveler, canner, jute mill operator, and laundry worker. Supported by a loan from a sympathetic Oakland saloon keeper, he studied philosophy for one semester at the University of California at Berkeley. In class, he was distinguished by his unkempt appearance, uncultivated manners, extensive reading, and wealth of personal experience.

Largely self-taught through his use of public libraries, he read Karl Marx, Friedrich Wilhelm Nietzsche, Charles Darwin, and social philosopher Herbert Spencer. On his own, London evolved a personal understanding of collectivism and the danger of fascism. In 1896 he joined the Socialist party; so profound was his allegiance to leftist philosophy that he ran a largely symbolic campaign as socialist candidate for mayor of Oakland in 1901 and again in 1905. During this period of political fervor, he was arrested for delivering an anticapitalist speech at City Hall Plaza.

Restlessness spurred London on a trip to the Yukon to prospect for gold in the late summer months of the 1897 Gold Rush and offered him a perspective on tales and novels about adventures in the wild. Just north of Skagway, with the aid of Indian guides and other adventurers, he and his brother-in-law scaled Chilcoot Pass and toured the Klondike. He took particular delight in racing their guides, often besting more surefooted mountaineers by sheer daring. He immersed himself so completely in the northland mentality that his later works identified him in the public mind with the stereotypical fearless, individualistic Yukon musher.

By the time London returned to California, he realized that, like most people, he would have to work for a living rather than discover a fortune by sheer luck. At this point, with his health depleted by scurvy, and because storytelling was a skill he felt sure of, he decided to dedicate himself to the sedentary job of writing. Ironically, his Yukon jaunt produced its own type of gold in proceeds from the chair-bound adventures he wrote for the *Overland Monthly* and the *Atlantic Monthly*.

A SETTLED MAN

At twenty-four, London married Bessie Maddern, a peevish, clinging woman with whom he had little in common. They had two daughters, and Jack London settled down to serious composition in a rented house in Piedmont, California. He taught himself how to write by studying forms of literary expression—anecdote, ballad, sonnet, tale, ghost story, and novel. Intent on mastering the writer's trade, he aimed to produce a thousand words each morning. By this determined method, he published his first novel two years later, *Daughter of the Snows*.

Marriage to Bessie proved more stifling than London could tolerate. To escape her cloying defenselessness and frequent domestic crises, he toured London's east end for information to use in *The People of the Abyss*, a sociological study of English slum dwellers. By 1903 their marriage had foundered, and London petitioned for divorce. He moved to Oakland, yet provided a good home for his ex-wife and daughters, whom he visited regularly. Bessie refused to stand on her own and clung to him for support throughout his life.

While still living with his family, London met and courted Charmian "Mate" Kittredge, the niece of a colleague. The strength of their love affair caused him to leave Bessie and marry his new love, to whom he was vastly more suited than Bessie. In adulthood, his daughters recalled the hurt and humiliation their mother suffered because of his cold, self-centered behavior, but they maintained their loyalty because he was so entertaining a father. London and Charmian honeymooned in Carmel, then moved to Beauty Ranch, an overgrown 130-acre farm in Glen Ellen, choice wine-producing land in California. There London dreamed of establishing a sizeable estate run by modern agricultural methods.

THE BATTLE FOR SOLVENCY

The farming venture strapped London for ready cash. In 1903, broke, ailing, and hounded by creditors, he accepted a $2,000 advance from Macmillan to produce *The Call of the Wild*, the story of Buck, a dog that discovers his feral roots. Although

London earned no more from it than from his other books, *The Call of the Wild* became his most famous work. He followed with energetic novels: *The Sea Wolf* (1904), *White Fang* (1906), the autobiographical *Martin Eden* (1909), *Burning Daylight* (1910), and *The Valley of the Moon* (1913), a back-to-the-land idyll. He also wrote forceful short stories, such as those in *The Son of the Wolf* (1900), *The God of His Fathers* (1901), *Children of the Frost* (1902), and "To Build a Fire," the classic tale he published in *The Century Illustrated Monthly Magazine* in August 1908 and two years later collected in *Lost Face*. This story, a moving view of survival through the eyes of a sled dog and man in danger of freezing in subzero temperatures, depicts London's most pervasive themes, the unpredictability of fate and the implacable forces of nature. He supplemented his royalties with lectures and commentary on the Russo-Japanese War for the Hearst newspapers and *Collier's* magazine. As a journalist, he wrote "The Story of an Eye-Witness," a description of the San Francisco earthquake of 1906, which shattered his birthplace.

While writing fiction, London also demonstrated an interest in writing pieces of social betterment, including *The War of the Classes* (1905), *The Road* (1907), *Iron Heel* (1908), *Revolution and Other Essays* (1910), *John Barleycorn* (1913), a detailed study of substance abuse, and *The Little Lady of the Big House* (1916). Fed by personal observations and his travels in the British Isles and the Orient, some of these works served as serious social commentary, especially the treatises on class warfare and poverty. He commiserated with human suffering because of his own wretched childhood, bouts of alcoholism, and addiction to tobacco, opium, and morphine, which he originally took for intestinal and kidney problems and muscle pain.

Although he sought financial independence, London's most serious faults were his inability to manage money and his disinclination to follow a goal to completion. In April 1907, he and his wife set sail on his home-built ketch the *Snark*, named for one of Lewis Carroll's characters, on an expensive voyage reaching as far as the South Pacific. Part of the journey included a side trip to the Hawaiian islands of Maui, Oahu, and Molokai. Roughing it with Charmian, London camped alongside a volcano, learned to surf, and photographed a leper colony, which he wrote about for *The Woman's Home Companion*. Two years later, still in the Pacific realm, he abandoned his plans to go around the world because of ill health and lack of funds for supplies.

In 1909, to shore up his faltering literary reputation, London determinedly returned to writing. He limited the remainder of his sailing days to short-term getaways to Mexico, the Caribbean, and Hawaii aboard the yawl *Roamer*. Hawaii is where London felt most at home and least encumbered by the worries of capitalist society. About this time, he made a singular statement concerning his discouragement with American life: "If I could have my choice about it, I never would put pen to paper— except to write a socialist essay to tell the bourgeois world how much I despise it" (*Encyclopedia Americana*, 702).

A MONUMENT TO SELF

In 1910, London again set out on a personal quest, this time to build Wolf House, a twenty-three-room $100,000 ranch house built of two rugged substances, redwood and lava boulders. The imposing edifice required three years of intense labor and most of his financial resources. As it neared completion in 1913, Wolf House burned, possibly by the work of an arsonist. The loss put London deeply in debt. Unable to replace the structure and realize his dream or even to support his children, he receded into alcoholism.

Scaling down the vision of a home, London and Charmian contented themselves with a ranch cottage, where he began writing with more speed and less artistry. He continued remodeling buildings and adding to his property by purchasing adjacent parcels of land. The additions of a modern hog farm, silos, and an orchard of 140,000 eucalyptus trees increased his net worth, although he never realized enough profit to cover his investment or the cost of upkeep. When necessary, he left the ranch and sought book material on location, such as his 1913 trip to a hotel and lighthouse in Port Orford, Oregon, which gave him information for *The Valley of the Moon*.

Still unsettled about his identity, London continued fighting the internal battle of what he represented and believed in. In 1916, his alliance with socialism came to an end. While battling cancer of the throat, London injected himself with a fatal dose of morphine and died at Beauty Ranch on November 21, 1916, at the age of forty. Family and colleagues debated about the nature of his overdose, which gave the appearance of suicide. Charmian interred his ashes under a rose lava boulder near the graves of two pioneer children. Two years after his death, his dystopian novelette *The Red One* was published. In 1922, Charmian set down her memories of traveling with him in *Our Hawaii*, a reflection on the couple's trip to Haleakala Ranch on Maui in 1907.

CRITICAL ACCLAIM

Critics and fans have remained loyal to London. A sizeable collection of London's works, photographs, and notes is displayed in the Huntington Library in San Marino, California. A trail at Kalaupapa on Molokai Island commemorates the visit of Jack and Charmian London in 1907. The 1,300-acre Jack London State Historic Park in Glen Ellen preserves fifty acres of his Beauty Ranch. On the grounds, the House of Happy Walls, Charmian's residence until she died in 1955, displays his Dictaphone and desk and the furniture he built for Wolf House.

London, a friend of Robert Louis Stevenson, Joaquin Miller, and Mark Twain, was the most widely read author of his age. Altogether, he earned more for his books than any of his contemporaries and dominated the literary world in the first decades of the twentieth century; however, his readership declined markedly after World War I. Against the journalistic realism of Ernest Hemingway, London's gold-mining days in the Yukon seemed dated.

London, who had achieved instant success with *The Call of the Wild*, his second novel, produced a phenomenal amount of writing—fifty books in fourteen years. His best novels demonstrate intense storytelling ability as well as the influence of Darwinism, particularly the concept of survival of the fittest. Literature classes return to his energetic works to study his ability to craft a plot and achieve a balance of theme, mood, character, and setting. His books are in constant demand in Russia, where readers of his works are numerous.

A crucial element in London's fiction is naturalism. Employing a scientist's meticulous examination of nature, London wrote a vigorous, detailed sketch of elemental instincts, which allowed his most famous nonhuman characters, White Fang and Buck, to survive in the wild against powerful odds of hunger, cold, accident, and the constant threat of predators, both human and animal. This dramatic intermeshing of environment and character resulted in a realistic study of behavior that continues to draw readers, especially those interested in the forces of nature.

Biographers have been intrigued by the unexplained drive that saw London through his work and adventures, despite serious illness and addiction. Most point to the lifetime of obstacles to which London, a believer in the superman myth, refused to cede. Depicted as the son seeking a father, the man in search of a patrimony, the writer rapt in creative effort, London seems all the more laudable for his success.

SOURCES

Beauchamp, Gorman. *Jack London.* San Bernardino, Calif.: Borgo Press, 1984.

Hedrick, Joan D. *Solitary Comrade: Jack London and His Work.* Chapel Hill: University of North Carolina Press, 1982.

"Jack London." *Encyclopedia Americana*, vol. 17. Danbury, Conn.: Grolier, 1987, 700-702.

Lundquist, James. *Jack London: Adventures, Ideas and Fiction,* New York: Frederick Ungar, 1987.

Perry, John. *Jack London: An American Myth.* Chicago: Nelson-Hall, 1981.

Sinclair, Andrew. *Jack: Biography of Jack London.* New York: Washington Square Press, 1983.

Stone, Irving. *Jack London: Sailor on Horseback.* New York: Doubleday, 1978.

Carson McCullers

Overcoming handicaps, particularly loneliness and alienation, because the meat of Carson McCullers's novels and short stories, famed for their unique blend of poignant and grotesque characters. An outgrowth of the southern literary renaissance, her fiction brought her acceptance with the in-crowd of New York, a boost that took her far from her roots and quickly weakened the source of her inspiration. Like her characters, she made a life's work out of establishing viable human relationships and for twenty-five years survived anemia, strokes, and a chronic respiratory disease that robbed her of strength and filled her with a sense of urgency.

SOUTHERN VIEWPOINT

Lula Carson Smith McCullers, born to Lamar and Marguerite Waters Smith on February 19, 1917, in the downtown section of Columbus, Georgia, was named for her maternal grandmother, Lula Carolina Carson Waters, with whom the family lived. Her father repaired watches in his jewelry store; Marguerite assisted him by selecting suitable stock for his clientele. The first of three children, followed by Lamar, Jr., and Margarita Gachet Smith in 1919 and 1922, Carson, nicknamed Tartie, was a big-eyed tomboy—lank and rather plain with straight brown hair, a soulful expression, and solitary habits. She attended kindergarten, then entered the Sixteenth Street School in 1923. When she was eight, her parents moved farther from town, where she attended Wynnton School and, in the family tradition, was baptized into the membership of the First Baptist Church.

Carson loved music, as is evidenced by frequent references to lessons and practice sessions in her fiction. With Marguerite's encouragement, she began studying piano with a local teacher and in 1930 decided to become a professional pianist. During early adolescence, she was invited to join a youth dance club, not because she was popular but because she was the only young pianist available. Bedfast at fifteen after a severe attack of rheumatic fever, which presaged a life of serious ailments, she began writing fiction and changed her career plans from music to writing but continued studying piano and concealed her new career goal from her teacher and friend, Mary Tucker.

Carson graduated from Columbus High School in 1933 and launched a home-reading program focusing on the significant novels and dramas from the canon of U.S., British, and Russian classics. Inspired by the works of Eugene O'Neill, she wrote *The Faucet*, her first drama, and cast her siblings in the parts. The next year, she made a significant break with the past when her piano teacher moved away from Columbus. At age seventeen, Carson convinced her mother that New York was the · place she should settle. There she could study music at Juilliard and creative writing at Columbia University. To pay the train fare to Savannah and the steamship passage to New York City, she sold the heirloom ring given her by her grandmother.

TO THE BIG CITY

The journey from Columbus formed a meaningful part of Carson's growing up. In later years, she joked about pinning $500 in traveling money to her underwear and taking a room at a brothel before she realized the nature of the late-night traffic and moved to the Parnassus Club and later to the Three Arts Club to obtain a more respectable residence. In her free hours, she haunted the waterfront to take in sights, sounds, and smells. While traveling by subway into town, she lost the proceeds from the ring and had to rethink how she would finance her education. She located jobs as typist, waitress, dog walker, accompanist for dance classes, and bookkeeper to enable her to attend creative-writing classes at Columbia by the second semester. She came home for the summer to study journalism by volunteering to write without pay for the Columbus *Ledger* before returning to New York to enroll at Washington Square College for two more semesters.

In June 1935, Carson met James Reeves McCullers, Jr., an Alabaman four years her senior who was serving a second hitch in the U.S. Army and was stationed at Fort Benning, Georgia. They formed a twosome in the winter of the next year after Reeves left the army to study journalism at Columbia. Because she became seriously ill with rheumatic fever, he escorted her home, where she spent the winter writing *The Heart Is a Lonely Hunter*, tentatively titled *The Mute*, and two stories, "Wunderkind" and "Like That," which were purchased by *Story* magazine. A return to Columbia and a second hurried trip south to recuperate from illness led Carson to agree to marry her rescuer, who searched for a stable job so that he could support a wife.

After Reeves settled in as credit investigator with a Charlotte, North Carolina, finance company, he married Carson in the Smith family living room on September 20, 1937. The bride, never a clothes horse, wore a suit, brown oxfords, and anklet socks. A neighbor provided hors d'oeuvres for guests, who followed the newlyweds to the depot and waved as their train pulled out. In Charlotte, the couple moved to his apartment, a shabby, ill-lighted place, but all he could afford on depression-era wages.

A transfer took Reeves and Carson to a seedier apartment in Fayetteville, North Carolina, where she ignored housework so that she could gad about town, chat with neighbors, and concentrate on her novel, *The Heart Is a Lonely Hunter*. After seeking two expert opinions, she entered it in the Houghton Mifflin Fiction Fellowship competition. Although she did not win first place, she placed the work with

Houghton Mifflin in 1938 and completed it to company specifications by April 1939. The sale fed her hopes that she and Reeves could earn enough to move away from the South, where poverty and racism depressed and discouraged them. Again pushed beyond her physical capacities, McCullers returned to her family, then came back to Reeves. Against the background of Fort Bragg, the army post outside Fayetteville, she began *Reflections in a Golden Eye*, a macabre voyeur's glimpse of perverse sexual practices near a southern military base, which she finished after two months of work and sold to *Harper's Bazaar* for $500. A later trip to Columbus brought two crucial concepts to her mind: First, she was beginning to work out the plot of a third novel, which she planned to name *The Bride and Her Brother*; second, she realized that her marriage had been a mistake.

SUCCESS AS A HANDICAP

McCullers published *The Heart Is a Lonely Hunter* in 1940 and achieved instant acceptance as a prodigy and probably too much attention too soon in her career. The novel, a complicated circular narrative, puts John Singer, a deaf-mute person, at the center of four down-and-out characters—a dying Black doctor, a widowed diner owner, a scruffy Socialist, and a teenage music lover, each of whom draws compassion and support from John's friendship. Critics considered it her most mature fiction. The success of the novel and other writers' attitudes toward her temporarily altered McCullers's desire to divorce Reeves. As biographer Virginia Spencer Carr described the change: "Life with Reeves was sweet-tasting all over again in New York City, and she thanked God that the ugly chapter of their wretchedness in Fayetteville was over" (Carr, 98).

Rather than ending her marriage as she had planned, she and Reeves abandoned the South and moved to a Greenwich Village apartment, where they enjoyed the ferment of literary friends. Pushed by her publisher, she accepted a grant to attend Bread Loaf, a writers' colony near Middlebury, Vermont, where she came under the influence of Louis Untermeyer, Eudora Welty, Katherine Anne Porter, Bernard De Voto, W. H. Auden, Robert Frost, and John Ciardi and earned a reputation for heavy drinking, chain-smoking, and independence. Her resolve to stay married lasted until September, when she left her husband and moved into two rooms in a large Victorian brownstone in Brooklyn Heights, which she shared with W. H. Auden, Gypsy Rose Lee, Richard Wright, and George Davis.

During that winter, McCullers's mother came to New York to tend her daughter during another bout of illness, then transported her home to Columbus. By 1941, McCullers had extended her published works to short stories for *Vogue* and the independent publication of *Reflections in a Golden Eye*, which brought threats on her family from the Ku Klux Klan. Her health faltered more seriously; this time a cerebral stroke resulted in diminished eyesight and migraine headaches. Friends noticed that she seemed driven, narcissistic, often talking at great length. She was terrified that declining health would destroy her ability to write and leave her permanently bedfast.

That spring, Reeves, intent on salvaging their marriage and rescuing his wife from an early grave, took her to New York, but this change did little to improve their home life. McCullers, during periods of intense concentration, relied on sherry and cough syrup containing codeine to ward off further respiratory illness. The couple began drifting apart as both drank to excess and Reeves pursued other women.

During a six-week workshop at the Yaddo Artists' Colony in Saratoga Springs, McCullers, surrounded by an exciting array of professional writers, completed *The Ballad of the Sad Café*, the story of a doomed love between an old maid and her cousin, a peculiar dwarf. She continued publishing essays, reviews, and stories for *Decision, Vogue, Saturday Review, The New Yorker*, and *Harper's Bazaar*. By fall, her career more firmly established and her health improved, she initiated formal divorce proceedings. That winter she returned to her parents to recover from pneumonia, pleurisy, and complications.

With her divorce settled and Reeves back in the army, McCullers accepted her first major award, a Guggenheim Fellowship, on March 24, 1942. Weakness and the potential recurrence of pneumonia hindered her from taking her dream vacation to Mexico. Instead, she returned to Yaddo to write. The next year was a repeat of the pattern of writing, publication, illness, and retreat to Columbus. In April, her career received a boost after she won a $1,000 grant from the American Academy of Arts and Letters, but her personal life remained a muddle with repeated attempts to reshape a relationship with Reeves, who departed in November for frontline duty in Europe.

UNSETTLED TIMES

The remainder of the war years left McCullers battered and weary. As she struggled to maintain her own modest gains in health, she fretted about Reeves, who participated in the landing at Normandy and the Battle of Brest. After the death of her father, she joined her mother and sister in renting an apartment in Nyack, New York, just north of the New Jersey border along the Hudson River. Reeves's safe return from fifteen months of duty ended with their remarriage in a civil ceremony in New York on March 19, 1945. By August, following a monastic stay at Yaddo, McCullers completed *The Member of the Wedding*, a story of a girl's obsession with her brother's wedding. Famed for its tender recreation of the insecurities of adolescence, the book was published in 1946 and led to her second Guggenheim Fellowship, which she and Reeves spent in Paris among appreciative fans.

McCullers's second stroke occurred in August 1947. Hospitalized in a U.S. facility in Paris, she suffered paralysis on the left side. She and Reeves, who suffered chronic alcoholism, flew home on stretchers and again parted. While accolades poured in to her bedside from *Mademoiselle* and *Quick* magazine, she struggled to regain control of her weakened body. With the encouragement of friend Tennessee Williams, she adapted *The Member of the Wedding* into a stage play in 1949 and saw it produced at Philadelphia's Walnut Theatre. The play, which ran for 501 performances, won the New York Drama Critics' Circle Award and the Donaldson Award for its Broadway run. The 1952 Columbia motion-picture version starred Julie

Harris, Ethel Waters, and Brandon de Wilde. Harris won an Academy Award nomination for her role as Frankie Addams, a thinly disguised version of McCullers in her early teen years.

MAKING THE BEST OF THINGS

For a short period, McCullers managed to enjoy both health and acclaim. She bought a three-story house in Nyack, continued publishing stories, poems, and essays, and visited Ireland, England, and France. Her circle of famous friends enlarged to include Elizabeth Bowen and Dame Edith Sitwell. Consultations with doctors on both sides of the Atlantic failed to restore life to McCullers's left arm. Again sick with pneumonia after a trip to New Orleans with Reeves, she returned to Nyack late in 1951 to recuperate.

By 1952, McCullers was able to sail aboard the *Constitution* to Italy. While touring Europe, she and Reeves purchased an old vicarage in Bachvillers, a village north of Paris on the Oise River. However, living together in their new residence did not lead to their patching up their differences. During this time, she published *The Ballad of the Sad Café and Collected Short Stories* and collaborated on a screenplay in Rome while coping with her drunken, spendthrift husband. Reconciliation with Reeves proved painful; in order to tolerate their failed relationship, she, too, drank heavily. Reeves, demented beyond her ability to cope with him, tried to convince her to commit suicide with him by hanging. After she fled the country, on November 19, 1953, he died from an overdose of barbiturates and alcohol.

FROM WRITER TO TEACHER

In her late thirties, McCullers wrote fewer new titles and spent more time thinking of ways to produce her works in play and ballet form. Accompanied by Tennessee Williams, she took up lecturing at Goucher College, then at Columbia University and the Philadelphia Fine Arts Association. The two journeyed to Williams's Key West home to vacation and work in privacy. Her idyll ended abruptly with the death of her mother, a mainstay during McCullers's chronic illnesses.

While fighting the pain and the withering effects of paralysis on her left arm, McCullers continued planning productions of her works and producing stories and poems for *Mademoiselle, Literary Cavalcade,* and *Botteghe Oscure.* Because staged versions of *The Square Root of Wonderful* fared poorly, she became depressed and worried that she might never write well again. Psychiatric care reduced her anxiety and renewed her confidence.

THE FINAL YEARS

In her final years, McCullers continued to battle infirmity as she strove to make the most of her talents. She blossomed into a major spokesperson for the arts and appeared at the American Academy of Arts and Letters and the National Institute of Arts and Letters with Danish writer Isak Dinesen, her longtime heroine. Continuing to work on a musical version of *The Ballad of the Sad Café*, McCullers twice opted for surgery on her crippled arm to ease her pain and, fearful that her leg would have to be amputated, abandoned her cane for a wheelchair.

By the end of 1960, McCullers, her health failing to the point that she could no longer hold a pencil, completed *Clock Without Hands*, worked with Edward Albee on a dramatic adaptation of *The Ballad of the Sad Café*, and continued publishing stories and articles. Exploratory surgery following a broken hip and crushed elbow left her gravely ill late in the summer of 1965. The final breakdown occurred August 15, 1967, when she suffered a third stroke and lay in a coma for six weeks from a brain hemorrhage. She died at Nyack Hospital on September 29, 1967, in Nyack, New York, and was buried in Oak Hill Cemetery.

CRITICS' VIEWS

Critics lauded McCullers's sensitivity to southern settings and themes, particularly those emanating from gothic perversities. She was admired for her compassion toward the estranged and isolated and gained a strong following among French and English critics, who placed her in the ranks of Faulkner and Hemingway. *Time* magazine considered her one of the top twelve writers of her time; shortly before her death, *Die Welt* in Hamburg, Germany, awarded her the Prize of the Younger Generation. In 1968, Warner Seven Arts produced the film version of *The Heart Is a Lonely Hunter*. Three years later, her early short stories were collected in *The Mortgaged Heart*. Her work, much stronger than her frail body, continues through her tender remembrances to reveal southern life from the view of one who lived it.

SOURCES

Carr, Virginia Spencer. *The Lonely Hunter: A Biography of Carson McCullers*. Garden City, N.Y.: Doubleday, 1975.

Wilson, Charles Reagan, and William Ferris, eds. *Encyclopedia of Southern Culture*. Chapel Hill: University of North Carolina Press, 1989.

Golda Meir

Golda Meir earned her place among the twentieth century's top women by pushing for a utopia, the creation of a free state of Israel. In an article in *The Ploughwoman*, Golda explained her belief in a woman's right to pursue her dream: "There is a type of woman who cannot remain at home; ... her nature and being demand something more; she cannot divorce herself from a larger social life. She cannot let her children narrow her horizon. And for such a woman, there is no rest" (Meir 1973, 42).

Like her ideal, Meir was a forceful, magnetic personality destined to sway people with her belief in self and Zionism. As Israel's fourth prime minister, she overcame preconceived ideas about a woman's place in politics and led her country during a serious attack on its sovereignty. For her, a fanatical zeal for a noble cause represented the essence of life.

BORN REBEL

The daughter of shopkeeper Bluma Naiditch and Moshe Yitzhak Mabovitch, a carpenter and furniture maker, Goldie Mabovitch Meir, named for her great grandmother, was born on May 3, 1898, in Kiev, Russia, where rumors of Cossack-led pogroms kept Jews in a state of fear. Her earliest memories of Russia center on terror, squalor, and hunger. She recalled in her autobiography that one of her sisters and four brothers died in infancy, one from smallpox, one from typhoid, and one from asphyxiation. Insufferable conditions drove the family to Pinsk on the Dnieper River to live with Bluma's father, Menahem, an innkeeper. To ease the family's want, in 1903 Moshe left to make his fortune in the United States; Bluma moved her daughters into a rented room and waited for the big move to a new country. The younger children studied at home.

Against parental orders, Shana, Meir's sister and idol, joined a forbidden Zionist-Socialist group. Because her connection with revolutionaries endangered the whole family, emigration was imperative. The rest of the Mabovitches, including eight-year-old Meir and baby Clara, sailed from Russia to Canada on falsified passports, then traveled by train to the United States.

At the direction of the Hebrew Immigrant Aid Society, a Jewish settlement agency, the family moved to Milwaukee, Wisconsin, where jobs were reputed to be plentiful. Moshe labored in a railroad workshop repairing train cars; Bluma ran a grocery store in the front of their rented rooms on Walnut Street; Shana made buttonholes in a tailor shop but refused to be Americanized. Eventually she was sent to a tuberculosis sanitarium in Colorado and married her Russian fiancé, but she secretly stayed in contact with her little sister.

A MIND OF HER OWN

From early childhood, Meir demonstrated willful, obstinate ways. She saved her earnings from giving English lessons to Polish immigrants so that she could be as financially independent as possible. When she lacked funds to buy schoolbooks, she organized a fund-raiser to impress on parents the absurdity of free education without books. After a fellow student victimized her, she mounted a campaign outside his home and made public his anti-Semitism. People began to expect exhibitionism from Meir.

At home, she raged most over being forced to tend the shop and carry out household duties while Bluma recovered from multiple miscarriages. Even worse, her mother disapproved of her choice of a teaching career, which would require her to remain single. Bluma insisted that she study secretarial skills so that she could land a husband. The height of Meir's home squabbles came after Bluma selected a thirty-year-old man as Meir's future husband. When Meir refused to consider the arrangement, Bluma ordered her to quit school.

In February 1913, unable to get along with her old-fashioned parent, Meir crept out the window with her small suitcase and hid in the bushes. Later, she walked to Union Station and boarded the train for Denver, where she lived with Shana, attended North High School, and worked in her brother-in-law Sam Korngold's dry-cleaning shop. Life in the Korngold house introduced her to free thinkers. From Shana's dissident friends, she learned of the Jewish homeland predicted in the writings of Austrian philosopher Theodor Herzl, a homeland she one day wanted to be part of.

Shana, more conservative after the birth of her own children, put a tight rein on her sister's many dates and frenetic social life. At sixteen, Meir, too independent to tolerate brow-beating, left, quit school, and took a job in a laundry stretching curtains. Into the vacuum of her lonely life came Morris Meyerson, a shy, sensitive sign painter five years older than she. They initiated each other into romance, but Morris realized that she was not ready for matrimony. At the urging of Morris and her father, she returned home. She was eager to finish school and more certain about the kind of life she wanted.

Determined to seize her dream, Meir joined the Socialist-Zionist Poale Zion in 1915 and worked at the Saturday Folkschule, where she taught children their cultural heritage. She graduated from the Milwaukee Normal School in 1916 and attended Teacher's Training College in Madison. The news of her increasing alliance with Zionism did not gladden Morris, who remained passive about politics. Undaunted, she continued to batter his resolve with her zeal. After meeting David Ben-Gurion, she knew that some day she would settle in the Jewish homeland. To pay passage to Palestine, she worked at the Lapham Park Library.

To encourage more Zionists to support the Poale Zion's goals, Meir became the party's mouthpiece, a job that tapped her natural talents. She moved to Chicago and supported herself as junior library assistant at the Chicago Public Library while helping the local chapter of Poale Zion proselytize more Jews. After statesman Sir Arthur Balfour announced Great Britain's interest in establishing a Jewish homeland in Palestine, Morris began to waver. He became Meir's toughest convert.

MAKING THINGS HAPPEN

On December 24, 1917, she married Morris in her parents' dining room and pursued her leadership in Milwaukee's Labor Zionist party. In September 1920, she and Morris moved to New York, that much closer to their goal of emigration. They lived in a six-room apartment in Morningside Heights, which they shared with a Canadian couple; Meir worked as a librarian and later at Gimbel's Department Store to earn their fares. On May 19, 1921, the Meyersons left the United States aboard the S.S. *Pocahontas*, a listing, poorly managed vessel sailing by way of Boston, the Azores, Naples, Brindisi, and Alexandria. They took the train for the last leg over the Sinai to Tel Aviv. Concerning their departure, she had little reason to be sad: "I took what I valued with me. So I had no regrets about leaving anything behind. I was leaving to participate in the setting up of independence and security for my own people" (Martin, 98).

Meir and her husband, accompanied by other Zionists, arrived in Tel Aviv July 14 and applied to live on the thirty-two-member Merhavya agricultural kibbutz. Until their acceptance, they found temporary jobs: She gave English lessons; he kept books for the British. Housing was meager, their baggage and mail were delayed, but Meir remained positive that she would one day help rebuild Israel. To prove her determination to stay, she gave up her U.S. passport and registered as an immigrant.

Finally accepted at Merhavya, Meir, at first ridiculed as a soft American, cared for chickens, threshed grain, planted trees, hoed tomatoes, baked bread, and superintended the laundry. In her letters to her parents, she abstained from describing the hardship of life in a desert land surrounded by hostile Arabs. Morris barely tolerated the lack of privacy; Meir, filled with energy and excitement, thrived on the atmosphere and earned a reputation as leader and idealogue. For once in her life, there was equality of the sexes.

LOSSES AND GAINS

Kibbutz life strained Meir's marriage. Morris refused to start a family there because children were raised by everyone, not just the parents. After he became seriously ill with malaria, Meir realized his inability to adjust to kibbutz life, and they left Merhavya and moved to Tel Aviv, where they lived in a squalid apartment without drinkable water, electricity, or plumbing. She worked as a cashier while Morris kept books in Jerusalem.

The birth of their son Menahem on November 23, 1924, did little to revitalize the dying marriage. For a few months, she returned to Merhavya to renew her enthusiasm but came home to Morris in despair. In May 1926, she gave birth to Sarah, a sickly child who often required medical care. To provide a nursery-school education, Meir agreed to do the school's laundry even though she had to boil water and scrub on a washboard. Later, she got a job teaching English at Miss Kallen's school.

The break in Meir's dismal life came when she was twenty-nine and was hired as secretary of the Women's Workers' Council. The challenge of readying women for a grueling job market required travel and separation from Morris and the children. The pull on her loyalties forced a crisis in her thinking. In her words, "A mother in public life—in her feelings—will never be the same as a man or a father in public life.... When the mother has to leave home ... and the child is down with a temperature, even if the best person is taking care it is not the same" (Martin, 148).

The Meyerson marriage remained intact even though she and Morris saw each other mainly on weekends and stayed together merely for the children's sake. She entered into several liaisons with leaders of the Zionist movement. Rumors circulated about her open adulteries. Meir, plagued by guilt that she neglected her family, suffered intense migraine attacks.

A promotion to secretary of Pioneer Women, a Zionist feminist movement, came at a grim time in Meir's life. Sarah was suffering from what doctors thought was terminal nephritis. Meir, stubborn as always, defied their diagnosis and took her children by steamer and train to New York, where Sarah was cured within six weeks. By the beginning of World War II, Meir had returned her children to Palestine, separated for good from Morris, and entered into the most intense part of her fight for a free Jewish homeland.

A FREE ISRAEL

At age thirty-six, Meir launched her political career by joining the labor committee of Histadrut, which ran Israel during its formative months. Her chief thrust in the establishment of a Jewish state was as fund-raiser in the United States and as head of the political department, which fought for the right to grant asylum to refugees. As spokesperson for Labor party leaders, she held her own against the British and, during widespread arrests, worked for the release of detainees and replaced Moshe Sharett, head of the political department of the Jewish Agency, after his capture.

Other assignments tested Meir's adaptability. One was to dissuade Jordan's King Abdullah, the Jews' only ally in the Middle East, from invading Israel. To accomplish the task, she dressed in the garb of a female Muslim and visited the king in secret to stop his alliance with more bellicose Arab statesmen. On May 14, 1948, she joined the signers of the state's declaration of independence and helped select a formal name for the country. Her tears flowed abundantly as she recalled fellow settlers who had not survived the difficult beginnings. That same year, Premier David

Ben-Gurion selected her as Israel's ambassador to the Soviet Union, where she lived until spring 1949.

Meir began a long career as member of the Knesset, Israel's parliament, and as minister of labor. She took pride in building roads and housing, supplying water from desalinization plants, diversifying industry, expanding free public education, and supporting a surge in Jewish immigration, which threatened to overrun the country's resources. In 1956, the year she renamed herself Meir, the Hebrew form of Meyerson, her focus shifted to foreign affairs, which she dominated until 1965, when she attempted to retire and moved to a pleasant tree-lined street in Ramat Aviv.

Because Israel suffered a deep recession, mainly because of Egypt's new restrictions on the Suez Canal, a forceful committee talked Meir into abandoning retirement after one month. She agreed to canvass the country for support for Israel's failing political coalition. One of her goals was the fostering of emerging African nations as a means of weakening the power of Muslims and gaining new supporters for Israel. In 1967 she was instrumental in the merger of two splinter groups threatening the solidarity of Mapai, the Labor party.

Meir was serving as secretary of Mapai on February 16, 1969, when Premier Levi Eshkol died of a heart attack. Chosen interim premier because of her experience and credibility, she moved even further from retirement to accept the post, which brought sixteen-hour days, a chauffeur-driven car, and less privacy than she had known as a member of the Knesset. She remained in office until June 1974, surprising world leaders who doubted that a woman in her mid-seventies could run a government effectively. Much of her service to Israel lay in travels to confer with other heads of state, including Romania's Nicolae Ceauşescu in 1972 and West Germany's Chancellor Willy Brandt and Pope Paul VI in 1973.

Her greatest challenge came in the Yom Kippur War of October 1973, in which Egypt and Syria launched an attack over possession of the Sinai, trouncing all hopes of a Middle East peace settlement. Critics lambasted her and her defense minister, Moshe Dayan, for delaying troop deployment, a decision that nearly cost her the war. More terrible perhaps was her self-criticism. In her words, "I shall live with that terrible knowledge for the rest of my life. I will never again be the person I was before the Yom Kippur War" (Meir 1975, 425).

The political infighting that resulted from the muddle endangered Meir's failing health and slowed the formation of a coalition government in the spring of 1974, although Israelis continued to love and support her with an 80 percent popularity rating. On April 10, with support for the Labor party ebbing rapidly, she resigned as prime minister but continued at the post until June, when Yitzhak Rabin replaced her. The last years of Meir's life were filled with party activities, visits with her children and grandchildren, and the composition of her autobiography. She died in Jerusalem on December 8, 1978, of leukemia, a disease she had concealed for twelve years.

A LEADER

From the outset, Golda Meir determined to prove that her vision of women in power was feasible: To her, women could achieve anything they set out to do. As a means of implementing her theories, she encouraged young women to be strong and to dare to make a difference with their lives. When dealing with power figures, she refused to kowtow or allow patronization from kings, popes, or presidents. While negotiating for weapons and loans, she made plain that Israel would stand on its own without help from outsiders.

Being a woman to Golda was merely a biological state, not a limitation. Her colleagues quickly grasped that she exhibited the strength of both sexes. As her political adviser, Simcha Dinitz, noted, she had "the best qualities of a woman—intuition, insight, sensitivity, compassion—plus the best qualities of a man—strength, determination, practicality, purposefulness. So we're lucky. We have double qualities—in one person" (Mann, 231).

Working to find homes and jobs for thousands of immigrants, many of them Holocaust survivors, Meir became a symbol of freedom and commitment. Her greatest fans spoke of her as "our Golda." The final words of her autobiography reveal her pride in Israel, "a country whose people have learned how to go on living in a sea of hatred without hating those who want to destroy them and without abandoning their own vision of peace. To have learned this is a great art" (Meir 1975, 459-460).

SOURCES

Mann, Peggy. *Golda: The Life of Israel's Prime Minister*. New York: Coward, McCann & Geoghegan, 1971.

Martin, Ralph G. *Golda Meir: The Romantic Years*. New York: Charles Scribner's Sons, 1988.

Meir, Golda. *A Land of Our Own*. Edited by Marie Syrkin. New York: G. P. Putnam's Sons, 1973.

_____. *My Life*. New York: G. P. Putnam's Sons, 1975.

Joseph Merrick

Remanded by his caretaker to a seamy professional freak show, Joseph Carey Merrick, a pitiable, unsightly outcast and wanderer, had little hope of acceptance in society until one man entered his life and offered him friendship and a tinge of human dignity. The hideously contorted frame, globular skin, and misshapen head, eye, and lip, which obscured verbal sounds and impaired his eating, continued to imprison Merrick for the remainder of his life, but for a brief span, he made normal contact with other human beings.

MISERY AND REJECTION

Repulsively deformed, Joseph Merrick (sometimes incorrectly identified as John or James), the first of three children of Joseph Rockley Merrick, a hack driver, and his wife, Mary Jane Potterton Merrick, a servant, was born August 5, 1862, in a slum off Lee Street, Leicester, England. His explanation of his deformity is an old wives' tale — that his mother, herself a cripple, was terrified while pregnant by a rampaging elephant in a traveling circus. When Merrick was born, the disfiguring condition was not yet manifest. By age twenty-one months, he had a large tumor on his lower lip; at age five, he fell and injured his hip, which developed a disabling disease. He bore a huge mottled head covered in warty masses of flesh. His right hand was equally massive and was paddle-shaped; one finger measured five inches in circumference. His left hand, which had more normal proportions, never grew to adult size. Protruding gray lumps of tissue, like dewlaps, covered his body, feet, and legs.

Merrick's unbalanced form seriously compromised normal movement. He could scarcely toddle, even with the assistance of a cane. He slept poorly because of the enormity of his head, which tended to fall backward and compress his spine and windpipe. In order to rest, he slept sitting up with his arms about his drawn-up legs and his cheek against his knees.

Owing to the love and support of his mother, whom he deified in his memories, Merrick managed to attend Board School on Syston Street until May 1873, when she died of bronchial pneumonia. His father moved to temporary lodgings and, in 1874, married his landlady, Emma Antill, a cruel, unsympathetic woman who could not cope with a monstrously handicapped stepson. In his autobiography, Merrick recounts his childhood misery and feeble attempts to escape it. Each time he ran away, his father returned the boy to the wretched domestic arrangement, where he could anticipate no love beyond the kindness of his uncle, Charles Merrick, a Leicester hairdresser and tobacconist.

Employed at Freeman's Cigar Factory for two years, Joseph Merrick had to give up rolling cigars after his right hand grew too clumsy for manipulating tobacco leaves. His stepmother deprived him of full meals and thrust him into the streets to earn his keep. Rather than return to her vile outbursts, he wandered about, hungry and dejected. For a time he peddled stockings and gloves door-to-door, but people found him such an intriguing curiosity that they gathered to gawk rather than to buy. His father ejected him permanently from home, and Merrick lived for two years with his uncle. After the local magistrate revoked the boy's peddler's license and proclaimed him a public nuisance, he moved out on his own and, shortly after Christmas 1879, joined nearly a thousand other unfortunates at the local workhouse.

To reduce the trunklike mound that obscured the right side of his head and impeded chewing and speaking, Merrick entered the Leicester Infirmary for oral surgery. The excision, unlike many medical procedures of his day, was successful, and he remained for nearly three years to recuperate. During his stay, he learned to read and familiarized himself with the Bible and the Book of Common Prayer, which served as the mainstay of his faith for the rest of his life.

SIDESHOW FREAK

In August 1884, when his head was sufficiently healed, Merrick left the workhouse and contacted Sam Torr, a local barker who dealt in freaks and variety acts. Torr sent him to J. Ellis at the Beehive Inn in Nottingham, where Merrick made his debut in show business and was, in comparison with his early years, well treated. He concluded his autobiography at this point, noting that he felt as much acceptance from strangers attending his public display as he did from family and acquaintances.

Sir Frederick Treves, an anatomy professor at the Medical College of London Hospital with a special interest in scrofula, picked up the thread of Merrick's tale in November 1884 from a staff surgeon who had visited the sideshow. Treves visited the exhibit and found a garish advertising canvas tacked across the door of a deserted shop on Mile End Road, opposite London Hospital. For two cents, viewers could enter to see the half-man, half-elephant inside. Treves's own response attested to his humanity: "There was nothing about [the advertisement] of the pitiableness of the misshapened or the deformed, nothing of the grotesqueness of the freak, but merely the loathing insinuation of a man being changed into an animal" (Howell and Ford, 170).

Because the exhibition had closed, Treves sought the owner, Tom Norman, in a pub, paid a shilling for a private viewing, and entered a dusty, damp, and bare suite of rooms. Behind a red tablecloth, crouched over a bunsen burner and shrouded in a brown blanket, Merrick, then twenty-two years old, sat on a tripod. Treves recalled that his "hunched-up figure was the embodiment of loneliness" (Howell and Ford, 171).

At the barker's terse command, Merrick displayed himself to Treves, who was repulsed by the extent of disfigurement on the so-called Elephant Man. Half clothed, Merrick, who was five feet two inches tall, wore cast-off pants and no shoes. Treves assessed the masses of scrofulous flesh that distorted his shape; he compared the front of the head to a loaf, the back to a sack of sponges, the right thumb to a radish, and the distorted lips to a rudimentary trunk. His pendulous skin had the texture of brown cauliflower. Marked by a frail tuft of hair, occluded right eye, formless nose, and pulpy growth distorting his mouth, Merrick's expressionless countenance could merely drool. In addition to suffering the gross skin disorder, Merrick had a hip impairment, which left him so lame that he could no longer contemplate escape. Totally isolated, he subsisted on indecent scraps of food. To add to his misery, his inadequate hygiene resulted in a foul stench.

Treves, in his evaluation of the bizarre symptoms, immediately thought of elephantiasis, or filariasis, the result of a threadlike larva that invades the human lymphatic system, migrates beneath the skin, and forms granular, fibrous swellings. The disease, usually associated with tropical climates, is particularly invasive in the groin and extremities and often blinds its victim. But Merrick's malady was probably neurofibromatosis, an untreatable disease that causes the random formation of unsightly tumors on peripheral nerves and bones and that may have been a congenital recurrence of the disease that crippled his mother.

DISCOVERY

Treves arranged for Merrick to cover himself in a disguise — a floorlength black cloak, baggy slippers, and an oversized cap with veil — so that he could cross the street to the medical building for professional examination of his abnormality. At Treves's office, he discovered his patient to be shy, confused, and incapable of comprehensible speech. The examiner measured the loose globs of tissue, charted aberrations of the skull, jaw, and frame, and concluded from garbled attempts at speech that Merrick was mentally defective.

Treves arranged for photographs of Merrick as well as for closer scrutiny by the London Pathological Society on December 2. Commentary in the *British Medical Journal* and *Lancet* indicated that the viewers, for all their medical sophistication, were appalled by the Elephant Man, whose particular anomaly surpassed the usual distortions of flesh by afflicting bone as well. Whatever Merrick hoped for from his exhibition to the greatest medical minds of his time, no curative measures resulted from the event.

The police closed Tom Norman's freak show, which moved to a new location in Belgium. Two years later in December, Merrick reached the end of his shameful exploitation. His keeper had found no ready audience in Belgium and, in June 1886, robbed and heartlessly jettisoned him. Merrick, with only a few possessions to pawn, purchased a ticket to London. Like a friendless dog, he shuffled along the streets near Liverpool Station, avoiding the curious. At length, the police found him, panic-stricken and drawn into a fetal position, escorted him to a waiting area, and debated how to assist so abject a lump of humanity. The remains of Treves's calling card gave them their only option.

Transported to the hospital by cab, Merrick fell asleep and seemed content that he was at last in capable hands. Against the rules of the hospital, which admitted only acute-care cases, Treves installed him temporarily in an isolation ward. The hospital chairman, F. C. Carr Gomm, held out no hope for a cure for Merrick's multiple ills and, on December 4, 1886, solicited funds for his care through a letter to the *Times*. Within a week, donors provided enough money to keep Merrick for life, a span Treves predicted would be short.

CARE AND TREATMENT

Since the initial diagnosis, Merrick's health had deteriorated from increases in his affliction plus the onset of bronchitis, a weakened heart, and premature aging. Under Treves's direction, he received care that had been denied him for a quarter-century—nourishing food, a comfortable bed, clean linen, and frequent baths, which removed his body odor. He thrived from the attentions of his first real friends, who endeavored to converse and make him welcome. To Treves's amazement, Merrick displayed not only sensitivity and intelligence but also read widely from textbooks, newspapers, and journals.

Treves surmised from Merrick's ramblings that he had compensated for his abysmal treatment by inventing romantic fictions about his beautiful mother. The truth of his life strayed far from his dreams. He had found no joy beyond crawling into the dark, safe from prying eyes. His notion of the ideal residence was a lighthouse or an asylum for blind persons, where no one would gape at him. Despite years of treachery and humiliation, he was surprisingly gentle and loving. He rose above the baseness of his former impresario to a nobility of character surpassing the ordinary.

Treves began treating Merrick with the most crucial of medicines and with decency and respect. While building confidence and calming his anxieties, Treves bolstered his self-esteem and allowed him to venture out by night for a stroll in Bedstead Square, the hospital grounds. Treves further bridged the chasm of years of solitude by introducing Merrick to a kind woman, the first to shake his hand and treat him civilly. Merrick became a cause célèbre, visited by notables who brought him gifts. His uncle heard of his return to England and offered him permanent residence yet was unable to follow through because his family could not duplicate the hospital's quality care.

Merrick remained at the hospital in a suite created expressly for him. Each day he perched in bed till noon, conserving his strength by reading and writing notes to a host of new friends. He enjoyed a private bath and small hearth, where he could sit in his armchair and warm himself. In security, surrounded by pictures, books, but no mirrors, he was grateful to his benefactors and blossomed into as complete a human adult as he was capable of becoming.

CURING THE SPIRIT

Although Merrick never anticipated recovery, he did achieve small bits of progress. His speech improved; but he was never able to shape a smile or whistle a tune. He delighted in basket-weaving, paper cutouts, and models, which his attendants helped him glue together. With painstaking accuracy he created a detailed model of St. Philip's Church, which he could observe from his window. As his strength ebbed, Merrick, no doubt mindful of his tenuous grip on life, became more spiritual. He often attended worship services and took communion. The local bishopric sent an emissary to christen him in the hospital chapel.

Merrick remained at the hospital and longed for contact with women, whom he idolized. He took particular delight in his acquaintance with Alexandra, Princess of Wales, and later the tsarina of Russia. Her visits brought him a sense of acceptance that furthered his recuperation from neglect and self-loathing. He kept her photograph in a place of honor. Soon, other noble ladies added their likenesses to his collection.

BECOMING WHOLE

Merrick displayed a childlike personality for much of his adult life. As a natural outgrowth of his nightmarish freak-show treatment, a land of make believe far from the realities of disease and deformity was his world. His mind was a clutter of romantic heroes and heroines dressed in glittering costumes and involved in outlandish lifestyles. For Christmas, he requested a travel bag filled with silver toilet articles. The brushes, cigarette case, toothbrush, razors, and shoe horn were unusable, but they delighted him as ornaments on his dresser, where he could finger them and dream of being normal.

The great emptiness of Merrick's life remained the lack of female companionship. His stirring emotional fantasies cast him in the starring role alongside lovely young ladies, rapt over his every word. To sublimate his normal urges, he focused on learning more about English homes. He visited Treves's residence on Wimple Street and seemed placated by contact with ordinary furniture and decorations.

Dame Margaret Kendal, an actress at Drury Lane Theatre, fulfilled one of Merrick's ardent desires by arranging for his attendance at a performance. With Treves's help, he was escorted to a closed carriage, up the private royal stairs, and into a box, where three hospital employees formed a screen in the front row while Merrick occupied the rear. Safely obscured, he thrilled to his first visit to a play and talked of it for weeks with reverent enthusiasm.

Another jaunt took Merrick on vacation to a country estate. He traveled by train to the home of Lady Knightley and shared her gamekeeper's cottage. From there, for the first time, he could ramble the woods, pick wildflowers, and enjoy nature. In his letters to Treves he marveled at bounding hares, birdcalls, and shadowy trout swimming in a stream. The outing improved not only his outlook but his health, which still remained frail.

A TREASURED LIFE

Merrick's life, which ended peacefully in his sleep on April 11, 1890, was over-balanced by grievous suffering. He had longed to sleep like other people, but owing to his deformity, had never been able to stretch out and rest his head on a pillow. On the afternoon the staff surgeon discovered him dead, his body appeared undisturbed by struggle or spasm; his head was back, his neck constrained. Cause of death was given as asphyxia from the weight of his head against his breathing passage. Treves concluded that he died from trying to imitate the position normal people assume when they sleep.

The mortal remains of Joseph Merrick were identified by his uncle rather than his father, who lived until 1923. Merrick was eulogized in the hospital chapel; his body was sent to the College Museum for study. There, casts, photographs, and tissue samples preserved much of the information that remains about his puzzling disease.

Joseph Merrick achieved much in his last four years by making the most of his experiences. In 1980, Treves's moving biography was the basis for Bernard Pomerance's award-winning Broadway play and film, in which John Hurt played the role of Merrick. Twentieth-century viewers and readers found such an uplifting personification of humanity in the Elephant Man's trials and rescue that they lionized him over a century after his birth.

SOURCES

Howell, Michael, and Peter Ford. *The True History of the Elephant Man.* London: Allison and Busby, 1980.

Montagu, Ashley. *The Elephant Man: A Study in Human Dignity.* New York: E. P. Dutton, 1979.

Gary Paulsen

Gary Paulsen, a writer whose life bears a resemblance to that of outdoorsman and survivalist Jack London, has overcome numerous barriers—poverty, alcoholism, and low self-esteem. As a writer and woodsman, he has created a better life for himself by coming to grips with his problems, including doubts about self-worth. Writing at feverish eighteen-hour stints, he has been known to complete a work in fifteen days. His steady outpouring of books—including twenty titles in 1979 alone—places him among the most prolific writers of recent years. His subjects vary from trucking, medicine, ranching, the Vietnam War, the environment, survival techniques, and Eskimos to animals and outdoor life, which are favorites with his youngest fans.

Paulsen's identification with the children who devour his books has led him to a strong commitment to this audience, who he feels may hold the answer to human survival. As he sums up their importance: "We have been passive. We have been stupid. We have been lazy. We have done all the things we could do to destroy ourselves. If there is any hope at all for the human race, it has to come from young people. Not from adults" ("Gary Paulsen," n.p.).

A complex, multifaceted outdoorsman, Paulsen, who lived an unfocused, unstable youth beset by the alcoholism of his parents, frequent uprootings, unsuccessful peer relationships, and little self-confidence, overcame his childhood misery by working in many fields—soldier, trapper, archer, truck driver, dynamiter, carpenter, ranch hand, migrant worker, sailor, folk singer, teacher, field engineer, actor, director, and editor. Out of his myriad careers came the one that made him whole—writing fiction and nonfiction about the outdoors, particularly for young adult audiences. Of his dependence on creative talent, he once said, "It's much like being a slave, I suppose, and in slavery there is a kind of freedom that I find in writing: a perverse thing. I'm not 'motivated,' as you put it. Nor am I particularly driven. I write because it's all there is" (*Something About the Author*, 76).

AN UNFAVORABLE BEGINNING

A native of Minneapolis, Gary Paulsen, born May 17, 1939, who is of Swedish-Danish-Norwegian descent, is the son of Eunice and Oscar Paulsen. His father, a career army officer, served with General George Patton in World War II. During the war years, Paulsen lived in Chicago, where his mother worked in a munitions plant. He was reared by his grandmother, uncles, and aunts. Later in his career, as he was writing *Madonna*, a collection of short stories about women, he examined the strength of the women in his life, from whom he learned to crochet and whose patience taught him to appreciate compassion.

In 1946, Paulsen traveled aboard a Liberty ship to live with his parents on a military compound in the Philippines. He spent the next three years getting acquainted with his father, who had been absent throughout the war years. Because of his parents' worsening alcoholism, he had to move in with relatives. To questions about this unpleasant era, he replies philosophically, "It happens. I had a rough run" (Handy, 4). He began supporting himself at age fifteen by delivering the *Grand Forks Herald* to bars and offices, hoeing sugar beets, and setting pins in a bowling alley. His earnings supplied clothes and spending money.

Schooling for Paulsen was the typical complaint of military families—he attended classes in every state, never longer than five months in any one system. A misfit and disadvantaged reader, he believed that teachers made fun of him. Nor did he fare well with other children because of his timidity, scruffy wardrobe, and ineptitude in sports. Ultimately, he came to despise school and downgraded himself for performing poorly in class. In his estimation, "I was not a person who used his brain very much" (Handy, 1). Because he missed a portion of the ninth grade, he had to shoulder a double load the next year in order to graduate on time. His grades were barely passing and his relationships unrewarding, leading him to consider suicide.

DEPENDING ON OTHERS

Paulsen's childhood was so abysmal that he came to depend on the public library as an alternative to a stable family. Because a kind staff member approached him one day when he entered the library to get warm, he received his first library card along with something even more welcome—acceptance. On the librarian's recommendation, he immersed himself in westerns, science fiction, and classics, devouring books at the rate of one a day. At home, he sometimes read in a decrepit armchair in the basement, where he drank milk and munched toast and peanut butter to escape the misery of drunken parents. He describes the experience with an appropriate image: "It was as though I had been dying of thirst and the librarian had handed me a five-gallon bucket of water. I drank and drank" (*Something About the Author*, 78).

In Bemidji, a small town 140 miles northwest of Duluth, Minnesota, Paulsen attended Bemidji State College from 1957 to 1958, paying his tuition by trapping predators for the State of Minnesota. As with his high-school training, he found little to excite or challenge him. He quit school and served in the U.S. Army the next three years, was assigned to missile duty, and attained the rank of sergeant. Through extension courses, he launched a career as field engineer. The first four years out of military service, he helped track satellites for Bendix and Lockheed, taking part in the *Gemini* moon shots, the *Mariner* voyages, and the design of a guidance system for the Shrike antiradar missile.

Paulsen disliked his work at the tracking station but compensated for his discontent by capitalizing on his writing chores, particularly drawing from reports for his fiction. To make up for his lack of professional composition training, he concocted a phony resumé and got a job on the editorial staff of a Hollywood firm that published fourteen men's magazines. Some of the work he edited came from top-notch writers, including Ray Bradbury, Ralph Ellison, and John Steinbeck. The ruse covered Paulsen's ignorance only a few days. However, even after his employers realized that he knew nothing about publishing, they decided to train him as an editor.

Through editing, Paulsen gained an in-house education in good writing. He notes, "I was there for about a year, and it was the best of all possible ways to learn about writing. It probably did more to improve my craft and ability than any other single event in my life" (Serdahely, 20). Among the stylistic details he incorporated into his own work were a clean manuscript with wide margins and readable typefaces, correct spelling and grammar, strong plot construction, tight transitions, and straight-forward language.

During his tenure in California, Paulsen wrote while he worked as a film extra in such movies as *Flap*. He also sculpted and carved wooden figures, for which he won a prize at a Santa Barbara exhibit. He eventually focused on writing and produced his first novel, *The Special War*, which he developed from interviews with returning Vietnam veterans. He quickly mastered fiction and produced 100 adult and young-adult novels, two plays, 200 magazine articles, nonfiction, and numerous short stories.

DARK TIMES

The 1960s brought a sense of accomplishment along with deepening despair. Paulsen's success with *The Special War* in 1966 resulted in an FBI investigation because of his detailed descriptions of missiles. Troubled by a failing marriage and liberal drinking, he gave up his son and daughter to the children's stepfather. While he lived in Taos, he was unable to write professionally because he drank to excess. When he bottomed out on alcohol, he had little choice but to turn his life around.

With his marriage to painter Ruth Ellen Wright on May 4, 1971, Paulsen made a new beginning. Still recovering from alcoholism, he faced years of economic privation. He confided to *Writer's Digest*, "I lived for two weeks on squash from the garden and a porcupine I killed in the backyard!" (Serdahely, 20). By 1973, while residing in Evergreen, Colorado, Paulsen realized that he would have to conquer his problem with drinking or else succumb to it. The effort cost him a painful admission that the problem was too large for him to manage, so he chose outside intervention in his approach to sobriety.

Newly released from dependence, Paulsen reflected on his early life and on opportunities that he had missed. Most painful was his realization that his daughter and son had grown up without much input from their father. To diminish his loss, he devoted time to James, born in 1971, who gave him a second chance at parenthood. It took another two decades before he could realign his relationship with his first family. By then he was a grandfather.

In 1975 Paulsen experienced his greatest despair. Facing poverty at the height of the oil crunch, he commented, "God, it was a rough year!" (Handy, 1). To shore up his failing self-confidence, he turned to friend and colleague Joe Foster, who warned him that poverty of things, money, relationships, soul, and life are the way of writing. Paulsen decided that he wanted a job as a technical writer. He interviewed with Philco and was accepted for the job but realized on the spot that it was not what he really wanted. Almost in tears, he rejected the company's offer and returned to creative writing. He decided that he would become "completely self-less" and devote himself to his work (Handy, 2).

A FINANCIAL BATTLE

Paulsen's dramatic rise in the publishing world came to a brief, but painful, hiatus with a lawsuit in 1977 following publication of *Winterkill*, a novel the plaintiff believed was based on his family. With the aid of attorney Margaret Troyer, Paulsen battled the libel suit in the Minnesota Supreme Court, defeating the charge in the final round but bankrupting himself with the effort. His family, opting for self-reliance rather than government handouts, moved into a tin lean-to. Embittered by the experience, especially his publisher's failure to assist him, he ceased writing for a few months, but then he returned to the only profession that gave him hope.

To support his wife and son, Paulsen traveled sixty miles on skis and trapped for the state to control the population of animals such as beavers and coyotes. He defends the grisly job with his claim that the snares killed instantly and humanely. Because he did not own a car, he accepted a gift of five Alaskan huskies and a sled to expedite his work. He learned to love the sight of frigid countryside by moonlight as he raced the team at better than sixty miles per hour over snowy terrain. The experience brought a oneness with nature and animals that caused him to give up trapping and vow never again to kill.

THE IDITAROD

Financed with a gift from Richard Jackson of Bradbury Press, in 1983 Paulsen worked up a racing team and entered the Iditarod, the grueling seventeen-day race over 1,049 miles of northern Alaska from Anchorage to Nome. To compensate Jackson, Paulsen gave Bradbury Press first option on his next manuscript. Training for the Iditarod required relentless back-to-back runs without sleep. In time, he learned to subsist on four-hour rest periods. His expenses mounted to $14,000, which he recouped in part by taking 750 photos of the event, from which he created a slide show for oral presentations at schools.

The Iditarod experience made a profound impression, leading the writer to abandon his earlier notions of masculinity and supplant them with an appreciation of compassion, endurance, and the intuitive nature of the dogs, which carry the entire responsibility for a human victory. In his words, "I used to say there was a state of primitive exultation that you enter into with the dogs. I still think that. I don't think you come back from the Iditarod. Ever. It affects you forever" (Handy, 4). Of the need for rapport with the team, Paulsen noted, "After about eight miles of navigating the Arctic Circle, you start to feel scared. After twelve miles, you realize that you are nothing and the dogs are everything. To survive, you must be in deep harmony with your team" (*Something About the Author*, 81).

The upshot of Paulsen's entry into the Iditarod was his 1983 book, *Dancing Carl*, which evolved from his original narrative ballet that appeared on Minnesota public television. While planning a second entry in the 1985 Iditarod, he learned that his friend and agent, Ray Peekner, was ill with cancer. Paulsen sold his team and diverted his focus to helping the dying man cope with his final three months.

REACHING AN AUDIENCE

Paulsen pushed on with his writing career and published *Tracker*, a metaphysical study of tracking, and *Dogsong*, the coming-of-age story of a teenage Eskimo who witnesses the suicide of a beloved old friend and aids a pregnant girl in giving birth. For this latter novel he won a Newbery honor in 1986, followed by a second award in 1988 for *Hatchet*, and a third in 1990 for *The Winter Room*. Concord-New Horizon Pictures filmed *Hatchet* in 1990 under the title *A Cry in the Wild*, and MGM turned the movie into a video to be shown on "Wonderworks," a children's television series. In addition, Paulsen won the Dorothy Canfield Fisher Award, the Society of Midland Authors Award, and the William Allen White Award and was featured in December 1988 during a CBS television interview with Charles Kuralt.

These honoraria came at a time when Paulsen lived in the wilderness in a cabin with no plumbing or electricity and eked out an existence from the sale of his wife's oil paintings and sketches. Managing on less than $3,000 annually, the family, still broke from their lengthy court battle, subsisted on vegetables from their garden. The success of the new books increased the family income to over $100,000. Their newfound wealth was unsettling to Ruth, who had to learn middle-class values and how to live a middle-class life-style. Paulsen, too, found so rapid a rise in spending power inconsistent with his former poverty.

A renewed interest in dogs and sledding brought Paulsen hope that he could compete in the 1991 and 1992 Iditarods. To train for these competitions, he bought forty-three dogs and accepted sponsorship from Lands' End, a mail-order clothing company, in whose catalog he agreed to appear. A clogged artery sidelined him from the race just before he boarded a plane at the Boston airport. His cavalier retort summed up the state of his body: "Too many pork chops" (Handy, 3). Seriously disabled and in great pain, he continued his flight home and went directly to a Minnesota hospital for treatment.

BACK TO BOOKS

From boyhood misery relieved by a librarian's kindness, Paulsen has come full circle to a writing career that contributes to the shelves whose contents once gave him hope. Gradually weaning himself away from the need to run dog teams, hunt, and camp out, he built an office near his Minnesota home and began experimenting with raw ideas on his computer. For material, he tried to experience firsthand how it feels to fly a bush plane, live off the land, and build a fire with nothing but a hatchet and wood.

Currently, in addition to publishing he gives public readings and tells stories for local audiences. Less driven than in earlier times, he meditates, gardens, rides horseback, delves into research projects such as the study of petroglyphs, and communes with the inner strengths that have helped him over rough times. Unstinting in his absorption in the task, he says of his schedule, "When I work—I *work*. I actually sit down and write. That's what they pay me to do, and that's what I do!" (Serdahely, 20).

To escape the frenetic pace, Paulsen enjoys a stroll to a neighboring hillside, where he fires his muzzle-loaders to relieve the tension. Another of his interests was ending the nuclear-arms race between the former Soviet Union and the United States. In collaboration with his son, James, Paulsen wrote letters urging an end to nuclear weapons. In 1986, his correspondence with writers in Soviet Russia produced a peaceful meeting with twenty Russian writers on the University of Minnesota campus. The following year, he delivered a stirring antiwar speech to a group of Russians at the Mayflower Hotel in Washington, D.C. The warmth of his reception brought him hugs and gifts. From the experience, he became even more determined to push for an end to USSR-U.S. hostilities.

Paulsen has established a comfortable, satisfying life for himself and his family in their residences in Leonard, Minnesota, and La Luz, New Mexico, where he moved to bolster his health and escape the confinement of long winters. Just as in boyhood, he loves books, particularly Dickens. As he describes his appetite for books, he reads "like a wolf eats. I still do. I read myself to sleep every night. I read constantly" (Handy, 1).

IN TUNE WITH KIDS

Paulsen continues to surround himself with young readers by visiting schools all over the country, although his heart condition has caused him to cut back from marathon sessions of four schools a day. Of this eyeball-to-eyeball method of confronting his audience, he once commented, "I believe in personal inspection at zero altitude. I don't think you can learn anything by listening to other people talk. You've gotta go be there" (Handy, 2).

One of the high points of his career came during a scholarly consortium when Paulsen and a handful of academics were discussing literary topics in a college amphitheater. A busload of middle-school children crashed the meeting and rushed their hero, demanding more information about *Hatchet* and *Dogsong*, two of their favorite books. The author chortled when recalling his relief, "Everybody had been so proper before, and the kids just blew it wide open! ... God it was great! They all cared. They really wanted to know about the stories!" (Handy, 2).

SOURCES

Contemporary Authors. New Revision Series, Volume 30. Detroit: Gale Research, 1978.

"Gary Paulsen." Publicity brochure from Dell/Delacorte Press, 1990.

Handy, Alice Evans. "An Interview with Gary Paulsen." From a reprint of *The Book Report*, May/June 1991.

Serdahely, Franz. "Prolific Paulsen." *Writer's Digest*, January 1980.

Something About the Author, Volume 54. Detroit: Gale Research, 1988.

Weidt, Maryann N. "Gary Paulsen: A Sentry for Peace." *Voice of Youth Advocates*, August/October 1986.

Claude Pepper

For people who live long enough, old age is the last barrier, the final frontier. For Claude Pepper, legislator and workaholic extraordinaire, fighting for rights for the elderly became an energizing crusade. He kept young despite damaged heart valves, failing eyesight, and deafness by staying in touch with his congressional constituents and battling for better economic conditions for the United States' elderly and retired citizens. Through nine presidencies, he championed issues that reflected human needs.

After his wife's death, Pepper, then nearing eighty, prepared for eight more years of government involvement in popular causes, which translated into full-time service in the U.S. House of Representatives on behalf of "Pepper's people." In the face of strong opposition he hurled fighting words: "I refuse to believe that a country as rich and powerful as ours cannot guarantee the basic comforts to its older citizens" (Langdon, 38). He maintained that uncompromising challenge to the end of his life.

SOUTHERN ROOTS

Well into his eighties, Claude Denson Pepper bore the stamp of his southern upbringing. Born on September 8, 1900, on a red-earth cotton farm in Dudleyville, Alabama, the first of four children of Lena Talbot and Joseph Wheeler Pepper, a farmer turned merchant and, later, police chief, Pepper absorbed in childhood the qualities that ennobled him. From his grandfathers, veterans of the Civil War, came pride in the South. From his Baptist, Democratic forebears he evolved a liberal philosophy grounded on fairness and compassion. As he characterized his outlook, "What worthier purpose could government serve than to make life a bit happier and a lot less arduous for its people?" (Fiedler, n.p.).

Pepper's early experiences plowing and picking cotton in rural Alabama prepared him for hard work, dedication, and humility. His family, which was numbered among the gentry because they owned land, lived far from paved roads and lacked both indoor plumbing and electric lights. Still, he maintained high expectations and in 1910 carved on a tree his name alongside the words "United States Senator."

Pepper taught public school in Dothan, Alabama, in 1917, the year he grad-uated from Camp Hill High School. At the University of Alabama at Tuscaloosa the following year, he earned tuition by washing dishes in the school kitchen, laboring in a steel mill, and stoking coal and hauling ashes at a power plant. He found time to balance labor with cross-country military training and writing for the school paper. The draft disrupted his education with a brief service in the army, which ended when he contracted a severe case of jaundice and suffered a double hernia. A Phi Beta Kappa graduate, he moved on to Harvard thanks to a government grant for his military disability, worked in the dining hall, and graduated in the top of his class with a law degree in 1924. The next year he taught law at the University of Arkansas before accepting a retainer from the Trumbo estate in Florida, his adopted home state.

From experience, Pepper appreciated a college education. When the depression drained his father of funds to send his brothers and sister to school, Pepper under-took the load himself. As his parents grew too old to care for themselves, he accepted that burden as well, making a home for his father until his death in 1945 and for his mother until her death in 1961. Later, on the public platform, he had every right to claim, "I know something about the poverty and problems of old people" (Langdon, 40).

LIBERAL POLITICS

Liberal politics stirred early in Pepper. While practicing law, he allied himself with grass-roots party workings, often making warm-up speeches and shaking hands. By 1929, he served in the state house of representatives, where he made his first move to aid the elderly. Because he refused to join house members in castigating Mrs. Herbert Hoover for inviting a black man to tea at the White House, he lost face with racist constituents and was voted out at the end of his first term. At the time, he feared he might be out for good.

During the 1930s, Pepper did not sever connections with politics; rather, he made himself useful on the public-welfare board, law-examiners board, and execu-tive council. By 1934, he felt that he was ready to run for the U.S. Senate but lost to the incumbent, Park Trammell. On this campaign trail, Pepper introduced the sound truck as a stumper's tool. He also endeared himself to voters by default when word leaked out that crooked Tampa businessmen had rigged the election against him.

In 1936, at the death of U.S. senator Duncan U. Fletcher, Pepper sought the vacated office and won it unopposed. While finishing Fletcher's term, he gained sup-port for the National Cancer Institute, one of his pet projects. He quickly established himself as a dapper, silver-tongued orator. He extended his successes into a full Senate term in 1938 and established himself as a formidable liberal voice. Many of his cherished issues were populist causes such as medical research, health insurance, an end to the poll tax, compulsory military training, and programs to support the arts and public works. In agreement with Roosevelt's platform, he helped initiate a fifty-cent minimum wage to help the poor. After Pepper's reelection in 1938, he declared himself an adversary of nazism, decried the rise of Hitler, and devised a lend-lease program by which the U.S. government loaned fighter planes and ships to England in exchange for leases on land in the West Indies.

At the beginning of World War II, Pepper was realistic about the spread of aggression. He backed U.S. efforts to remain neutral yet anticipated that the country would eventually be drawn into the conflict. His call for a draft made him unpopular with pacifists, but he stuck to his vow to see the nation through the war years, even when mothers branded him a hawk and a warmonger and hanged him in effigy on the Capitol lawn in stuffed denims with a coconut head.

CHANGE OF COMMAND

In the postwar era, Pepper maintained political momentum by spearheading support for the World Health Organization and the National Institutes of Health. As the liberal cause began to weaken during Roosevelt's declining years, Pepper came close to being unseated by Edward Ball during the 1944 campaign. As a result of Pepper's sympathetic support of Stalin's rebuilding effort in the USSR, detractors branded him a "commie lover," a label that led to his defeat.

During the Truman years, Pepper stayed in the president's favor by pressing for improvements for the average American—for stabilization of prices, better schools and housing, dismantling of slums, and an end to sex discrimination. He lost favor with Truman during the 1948 Democratic convention after Pepper supported first Wallace, then Eisenhower, then himself for the nomination. Late in his career, when asked to address the Cosmos Club on his association with Truman, Pepper reminisced fondly about his old friend and colleague and generously forgot the animosities that had created a gulf between them.

UPS AND DOWNS

Pepper's lengthy political career came to an inglorious hiatus in 1950 with his run against George Smathers for the Democratic nomination. Smathers's degrading and libelous speeches, by appealing to the lowest common denominator in Florida's backwoods, jerked Pepper out of the legislature and mothballed him for twelve years. In Smathers's parlance, Pepper stood for "Northern labor bosses, all the Communists, all the socialists, all the radicals and the fellow travelers" (Fiedler, n.p.). The ensuing racial slurs, below-the-belt insinuations, and red-baiting, harking back to Pepper's attempts to lessen hostilities between the USSR and the United States after World War II, led to a groundswell of negative votes. Chief among powerful detractors was Joseph Kennedy, who donated $125,000 toward achieving Pepper's downfall.

Unable to circumvent the effects of names like "Red" Pepper and the "spellbinding pinko," Claude retreated to his law office. He carried an onus of debt and the bitterness of an unfair fight, but he refused to give political ground. He recalled with particular acrimony a Republican trick of photographing him with black actor, opera singer, and Communist sympathizer Paul Robeson, thereby signaling to southern voters that Pepper courted blacks and Communists. His adamant retort illustrates his refusal to be manipulated: "I knew just what they were doing. But I thought I'd be damned if I'd move" (Langdon, 40).

Gaining his second wind in 1962 after an abortive comeback against Senator Spessard Holland four years earlier, Pepper took the challenge of Miami's newly established seat in the U.S. House of Representatives. For thirteen elections, he regularly won 65 percent of the constituency. The new home base gave him a focused outlook: He represented a largely retired population containing Jewish, Cuban, and black constituents. When Democrats voted Kennedy and Johnson into office, they injected new life into Pepper's liberalism. His platform remained largely the same as it had been during the 1930s and 1940s — better health care, a revitalized educational program backed by federal moneys, stronger anticrime measures, and an affirmation of the place of nonwhites in the nation.

In a reflective perusal of his years out of office, Pepper took comfort in the change from senator to representative. He asserted that the loss of the Senate seat brought him a more profitable legal business in Miami and Tallahassee. It also removed him from an inevitable stint as chairman of the Foreign Relations Committee and second in command of the Senate. As he saw it, "What would I have accomplished? I've come back to the House and been able to raise the hopes of older people. You don't better the lives of ordinary people as the chairman of the Foreign Relations Committee" (Langdon, 40).

During the opening stage of the Vietnam War, Pepper supported troop placements. As the war led to a miasma of carnage and waste, he, along with other courageous spokespersons, reversed his stand and advocated an end to the conflict. Another unpopular stance for Pepper was his role in combatting the House Un-American Activities Committee during the McCarthy era. At the same time that he waged war on red-baiting and promoted First Amendment rights, he chaired the Committee on Crime and increased his clout with Miami voters who were intimidated by drug shootouts, illegal Cuban immigrants, and the early release of criminals.

The doughty congressman moved with the popular flow toward Johnson's visionary Great Society. By sponsoring the Older Americans Act, Pepper harnessed "gray power" and assisted aging citizens, whose representation in the overall population was increasing in the 1970s and 1980s. He catered to older voters by supporting beefed-up military hardware, a rebuff of Fidel Castro's overtures, increased medical research, abolition of forced retirement, and, most significantly, an end to ageism, which he defined as a shameful waste of human talent on a par with racism and sexism.

A LATE-SPRUNG HERO

As his own health began to deteriorate, Pepper moved into a golden era of advocacy for older Americans. During this period, he learned a harsh truth shared by many elderly people, that living as a childless widower required painful adjustment to loneliness and loss. After his wife of forty-three years, Mildred Irene Webster

Pepper, died of cancer in 1979, he preserved her memory by keeping his residences as she had arranged them, even to the clothes in the closet and a little love note taped to the bathroom wall reminding him about closing the shower curtain. On her tombstone, he inscribed his own love message: "She was a perfect wife; lovely of person and beautiful of spirit. Her beautiful life has left a glow that will illume and inspire others for generations to come" (Sinclair, 25).

Subsisting on thrown-together breakfasts and snacks, cafeteria lunches, and club dinners, Pepper kept active. He played golf at Burning Tree Country Club, worked out on his stationary bike, attended the necessary social events and danced with the "ladies," and continued the regular commute between Washington, D.C. and Miami. A spiffy dresser in tailored three-piece suits, he carried his five-foot-eight-inch frame with pride and energy, giving no indication of wanting to retire despite his reliance on a pacemaker, synthetic heart valve, trifocals, and two hearing aids. He jokingly suggested the year 2000 as an appropriate end to his public career, then added, "But I may have to reconsider and stay on longer in the House depending on the political situation at that time" (Sinclair, 27).

Some of Pepper's fiercest speeches came in his last days in office when he refused to mince words with right-wing adversaries. In his address to the Conference on Aging, which he chaired for three terms, he averred, "I'm not grandstanding.... This isn't a matter of vanity with me. I don't think of myself as an old person. But these people need someone to listen to them. They need a voice" (Langdon, 38).

Pepper attacked entitlement slashing during the Reagan years and lambasted legislators for allowing the poor condition of the elderly to reach catastrophic proportions while changing the tax structure to favor the rich. With great acrimony, he fought Reagan's proposed reduction in Social Security benefits. In 1981, Pepper refused a puppet role, which would have taken him out of frontline action on behalf of the United States' oldest citizens. For them he became a living symbol and the epitome of age refusing to bow to an uncaring younger generation.

Before his death on May 31, 1989, Pepper, the oldest U.S. legislator, effectively challenged the conservative faction, notably as chairman of the Rules Committee, which oversaw the internal workings of legislation. Teaming with House Speaker Tip O'Neill, he pressed for a strengthening of Social Security, which at that time was in danger of collapsing. To replenish failing coffers, he moved for a transfer of funds from tax revenues. As a final gesture toward his idol, Franklin D. Roosevelt, Pepper, only a month before his death from stomach cancer, urged colleagues to put aside money for an F.D.R. memorial.

On a personal level, Pepper remained available to people in need. He published his Miami and Washington telephone numbers so that voters could contact him directly with their needs and frustrations. As he anticipated, they used the service and petitioned him at the rate of 400 calls and 3,000 letters per day. In addition, he penned a syndicated column, "Ask Claude Pepper," which extended his influence across the country.

ASSESSING A LIFE

At his passing, U.S. politicians, both liberal and conservative, paid homage to Congressman Claude Pepper, feisty advocate of the elderly, minorities, youth, and women for six decades, including fourteen years in the Senate and twenty-seven in the House of Representatives. Encomiums listed his honorary doctorates alongside the Mary and Albert Lasker Public Service Award, Eleanor Roosevelt Humanities Award, United States Chamber of Commerce "Man of the Year" Award, Jefferson Award of the American Institute for Public Service, two *Time* magazine cover stories, and the Medal of Freedom. Floridians took special pride in the Claude Pepper Eminent Scholars Chair in Gerontology at Florida State University. The nation honored him by placing his body in the Capitol Rotunda, in the style reserved for heroes and presidents.

More telling than these formal honors were the testimonials to Pepper's personal attention to people's needs. Whether dropping fishing-license requirements for aged Floridians, investigating shoddy nursing homes, or restoring disability to an amputee who was ruled ineligible by a computer error, Pepper found time to listen and serve. The inscription on the Medal of Freedom, which Bush presented to Pepper on his last public appearance, summed up his greatest achievement: "The champion of the most vulnerable among us" (Fiedler, n.p.).

SOURCES

Contemporary Biography. New York: H. W. Wilson, 1983.

Fiedler, Tom. "Cancer Claims Champion of the Elderly." *Miami Herald*, May 31, 1989, n.p.

Langdon, Dolly. "Claude Pepper, a Southern Gentleman with a Fist of Iron, Takes on the President to Defend the Elderly." *People Weekly*, June 21, 1982, 38-40.

Magnuson, Ed. "Champion of the Elderly: At 82, Claude Pepper Is at the Peak of His Career." *Time*, April 25, 1983, 20-26.

Sinclair, Molly. "Keeping Up with Claude." *50 Plus*, October 1984, 23-27.

Renée Richards

Richard "Dick" Raskind, child of a privileged family, star athlete, and scholar, gave all appearances of success with a medical degree from Yale followed by high rank in the U.S. military and a satisfying career in ophthalmic surgery. There are plenty of people who allow barriers to grow out of bounds before attempting to breach them. Outwardly, he was content; on the inside, he faced a bizarre crisis—from early childhood he had known that his inner self was female. As the hidden persona struggled for actualization, Raskind risked his earnings and self-esteem on an operation that would transform his sex.

BATTLE OF WILLS

Raskind's birth was difficult. His mother, Dr. Sadie Muriel Bishop, a psychologist, was intent on the propriety of a Manhattan hospital and a female obstetrician. She ignored a massive hemorrhage and drove herself from her summer quarters across New York City so that her infant could be born in the Infirmary for Women and Children. His father, Dr. David Raskind, was working at his Long Island medical practice on August 19, 1934, as Richard Henry Raskind was being born by caesarean section. Of Russian heritage and named for Richard the Lion-Hearted, the boy baby, destined to do his own great deeds, completed the family, which already had a five-year-old daughter, Michael "Mike" Bishop Raskind.

Surrounded by females, including his aunt, grandmother, nurse, and a housekeeper at the family's home on Forty-fourth Street, Raskind marveled at his gruff, ursine father, who would stand his ground against the women who dominated the household, then, at a crucial moment, acquiesce to Muriel and retreat into brooding diffidence. Muriel, a power not to be trifled with, ran not only her patients' lives but her children's and husband's as well. The family residence served Muriel as an office, although her major sphere of interest was a residency at Columbia Presbyterian. From his toddler years, Raskind identified with her courage, strength, and feminity and at age three accepted her decision that he should become a brain surgeon.

Both Mike and Richard Raskind, unhappy with their sexual identities, experimented with changing personae. Richard, who despised the formal, old-fashioned rompers and white stockings his mother chose for him, enjoyed watching his mother put on lacy lingerie and hose each morning before work and sometimes allowed her and Mike to dress him in female attire. Although supported by his mother and sister in these episodes, he suffered severe guilt for his aberrant behavior. In later years, he pondered the unspoken meanings of his family's power structure—the weak-willed father, dominant mother, and cruel, tomboyish sister.

In 1939, the Raskind family moved to a tony fifteen-room mansion in a restricted area of Forest Hills but failed to rid themselves of the undercurrent of family dysfunction. In the privacy of his own room and bathroom, Raskind, then aged six, sought his own escape from familial unrest by initiating secret cross-dressing episodes. In his autobiography, *Second Serve*, he recorded the comfort he received from wearing women's clothes: "The feeling of wrongness ... was much diminished. In that regard I felt surprisingly at ease.... It had the taste of serenity about it, of rest" (Richards and Ames, 23). The girl he perceived inside himself he named Renée. For maximum enjoyment of Renée's emergence, he made lengthy forays in public, sneaking home when no one was present and avoiding the watchful eyes of neighbors.

The battle of wills between mother and son escalated as Raskind approached his teen years. He still wore the hated formal wear and longed for a more relaxed, all-American look. His mother, who read aloud to him from the classics, enrolled him in piano, oil painting, boxing, violin, and tennis lessons. To offset these structured activities, he began to cross-dress more often, to gaze at his transformation in the mirror and fantasize about life as a girl. The possibilities seemed more normal than the charade he lived as Richard Raskind.

THE TEEN YEARS

By 1944, Raskind was making a name for himself as a budding tennis star and later as pitcher for his high-school baseball team. These opportunities to outshine his sister brought him much comfort. Likewise, he derived contentment from the relative simplicity of the athletic arena, so clear-cut in comparison with the complexities of life in a cruelly competitive family. In his words, "I treasured my times on the court as periods of clarity in the midst of an often terrifying muddle of conflicting signals and impulses" (Richards and Ames, 36).

Although he showed a small spark of interest in girls his age, Raskind's evolving sexuality revolved mainly around Mike. Their physical explorations in early childhood grew into more titillating encounters in the teen years, brought on by sharing a bed. During these episodes, Raskind, who felt no lust for his sister, experienced a stronger push to act out his female persona.

He enrolled at the Horace Mann School in 1946, where he excelled in literature and history, played on the tennis and baseball teams, and earned the Eastern States Tennis Championship. His cross-dressing, kept up along with boyish activities, was unhampered by secondary sex characteristics until he reached sixteen. His fantasies burgeoned, with Renée at the center of erotic dreams of marriage and family. To his dismay, he also displayed an interest in girls as his body began its growth to above six feet.

Raskind's bar mitzvah, the ceremonial pinnacle in his emerging adulthood, gave him the opportunity to exclaim proudly and publicly his masculinity. The emotional high clashed with negative reactions to cross-dressing, which continued unabated. Distressed to the point of paralysis, he longed for a different handicap. He surmised, "If I had had a heart condition at least I would have had some company, and that would have made it more bearable. As it was, I felt that I was the focus for some singular nastiness, the carrier of a germ specific to me and only me" (Richards and Ames, 39).

As an outgrowth of Renée's strength, Raskind surrounded himself with handsome, tall young males who mirrored his own smooth good looks. He and his friends spent time in worthwhile pleasures, reading poetry, attending games at Yankee Stadium, and watching action movies. The moral standards of the times impeded him from sexual involvement with dates, but later, in the company of Josh Frick, he combed the shady areas of Mexico and the Caribbean and sampled brief moments with prostitutes.

MANHOOD

Raskind obeyed family tradition by attending Yale. Various activities took him to a national tennis tournament and on expeditions to Greenwich Village, where he indulged Renée by dressing up in coed outfits and flaunting his good looks. He applied for work in the Satin Slipper Revue at Harlem's Apollo Club, where he lost his virginity to Jimmy, the impresario who auditioned him as a transvestite stage performer. To Raskind, the affair, because it was unsatisfying, proved that he was not gay. The affair and audition faded from his memory as he forced himself to think of school and tennis.

By his junior year, fearing suicidal urges, he confessed his dual sexuality to his mother and began psychotherapy. His doctor urged him to forget an athletic career and to opt for medical school at the University of Rochester, far from family control. Near the end of his training he chose to specialize in ophthalmic surgery, an endeavor he found challenging and rigorously controlled, as contrasted with the chaos of his personal life. During this time of professional growth, he moved closer to various women, one of whom conceived a child and accompanied him to Puerto Rico for an abortion.

In the midst of Raskind's continual vacillation concerning his sexual identity, psychotherapy failed to relieve his urge to give Renée full power over his life. The therapist, repulsed by the idea of an irreversible sex change, dosed him with tranquilizers and sent him to another doctor, one equally averse to the idea of genital removal. The antidote came instead from nature, which caused Raskind to grow a beard. The change enabled him to take decisive strides toward masculinity. By 1959, he became the fourth doctor in the family and joined the U.S. Navy.

CAREER SATISFACTIONS

Serving as a lieutenant commander and head of eye treatment, Raskind was able to wangle assignment to Long Island so that he could stay in psychotherapy. He participated in navy tennis competitions, but his chief satisfaction lay in tying and taping down his genitals and walking the streets in female attire. Freed at last from his parents' domination, he kept to himself. Following his mother's death, he maintained a workable relationship with his father, from whom he withheld the secret of his confused sexuality.

At his father's suggestion that he needed a vacation, the two traveled to Europe in 1976. Raskind moved on alone to Paris and roomed at the Hotel de la Paix, a gathering spot for transvestites, who befriended him and took seriously his identity crisis. The information he gathered from these experts put him on the right track for the first time, although many hotel residents doubted that a man as tall as Raskind could ever make a successful transition. Back in the United States again in his naval persona, he continued reading articles on transsexualism, particularly concerning Christine Jorgensen, a pioneer in the field.

A significant break from nine years of therapy came after Raskind's first appointment with Dr. Harry Benjamin, the U.S. authority on transsexualism. The outcome of that first evaluation left Raskind with a dilemma—whether to risk a surgical procedure that might leave him a freak of indeterminate sex or continue living his off-again, on-again female impersonation. Plunging into the unknown, he chose to submit to hormone injections, electrolysis, and group therapy with others trapped by the same accident of birth. By the time he mustered out of the navy, he was ready to become Renée. A considerable obstacle was Dr. Benjamin, who, out of fear for Raskind's mental state, forced him to take a break from hormone therapy.

During the interim, Raskind received the Head Fellowship for intense specialized ophthalmic training in Oregon. While he studied, he continued posing as Renée in his off-hours. On his return to New York, he developed keener expertise in his field, particularly in the teaching end. Buoyed by greater professional confidence, he sought psychological strength in Copenhagen from Dr. Christian Hamburger, who prescribed a new round of hormones. To create a more feminine profile, Raskind underwent larynx reduction to lessen the bulge of his Adam's apple. Further search for a suitable surgeon to complete the changeover took him to Chicago, Los Angeles, and New York. Ultimately, he settled on Casablanca, the one place where he could register for sex-change surgery without tedious and probing formality.

FACING AN IRREVOCABLE CHANGE

In 1968, at his doctor's suggestion, Raskind dropped out of sight and lived as a woman in Europe before changing forever into Renée. After some necessary razzle-dazzle with identification, he wandered France, Italy, and Spain in a racy Maserati, then moved on to Casablanca to complete the transformation. At the steps of the clinic, his nerve gave way. The uncertainty of so great a decision forced him to flee

Africa and embrace life as a male. He returned to New York, married in June, and honeymooned in Europe.

Marriage presented a new problem—Raskind's declining virility from abuse of hormones and the need for breast-reduction surgery. Shortly afterward, Meriam, his wife, gave birth to a son, Andrew "Andy" Bishop Raskind, but fatherhood failed to reassure Raskind of a clearly defined male orientation. The charade of masculinity ended in separation in 1973. With Renée's resurgence, he again sought transsexual counseling and immediate surgery, which was performed by Dr. Roberto Granato.

The radical reshaping of his own tissue into female genitals required four hours. On awakening from the procedure, Richards suffered intense aching, searing pain, both from her newly molded sex organs and in the area of her thigh from which the surgeon obtained a necessary skin graft. Mirror inspection of her new organs compensated somewhat for the weakness and suffering that caused her to pass out on her first venture out of bed. During recuperation, she dressed as a man during business hours, then relaxed at the beach in women's clothes. To achieve a new identity, she moved to an apartment west of Central Park and began making friends.

INTRODUCING RENÉE

Employed on a medical staff in Irvine, California, as Dr. Renée Richards, she canceled the life of Dr. Richard Raskind and bid farewell to friends and son, Andy, who continued to call her Daddy. Drawn to the tennis courts, she nevertheless skirted sports until her professionalism was established on the West Coast lest some tennis buff identify her well-known tennis form and reveal her former identity. In time, as her confidence grew, she agreed to a doubles match with Bobby Riggs.

Richards made her formal sports debut at the 1976 La Jolla Tennis Tournament, where an umpire recognized her immediately. Renée won the women's singles championship, then returned to her practice. A sharp-eyed reporter, tipped off by the double name on her medical license, ran down crucial information, then confronted Richards with the facts: "Isn't it true Dr. Richards that your identity was once that of Dr. Richard Raskind, a prominent ophthalmologist and an amateur tennis player from New York City?" (Richards and Ames, 319). Renée appealed to him to be fair to Andy, the person most at risk, but the reporter insisted that a revelation would appear on the eleven o'clock news.

Unmasked at last, Richards struggled through the week with no help from the press, who watched her home and office. But a flood of letters from the public, mostly supportive, brought her new confidence. The writers—some minorities, some handicapped—understood the feeling of life on the dividing line, neither in nor out. The commiseration of these new friends helped her cope with the media circus that followed her exposure.

A NEW PERSON

With much hesitance, Richards at first gave up medicine and forged a new career in sports. Countered by the tennis hierarchy, who wanted to protect women players from unfair competition via chromosome testing, she rejected their ploy and accused them of discrimination. However, without their cooperation, the likelihood of monetary return was severely limited. Other factors weighed heavily, not the least of which were age, a history of smoking, and haphazard past training. Against the odds, she proved on the Lionel Cup circuit that she was ready for competitive play. With the encouragement of old buddies like Billie Jean King and Bobby Riggs, she played well.

The U.S. Tennis Association's refusal of Richard's credentials forced her into litigation. With the aid of lawyer Roy Cohn, she won her case and pursued a career in tennis. By 1981, at the age of forty-seven, she retired from the court and returned to her medical career. While participating in a final tournament, Richards allied with Martina Navratilova and offered to develop her tactical game. The winning pair breezed through Wimbledon in 1982, whipping Chris Evert Lloyd.

Even in victory Richards continued to fight old battles. Her relationship with her sister reached a breaking point after Mike admitted her discomfort with the sex change. Her father, never one to face up to problems, ignored the controversy over Richard-Renée. Problems with Andy also presented a challenge, but Richards managed to cope. With her new identity, she at last felt firmly situated in the self she was meant to be.

SOURCES

Richards, Renée. "A Blueprint for Winning the Open." *World Tennis*, September 1984, 52-58.

Richards, Renée, and John Ames. *Second Serve*. New York: Stein and Day, 1983.

Nelson Rockefeller

Dyslexia—battled by notable achievers such as William Butler Yeats, Albert Einstein, Hans Christian Andersen, Woodrow Wilson, King Karl XI of Sweden, Gustave Flaubert, and Nelson Rockefeller—is a disorder affecting the processes of sorting data to such a degree that it renders many victims illiterate. Labeled "word blindness" in the nineteenth century and still undiagnosed in Rockefeller's childhood, dyslexia is an inherited malfunction in the brain's ability to interpret language. Dyslexic persons, often stymied by high intelligence and a frustrated will to succeed, tend to reverse or rotate letters. Their lack of spelling skills causes them much dismay, as does their inability to encode and decode language cues. These flaws, while not untreatable, require a type of retraining available only in recent decades.

Nelson Rockefeller, among the distinguished coterie of public figures who have mastered or at least coped with dyslexia, learned not only how to untangle scrambled neurological signals but also how to quell the fear of failure and the need to conceal his handicap. Astute, extroverted, and self-assured, he spoke publicly of his malady, thus furthering educators' attempts to reach and reassure the number of fellow sufferers who "pass" into literate society by pretending to function normally.

ELITE BEGINNINGS

On the day that Rockefeller entered the world, the front page of the *New York Times* reported the event, which stole the limelight from William Jennings Bryan's nomination as the Democratic candidate for president. The coincidence presaged Rockefeller's future as power broker for the Republican party, which under his influence successfully outclassed Democrats for a quarter-century by brilliant manipulation and financial force. Born July 8, 1908, in Bar Harbor, Maine, summer playground of the United States' wealthiest and most privileged, Nelson Aldrich Rockefeller, second son among John Davidson and Abby Green Aldrich Rockefeller's six children, came from one of the nation's most prominent families and was named for his maternal grandfather. His paternal grandfather, John D. Rockefeller, Sr., the United States' first billionaire, had wrested a $2 billion fortune from Standard Oil Company and established noteworthy philanthropies. The Aldrich side of the family, equally admirable, claimed kinship with the founder of Rhode Island and boasted a powerful U.S. senator, Nelson W. Aldrich. Abby Rockefeller, herself deeply involved with public trusts, helped found New York's Museum of Modern Art.

Rockefeller, who lived alternately at family residences in New York City, Pocantico Hills, and Bar Harbor, was ruled over by governesses and weaned on strict, conservative philosophy. He once boasted of his background, which dated to French Huguenots named Roquefeuille: "The roots of our family ethic were deeply implanted—an ethic based on the fundamental American values which have come down through the generations since then" (Kramer and Roberts, 34). In accordance with his grandfather's Baptist faith, he was reared to avoid smoking and alcohol, to pledge part of his allowance to the church, and to revere the Sabbath. Daily, his father led the children in prayer and catechized them in duty, self-reliance, sobriety, frugality, and responsibility, the tenets he deemed most appropriate to young scions of a dynasty. His mother injected the warmth and humanity that made her son a unique cultural and political lion with a taste for beautiful things and a drive to incorporate them into his daily life.

Affectionately known to siblings and pals as "Nell," Rockefeller frolicked with his four brothers, who became his best friends. The boys pursued a friendly rivalry but in general accorded family leadership to Nelson, who cheerfully accepted the honor. He attended New York City's Lincoln School, a progressive educational experiment financed with Rockefeller money. A puzzle to the family was his inability to excel in his studies. He obviously possessed the intelligence and drive to achieve, but his reading and spelling skills were abysmal. His father, believing that righthandedness was the normal orientation, blamed Nelson's lefthandedness and attempted to correct the fault by tying an elastic string from his left hand to his waist and snapping it to emphasize use of the right hand. Consequently, the boy never developed athletic skills, as demonstrated by his poor showing in soccer.

CROSSING THE HURDLE

By ninth grade Nelson had sunk to the bottom of his class, particularly in French and math. Despite money, family pull, and regular tutoring, he was denied entrance to Princeton University, his first choice of alma mater. Endowed with personal magnetism and more verve and potential than older brother John III, Nelson Rockefeller, at age eighteen, entered Dartmouth College and, ignoring past indicators, set his sights on a first-class college experience. True to Grandpa J. D., Sr.'s elan, he called on the college president the first day to announce his arrival.

Rockefeller followed a well-rounded program of studies that extended to sports and creative writing and also included frequent visits to neighboring girls' colleges in his zippy Buick roadster, which he wangled from his tight-fisted father. During his college years, he matured in his attitude toward success and how to achieve it. In a letter to his parents he cited strong idealism: "I've lost my feeling of incompetency, of not being able to handle a job without relying on someone else" (Kramer and Roberts, 40). This newfound self-esteem brought him courage and the ability to speak in public, both of which served him well in public life. An economics major, he was elected to Phi Beta Kappa, completed a forty-five page senior thesis detailing his grandfather's rise to wealth and prestige, and graduated cum laude in June 1930.

His social tastes as carefully managed as his intellectual and moral under-pinnings, Rockefeller was encouraged to mingle with the offspring of the most distinguished clans. Following his family's preference, he married Mary Todhunter "Tod" Clark, a Philadelphia debutante, in June of that year. Still undecided about a career, Rockefeller took his bride on a year's round-the-world tour, stopping off to visit writers, political leaders, Standard Oil officials, and the king of Siam. The marriage proved satisfying. He fathered five children, Rodman, Ann, Steven, and the family's first twins, Mary and Michael, and renewed himself through constant contact with his young family. Later evidence suggests that he did not maintain his earlier enthusiasm for parenthood. As his daughter Mary summarized, "My father, well, I love him for his warmth. But he stands for power" (Persico, 154-155).

THE WORLD OF WORK

Rockefeller's first jobs centered on public service, which remained his primary interest throughout a varied career. He defied his father and assumed a trusteeship of the Metropolitan Museum of Art and membership on the Westchester County Health Board. Later, as a clerk at the London and Paris branches of the Chase National Bank and as a representative for Rockefeller Center, a family-owned and -managed concern, he performed well, renting office space at bargain prices during the depression and giving indications of future greatness. Expanding to other interests, he directed the growth of the Creole Petroleum Corporation from 1935 to 1940 and developed an affinity for Latin America, which he touted in U.S. political circles. As a result of his enthusiasm, President Franklin Roosevelt created the Office of Inter-American Affairs and placed Rockefeller in charge. During his tenure as coordinator, Rockefeller furthered the growth of developing Latin American countries with loans, a lively import-export trade, cultural exchange, and betterment of living standards. Refinements of his campaign to ally powers of the Western hemisphere led to the creation of the American International Association for Economic and Social Development and the International Basic Economy Corporation.

A bonus to the Rockefeller name was Nelson's part in the establishment of the United Nations. He influenced not only the creation of the charter but was the deciding factor in the selection of seventeen acres of Manhattan's Lower East Side for its headquarters. In a single day of negotiation, he sealed the proposal by convincing his father to donate $8.5 million to pay for the land and convinced the U.S. government to declare the property tax-free.

UP THE POLITICAL LADDER

In November 1950, Rockefeller worked effectively with President Harry Truman to upgrade underdeveloped nations and thereby stabilize international relations. A primary Rockefeller project was the Point Four foreign-aid program, which sought to stifle Communism by helping poorer countries fend for themselves economically and socially. Restless and unfulfilled in this job, he withdrew a year later to concentrate his efforts in the private sector, where he could be more effective.

Averell Harriman suggested that he rethink his political future and run for an elective office. By 1958, Rockefeller had honed his political savvy well enough to snatch the governorship of New York away from Harriman. Quipping about the change in his goals, he said, "I had two choices.... I could have become a gigolo or a governor" (Kramer and Roberts, 72). Neither too fastidious nor too aristocratic for the role, as some had predicted, he navigated expertly through nearly four terms, fluctuating from hardline right-winger to a more moderate pose. One of his most useful talents was the ability to discern creativity in others. With no fear of competition, he hired outstanding young moguls and granted them freedom to apply creative solutions to nettlesome problems.

The ups and downs of Rockefeller's tenure in state government found him able and adaptive. Major events of his governorship were the forceful quellings of a New York City garbage strike and racial warfare at Attica Prison in 1971. Less volatile and more to his tastes were generative efforts, including his bolstering of the state university system; the addition of needed public housing, hospitals, mental-health clinics, and nursing homes; and his construction of the twin-towered World Trade Center. So frequently did he plan and execute new buildings that his enemies criticized him for his "edifice complex."

This period of Rockefeller's life saw multiple unhappinesses, not only his failure to land a presidential nomination but also the failure of his thirty-one-year marriage, which had been drifting toward total estrangement since he had chosen to run for public office. Amid much media hoopla, on May 4, 1963, he married Margaretta Fitler "Happy" Murphy, a woman more suited than his first wife to coping with the media curiosity about his public and private life. The abruptness and secrecy of their marriage did not further his political career. Upon his return from a two-and-a-half-week honeymoon at his ranch in Venezuela, he found his bid for the presidency almost moribund.

Rockefeller's second marriage did revitalize him personally. He and Happy produced two sons, Nelson, Jr., and Mark, whose upbringing he directed more carefully than he had his first set of children. Like his own father, he led his sons in morning prayer at breakfast, participated in the running of electric trains and the raising of hamsters, and watched their favorite television programs with them in the evening. Another aspect of his regeneration came from his brother David and sister, Abby, who lent their moral and financial support after his remarriage, a time when political forces were elbowing Rockefeller out of the running. Matter-of-factly, he commented, "Despite the fact that I was under bitter attack on many sides, because I had gotten remarried, this was a gesture of friendship and love and affection from two members of my family who had been upset. I am embarrassed to say this, but it is a fact" (Kramer and Roberts, 271).

In two campaigns—Richard Nixon's in 1960 and Hubert Humphrey's in 1968—Rockefeller opted not to seek the vice presidency. Then, as power shifted to the Washington scene, he changed his mind about the post second to the president. Selected forty-first vice president in 1974, he served during President Gerald Ford's disjointed term of office. His tenure was marked by his own brand of political chutzpah. Dubbed Rocky by an admiring media, he overcame the stigma of privileged rich boy by reaching out to all levels of U.S. society. Handsome, voluble, self-assured, he represented the Republican party and the nation during tenuous times following Nixon's Watergate fiasco.

The experience was a mixed blessing for Rockefeller's career. His proposed partnership with Ford, which took as its foremost task lifting the mangled Republican party from its public humiliation, began with four months of probes into his personal and financial dealings. The result was the payment of a $900,000 discrepancy in his income tax. From inauspicious beginnings, he worked toward a stronger domestic policy and greater control over the CIA. A stickler for details, particularly in matters of art, he redesigned the presidential seal so that the eagle's wings projected up rather than down. Gradually, however, he fell into the malaise that dogs the office of vice president—he attended state funerals, oversaw lesser details, and grew stale in the job of second in command. "I don't think I'm cut out to be a No. 2 type of guy," he explained (Goldman, 29). When Ford selected a running mate in 1976, he overlooked Rockefeller.

RETURN TO PRIVATE LIFE

In 1977, Rockefeller, at the age of fifty-nine, gave up political office and returned to the philanthropic and cultural interests that garnished his career. An optimist at heart, he declined to see the move as acquiescence to failure. Following his great love of painting and sculpture, he authored *Masterpieces of Primitive Art*, published high-quality art prints, and busied himself with his family's foundations. Not one to conceal his emotions, he admitted candidly that his chief regret was retiring without ever having been nominated for the presidency.

Rockefeller's benevolence did not go unpraised. He received honorary degrees from Dartmouth, Fordham, and the Jewish Theological Seminary. Chile, Mexico, and Brazil awarded him special orders of merit. In 1949, climaxing his work for the National Conference of Christians and Jews, he had chaired Brotherhood Week. Yet these numerous plaques, titles, honors, and ribbons failed to fill the slot he had reserved for an achievement he thought he had earned.

Typical of his ebullient, go-getting style, he neglected his health in his last two years, gained weight, and died of heart failure on January 26, 1979, while working late one evening on a book about modern art. In classy Rockefeller style, his funeral at Riverside Church was led by Dr. Sloane Coffin and Martin Luther King, Jr., and was attended by former colleague Henry Kissinger, ex-president Ford, and incumbent president Carter. Music was provided by Metropolitan Opera star Roberta Peters and jazz great Lionel Hampton, who concluded the service with Rockefeller's favorite tune, "Sweet Georgia Brown." Rumors previous to his death hinted that running for public office had sapped his financial strength, as suggested by the sale of several residences, including his summer home in Seal Harbor, Michigan. Insiders, quick to champion Rocky, declared that a late-in-life attempt to consolidate holdings came nearer to the truth.

A clear assessment of his goals and ambitions came after age sixty, when Rockefeller bridled at allegations that he had never had to work hard. He reminded a critic that he had never missed more than three days for sickness in twenty-five years of public service. He declared that he had always wanted to be an architect but chose otherwise because he could not justify that particular profession in terms of community service. Instead, he followed serendipity, grasping opportunities that came his way and making himself useful in a variety of endeavors. As he characterized his efforts, "If you've got patience and persistence, even though you may be thwarted at one point, you can [succeed]. And I'm a great believer in that" (Kramer and Roberts, 75).

SOURCES

Current Biography. New York: H. W. Wilson, 1951, 531-533.

Goldman, Peter, with Tom Mathews and Susan Agrest. "Death of a Public Man." *Newsweek*, February 5, 1979, 27-30.

Kramer, Michael, and Sam Roberts. *I Never Wanted to Be Vice-President of Anything!* New York: Basic Books, 1976.

Persico, Joseph E. *The Imperial Rockefeller.* New York: Simon & Schuster, 1982.

Simpson, Eileen. *Reversals: A Personal Account of Victory over Dyslexia.* Boston: Houghton Mifflin, 1979.

Anwar Sadat

For a humble village boy, advancing from a military career to president of Egypt was unlikely, but Anwar Sadat achieved the transition by filling his imagination with deeds of heroes and by holding fast to a dream of freeing his nation from tyranny. While in prison, the leading dissident among Egypt's young army officers developed into a leader, a viable force for change. Because he was a man gifted with the rare qualities of honesty, directness, and a love of peace, President Sadat helped restore Egypt by renewing the people's lives and rebuilding their confidence.

SMALL BEGINNINGS

Muhammad Anwar el-Sadat was born the third son of his father's second wife, Sitt el-Barrein, on December 25, 1918, in the village of Mit Abul-Kum on the banks of the Nile halfway between Cairo and Alexandria. Sadat lived comfortably and felt a part of the community, which served as an extended family. He recalled in his autobiography the respect villagers accorded his illiterate grandmother, Um Muhammad, the local herbalist. Much of his early life connected him with nature, especially her herbs, fresh dates and vegetables from neighboring fields, and the cattle and water buffalo he and other boys drove to communal grazing areas near the canal.

Sadat grew hardy from lack of luxuries such as electricity and plumbing. The beds of his simple house were brick slabs extending from the wall. In an indolent moment, he perched atop the mud oven and warmed himself. He made regular meals from crusts of bread and bits of cheese. For a nighttime treat, he often roasted an onion and slipped away to eat it in solitude.

Muhammad, Sadat's father, the local effendi, or educated man, had received certification in primary education and secured a place within the British-controlled system. He and Sadat's grandmother pushed the boy to a similar height by sending him to the local Koranic school, then to a Coptic, or Christian, school in Toukh, a half-mile from the village. After opening his mind to literature, Sadat sat still for stories told by his mother and grandmother. One theme permeated much of the lore he absorbed—the cruelty and rapaciousness of British overlords.

In 1925, Sadat, his elder brother Tal'at, eleven other sisters and brothers, and his parents moved to Kubri al-Qubbah near Cairo after his father returned from the Egyptian army, which had withdrawn from the Sudan, and took a job as senior clerk at the health department. Sadat enrolled at the Islamic Benevolent School in Zaytun, walking distance from home. A top scholar, he reached the Fuad I Secondary School in 1930 and came to value his father's efforts to educate him despite their poverty. In this urban setting, he confronted for the first time the fact that some children were rated above others on the basis of what their fathers owned or did for a living. Because of his ragged clothes, he found himself at the bottom of the class ranking.

Sadat, easily moved by accounts of leaders such as Kemal Ataturk, Napoleon, and Gandhi, fell prey to a hatred of all outsiders who endangered his homeland. After the Anglo-Egyptian treaty of 1936, an increase in the size of the army coincided with Sadat's surge of patriotism. With references from some of his father's army acquaintances, he, along with other lower-class boys, entered Abbasiyah Military Academy. He graduated as a second lieutenant in 1938.

PLOTS AND PRISON

Stationed with the infantry in Manqabad, Sadat spoke nightly to less-spirited colleagues about Egypt's majestic history and its abysmal future under British tyranny. In his free time, he sat contentedly at his books, oblivious to the rowdier pastimes of the other soldiers. In 1939, he, along with classmate Gamal Abdel Nasser, studied at the Signals School of Maadi. Because of his excellent work, Sadat was chosen to serve with the signal corps. During this productive period, his evening sessions with other dissidents led to the formation of the secret Free Officers Society, a group pledged to free Egypt from colonialism.

In the summer of 1941, Sadat put his revolt into motion by first refusing to hand over weapons to the British, who were embroiled in resistance to the Axis powers, then by marching toward Maadi to topple the colonial government. The plan failed, yet daily more converts, disgruntled by British high-handedness, joined the Free Officers. As Rommel's German forces pressed Britain's army of occupation, Sadat and his coterie, who had a secret transmitter, formed an underground network to advise the Germans.

Word of their cabal leaked to the authorities; Sadat was placed under house arrest. He was at first threatened with death by firing squad, then stripped of rank and incarcerated in the Aliens' Jail. In no way dismayed by the interruption of his plans, he asked for books and spent his time reading, reflecting, and walking in the exercise yard. His family visited him monthly and sent parcels when they could afford them or when army buddies assisted them with gifts of money. In December 1942, he was transferred to the Upper Nile and lodged in the Maqusah Palace, which served as a detention center for political detainees. During this phase of his sentence, he mastered German by reading aloud with the help of a native speaker.

In early November 1943, thin and drawn, Sadat was again moved, this time to Cairo's Zaytun Detention Center, where he passed his days tending and breeding rabbits. As World War II drew to a close, he organized a mutiny and escape to publicize prison maltreatment. Returned to his cell, he took part in a hunger strike in September 1944, then escaped for good in October, remaining a fugitive until September 1945. To earn a living during this period, he grew a beard and, under the alias of Hadji Muhammad, worked as a porter for a millionaire trader, then as a transporter of quarried marble for King Farouk's resthouse.

BECOMING HIS OWN MAN

Relieved of the need for secrecy, Sadat rejoined his cell of dissenters and was recaptured and returned to the Aliens' Jail on January 11, 1946, this time put in solitary confinement relieved by two short breaks a day for walks with other prisoners. Numbered 2151 and transferred to cell 54 in Cairo Central Prison, he endured unspeakable hygienic conditions and coarse meals that undermined his digestive system. The Muslim Brotherhood, learning of his family's economic distress, paid prison purveyors £10 per month to supply him with decent food, furniture, and clean linen.

Although the period of bombing during the Arab-Israeli War of 1948 distressed him severely, the final eight of his thirty-one months of imprisonment put Sadat in touch with his inner self and brought him understanding and a stronger belief in Allah. On his acquittal and release in July 1948, Sadat took firmer control of his life. Because his wife and their three daughters, Rokaya, Rawia, and Camelia, no longer represented the life he wanted to live, he divorced Ekbal Madi, a distant relative in his village whom he had been obliged to marry in 1940. While visiting a colleague, he met Jehan Raouf, an English-Egyptian sixteen-year-old enamored of his swarthy good looks and military bearing. In a traditional Islamic ceremony, she became his second wife on May 29, 1949.

Sadat got a job as rewriter for a publishing house, then moved up in the business world as a water contractor. He and Jehan lived frugally in a small hotel and waited until his company earnings were substantial before claiming them. Because his partner cheated him and accused him of embezzlement, Sadat grew to dislike business and had himself reinstated in the army with his former rank of captain. Still dedicated to the cause of Egyptian freedom, he was pleased to learn that the Free Officers Society had prospered during his absence.

Sadat rose in the power structure alongside Nasser, his idol. On July 23, 1952, Sadat helped lead a revolt against King Farouk, the incompetent, profligate despot who survived and fled to exile in Rome. Without its puppet ruler, the British superstructure collapsed. In his memories of the upheaval, Sadat spoke majestically of his ideal: "The dream on which I had lived for years—a dream to which I devoted my entire life—had finally materialized. It was now a reality, surging in my heart, possessing my being and dwarfing it" (Sadat 1978, 107). Moved to share his joy, he spoke at dawn over the radio, announcing Egypt's liberation.

REWARDS AND RESPONSIBILITIES

Rewarded with a seat on the Revolutionary Command Council, Sadat helped negotiate arms purchases, confiscate royal property, establish schools and hospitals, shore up foreign alliances, and plan the Aswan Dam, a lengthy project that was not completed until 1960. He was indispensable as the only member of Nasser's advisory board to speak knowledgeably about poverty and imprisonment. Before the dissolution of the council and Nasser's formal election in 1956, Sadat rose to minister of state and chairman of the assembly. In turn, he served as editor of *al-Jumhuriya*, an influential newspaper, broadcaster for the "Voice of Arabs" radio program, and vice president of Egypt.

Facts from Sadat's personal life during this period suggest the stress of dealing with the vast changes that brought Egypt and Syria into the United Arab Republic and resulted in the nationalization of the Suez Canal, an overt threat to both England and the United States. More damning to the revolution was the counter-productivity of corrupt commissioners, which violated Sadat's sense of mission. Frustrated and disgusted, he blamed Nasser for allowing weak men to assume too much power. To maintain his perspective, he kept his distance and worked alone. On May 15, 1960, an overload of plans, meetings, and travel and the disillusionment he experienced from political squabbling brought on a heart attack, which sidelined him temporarily.

By 1966, Egypt was well on its way toward recouping its pride in nationhood. Having damaged relations with the United States by dealing with the Soviets, Nasser sent Sadat on a conciliatory state visit to Washington, D.C. The next year, another mishandling of foreign relations resulted in war with Israel and Egypt's first significant defeat as a free nation. As was his pattern, Sadat internalized the loss: "It sank into the very fabric of my consciousness so that I relived it day and night. As its real dimensions were daily revealed to me, my agony intensified — and my sense of helplessness" (Sadat 1978, 184). To cope with his emotions, for three weeks he shut himself in his house near the pyramids.

PRESIDENT OF EGYPT

With Nasser's sudden death from heart failure on September 28, 1970, Sadat, in a state of collapse at the loss of his friend, was suddenly pushed into the presidency of Egypt. Before the people made his position official with their vote on October 15, he mulled over second thoughts, particularly about the hidden maneuverings and rivalries that accompany power like twin consorts. The unrest that followed the death of so great a leader as Nasser resulted in a coup, led by Ali Sabri, his vice president. Counter to this incident, Sadat received an outpouring of goodwill from Egyptians, spurred in part by his unparalleled popularity with the military.

Sadat, alarmed by repressive measures still in operation at the time of Nasser's death, returned the support of Egyptians by liberalizing government rule, ending wiretaps and punitive arrests, bringing in more diverse manufacturing and foreign investors to boost the job market, and supporting tourism to improve foreign exchange. At the same time, he abandoned Nasser's pro-Arab agenda in favor of more democratic goals and began cultivating a fuller panorama of world leaders. Still more important to his people's self-image, he strove to offset the humiliating defeat of the war with Israel in 1967.

A STRONG ARM

Although world leaders gave little credence to his bellicose rhetoric, Sadat quickly proved to be more pragmatic than visionary. In 1972, he forced 20,000 Soviet advisers from Egypt, claiming that their presence deterred his plans for a confrontation with Israel because they refused him the armaments needed for victory. He explained: "I wanted to put the Soviet Union in its place — in its natural position as a friendly country, no more, no less.... I wanted to tell the whole world that we are always our own masters" (Sadat 1978, 231). His abrupt move stirred discontent among students, who clashed with police. In October 1973, he led a costly surprise strike across the Suez Canal on the Sinai Peninsula, the triangular territory traditionally claimed by Egypt that Israel had usurped in 1967.

Backed by Syrian insurgents from the Golan Heights, the three-week war impressed on Israeli leaders Sadat's intent. Quickly, Israel, which reclaimed most of the Sinai strip, opened the way for more candid negotiations with a fierce enemy it had discounted as negligible. One of the major upshots of the war was Sadat's leverage with Arab oil magnates, who countered the United States' pro-Israel stance with an oil embargo.

By 1974, Sadat was ready to negotiate more candidly with President Richard Nixon, his successor, Gerald Ford, and Secretary of State Henry Kissinger. By the end of their productive talks, Sadat had cemented his control of a strip of the contested Sinai territory. The success of his carefully choreographed meetings with world officials, along with his disavowal of a Soviet treaty, enhanced his stature in the Mediterranean world.

Within two years, Sadat, in the face of widespread Arab opposition, was ready for more aggressive peace overtures. On November 19, 1977, he spoke before Israel's Knesset, boldly demanding that Israeli troops gradually cede the western portion of lands taken in the 1967 conflict, where rich oilfields could once again fatten the Egyptian economy. By 1978, further talks with President Carter and Israel's Menachem Begin produced economic and military commitments and a peace agreement, which climaxed in a historic treaty signed in Washington, D.C., on March 26, 1979. For his persistence in the settlement of a Jewish-Arab crisis, Sadat shared the 1978 Nobel Peace Prize with Prime Minister Begin.

By 1980, the projected cessation of hostilities between Israel and Egypt became fact. Israeli ships once again passed through Suez waters. The two neighbors established diplomatic niceties, although actual progress toward settlement of Middle Eastern tensions existed primarily on paper. Yet to be negotiated were government of the Gaza strip and home rule for Palestinian refugees.

A BITTER CONCLUSION

Few local voices cheered Sadat's role in restoring peace to the eastern Mediterranean by bringing two cataclysmic forces toward a more peaceful future. Arab leaders, infuriated with what they interpreted as an act of betrayal, booted Egypt from the Arab League. Immediately, dissidents seized the opportunity to foment sedition. To control local unrest, in September 1981 he detained a group of 1,600 extremists, including Communists, Arab nationalists, and Islamic fundamentalists. This move quieted Egypt but depleted support from one of his strongest allies, the military, which no longer backed him with unquestioning loyalty.

In 1978, Sadat, cheered by his second family—daughters Loubna, Noha, and Nana, a son, Gamal, and grandchildren Sherif and Yasmin—expressed contentment with his pragmatism: "Nowadays I am never happier than when I am on the banks of the Suez Canal. I sit there for hours on end in a small log cabin watching the progress of work on new projects and the ceaseless reconstruction effort" (Sadat 1978, 271). Three years later, on October 6, 1981, during a military parade in Nasr City to honor Egyptian reclamation of lands taken by Israel, a band of Muslim fanatics infiltrated the army and shot Sadat and eight others before his horrified family and staff. He was flown by helicopter to Maadi Hospital, but his chest wounds were too severe for surgical repair.

Buried symbolically in the Sinai, site of his great victory, Sadat left behind a grieving nation. The gathering of mourners included three former U.S. presidents, Charles, Prince of Wales, and Prime Minister Begin. In her autobiography, his daughter Camelia said in tribute: "World leaders have called you great; historians are calling you a man of courage and wisdom. Your story, like that of your hero Zahran, may yet be told to some impressionable child who yearns for tales of courage and sacrifice far beyond the village horizons" (Sadat 1985, 190).

SOURCES

Sadat, Anwar. *In Search of Identity: An Autobiography.* New York: Harper & Row, 1978.

_____. *Those I Have Known.* Foreword by Jimmy Carter. New York: Continuum, 1984.

Sadat, Camelia. *My Father and I.* New York: Macmillan, 1985.

Sadat, Jehan. *A Woman of Egypt.* New York: Simon & Schuster, 1987.

Sequoyah

Sequoyah, a notable Cherokee linguist and self-made scholar, overcame native superstition by transforming symbolic markings into readable language. He surmised that Cherokees were less sophisticated than whites because they could not pass their achievements on to later generations through the written word. Famed for his "talking leaves," a syllabary that rendered the Cherokee language in written form, Sequoyah taught his people the magic of writing and became the only person in recorded history to create an alphabet. Within months, he transformed his people into readers and writers.

A poor, crippled man who lived a sequestered life, Sequoyah accomplished what linguists of the Cree, Winnebago, and Athabascan language groups failed to do — complete a language system that enabled natives to translate spoken sounds into letters. But in order to create the miracle of written words, he had to buck native superstition that only whites could make books. His reward came from the praise of one of his own people, who referred to Sequoyah as a "native genius [who] has struck light from darkness — conferred inconceivable blessings upon his people and achieved for his own name an enviable distinction among those few truly great names, with which are connected imperishable honor" (Foreman, 68).

UNCERTAIN BEGINNINGS

Of mixed parentage, Sequoyah — spelled Sik-wa-yi in the Cherokee sound system — was born around 1760 to 1770 in Taskigi, Tennessee, a village near Fort Loudon on the Tennessee River, five miles from the tribal capital of Echota. Some accounts indicate that he was lame from birth. He never knew the identity of his father and was raised by his mother, a Cherokee princess and daughter of Chief Echota, who was part Shawnee.

Sequoyah adopted the name George Guess or Gist from Nathaniel Gist, a British frontiersman he assumed was his father, although other sources name an American and a German trader as possible sires. Sequoyah's white half-sisters rose in prominence: Eliza Blair married the editor of the Washington *Globe*; Sarah, a U.S. senator; Anne, a doctor; and Maria, an entrepreneur from Kentucky. Sequoyah's nephew, Montgomery, was Abraham Lincoln's postmaster general; a second nephew, Francis, was a U.S. senator and brigadier general during the Civil War.

Sequoyah, a contemplative, creative man and a skilled linguist, never attended school or studied English. A noted essayist, Samuel Lorenzo Knapp, recalled that he was stoic but affable, engaging, and reflective. In his words, "Early in life he was gay, talkative, and ... from the strength of his memory, his easy colloquial powers, and ready command of his vernacular, a story teller of the convivial party" (Foreman, 19).

During the Creek War, Sequoyah served as a private in a Cherokee cavalry regiment of the U.S. Army, which defeated invading Creeks during their alliance with the British in the War of 1812. He fought in one of the most decisive engagements, the Battle of Horseshoe Bend. Later, he worked as a trapper, trader, and hunter until an accident maimed his knee, shortened his leg, and prevented an outdoor livelihood. Under the patronage of Chief Charles R. Hicks, he labored among Georgia Cherokees as a painter and silversmith and was widely acclaimed for his use of animal-hair brushes and the beauty of his handcrafted spurs and spoons.

In 1815 in a tribal ceremony, Sequoyah married Sarah, or Sally, as she is sometimes called, who survived him and claimed a land bounty as rightful reward for his military service. In September 1816, while a member of a deputation of fifteen chiefs and warriors at Willstown, Alabama, Sequoyah refused to sell land to a delegation from President Jackson. Eventually, by gifts and expert wheedling, white diplomats managed to purchase 1,300,000 acres in southern Tennessee for $65,000. Two years later, following the treaty of 1817, Sequoyah and his son Tessee joined a group of Cherokees emigrating to Arkansas to escape white domination. The group of 331, who headed into uncharted territory to the west of Skin Bayou, launched nineteen flatboats on the Tennessee River for the modern city of Sallisaw.

CREATING A WRITTEN LANGUAGE

To help his people establish their independence in an increasingly white-controlled world, in 1809 Sequoyah announced to tribal leaders that he intended to duplicate the white world's magic by creating a Cherokee book. He evolved the idea from a nephew who had observed white people reading and writing in Sauta, a neighboring village. Sequoyah's ambitious plan introduced a concept for which the tribe had no words—communicating through letters.

The graybeards of the tribe replied with a myth: The Great Spirit originally created a white child and a red child. He gave the white child a bow and arrow; to the red child he gave a book. The white, who was aggressive and warlike, stole the red child's book and left in its place the bow and arrow. Thus, the elders deduced, the matter of literacy was divinely determined. In their eyes, the burden of the red race was to acquiesce to nonliterate ways, which were ordained by the Great Spirit.

Sequoyah, believing that white people had merely stumbled on the method of symbolic communication, remained adamant against the elders' superstition. Scribbling away with pokeberry juice on slabs of bark, he began writing. He perturbed his family and neighbors, who shook their heads at his unhoed corn and called him a lunatic. His wife used his scribblings as tinder to start cooking fires. Fearful tribespeople burned him out of his hideaway and destroyed two years' work on the alphabet, but Sequoyah persisted. Even on his river journey to Arkansas, he continued testing his concepts and discarding false starts. After settling at his new farm, he eked out a meager living by making salt while conducting laborious linguistic study.

At first, working by firelight in a cabin apart from his family's dwelling, Sequoyah composed pictographs similar to Egyptian hieroglyphs. By 1821, after years of trial and error, he abandoned pictographs and conceived a simpler method of writing Cherokee words—through 200 characters, which he pared down to an even handier 86. He adapted shapes for his letters from a scrap of newspaper he found on a nearby road. Thus, in one month's time, with the help of his six-year-old daughter, he simplified his method by isolating each distinct sound and creating characters to represent consonant/vowel combinations.

The crude letters required some modifications. Sequoyah, carving with a nail or knife on bark, adapted his letters from Hebrew, Greek, and English alphabets but found that a unique method was the only answer to the peculiarities of Cherokee semantic structures, which contain no pronouns, prepositions, or auxiliary verbs and employ three numbers—singular, double, and plural. In time, he acquired pen and ink and began writing in imitation of white people.

When Sequoyah had depicted all Cherokee sounds and mastered them, he tested his hypothesis first on his daughter, then on six dubious tribespeople. He asked each participant to deliver a speech. He scribbled down arcane markings and then, to their amazement, read back their exact words. The doubting Thomases of the tribe were forced to admit that Sequoyah had done just what he set out to do—write a book. And they were especially proud of the fact that the material in the book was their own oratory.

ACCEPTANCE AT LAST

Sequoyah returned to the Cherokee nation in Tennessee to introduce his writing system as a valuable tool of tribal communication. The Cherokee General Council approved his syllabary in 1821. Under the aegis of tribal authorities, who set up a school, he enabled many tribespeople to become literate. Having been labeled an eccentric, miscreant, liar, even a wizard, he quickly compensated for years of alienation and became a local hero.

Unlike English, which contains many orthographic pitfalls, Cherokee is completely phonetic. The syllabic system is so easy and self-explanatory that any native speaker of the Cherokee language can master reading and writing after a few days' study. Among those who first embraced this concept of literacy were Sequoyah's daughter, sons, and a number of youths who proved more malleable than older, stodgier natives.

In a matter of months, over a thousand Cherokees became literate. They began putting up directional signs to paths and villages. Sequoyah assisted eastern tribespeople in writing messages to their western kin. When he returned to Arkansas in

1822, he bore an unheard-of luxury—letters from easterners in Wills Valley to westerners beyond the Mississippi over 500 miles away. By carrying mail written in the Cherokee language, he demonstrated to his nation the utility of literacy.

Within two years, he spread his method westward to the 6,000 emigrant Cherokees in Arkansas, where he took up permanent residence to avoid extensive contact with whites. By 1824, Atsi, a Moravian convert, translated the Gospel of John. That same year, David Brown, a member and key advocate of the Cherokee nation, translated the New Testament into Cherokee script. Within four years, American Indians as far away as Oklahoma recognized the Cherokee syllabary and used it to send messages among tribespeople.

The method also assisted Moravian missionary Samuel A. Worcester, who took up residence at Park Hill in the Cherokee nation in 1825 and valued Sequoyah's invention as a vehicle to educate and convert American Indians to Christianity. He increased his outreach by bypassing instruction in English and moving directly to the Cherokee tongue. In like manner, Sequoyah's alphabet earned praise from legislators, translators, hymnologists, teachers, textbook publishers, temperance leaders, and journalists, who ordered a set of printing characters to be cast in a Boston foundry.

SETTING UP A PRINTING PRESS

The equipment was shipped by water to Georgia and overland 200 miles by wagon. It arrived at New Echota, Georgia, in 1827; Dr. Worcester christened the equipment by printing the first five verses of Genesis. In February of the following year, local people, with the help of teacher and editor Elias Boudinot, produced the *Cherokee Phoenix* and the *Cherokee Advocate*, weekly four-page bilingual newspapers created for both white and American Indian readers. The original purpose of the newspaper was to defend American Indian rights, advance general knowledge, report news, and promulgate information about tribal law. The *Phoenix* remained in print until 1834, when Georgia authorities seized the press and employed it to print propaganda aimed at subverting tribalism. The *Advocate* continued until 1853, halted for lack of funds, then resumed operation in 1870. It ceased permanently in 1906.

Through the *Advocate*, Sequoyah influenced his fellow tribespeople with journalistic essays. He urged his readers to work with the Bureau of Indian Affairs in the reorganization of the Cherokee Indian Territory but vehemently opposed the intrusion of white culture into Native American lands. With equal enthusiasm, he advocated internal communication within the Cherokee nation, which by his day had spread over a vast tract of land and suffered from loss of unity and cohesion. To stave off fragmentation, Sequoyah reviewed and published tribal affairs occurring over the preceding twenty years.

Having overcome barriers to literacy, Sequoyah next set out to supply his people with arithmetic skills. With no knowledge of Arabic or Roman numerals, he conceptualized a mathematical system of numbers up to a million. This led to a method of performing simple computation and expressing fractions.

THE TWILIGHT YEARS

Sequoyah remained remarkably active and influential in American Indian affairs in his old age. In 1839, 17,000 Cherokees were forcibly uprooted from their tribal home, and only 13,000 survived the ignoble Trail of Tears. Sequoyah distinguished himself by calling the Cherokees to an assembly on July 1 at the Illinois Camp Ground and helping to create a new government. In the face of bitter internal opposition, by July 12, he and his associates realized a pact reuniting the Cherokee nation.

Although there is little personal information about Sequoyah, a book published during the late 1830s details some of his physical characteristics. Late in life, he bore himself with dignity and affability. A modest man, he was above average in height, slender, and quite lame. Dressed in his characteristic flowered turban, leggings, and open-necked tunic, he had gray hair and puffed on a long-stemmed calumet, or ceremonial pipe, which he filled with dried sumac. His bespectacled, professional image, like that of a Greek philosopher, commanded deep respect and became a symbol of Cherokee eclecticism, independence, and pride. Most acquaintances remember him for his intellectual talents, particularly his meticulous journal and realistic drawings of animals.

A diary entry from January 1840 gives more details about the life of Sequoyah. He was married five times, had twenty children, and lived on a ten-acre farm in a three-cabin compound. He kept mules, oxen, cattle, and hogs, but his farming skills took second place to his boundless intellectual curiosity.

A FITTING MEMORIAL

While following the trail of the "lost Cherokees," who migrated west during the American Revolution, Sequoyah, in the company of his son Chusaleta, died of dysentery in August 1843 near San Fernando in Tamaulipas State in Mexico. He was buried in an unmarked grave beside the Red River. His friends questioned the authenticity of the news and sent a party to search for him two years later before accepting the fact of his death. His writing system remained in use until government agencies forced tribe members to abandon it in favor of English. Attempts to revive the Cherokee syllabic system as a source of ethnic pride and oneness continue into the present.

A giant among his race, Sequoyah is memorialized in the Latinate spelling of elegant redwoods, *Sequoia sempervirens* and *Sequoiadendron giganteum*, which are deciduous redwood trees native to the Pacific region. Also, the Sequoia National Forest at the southern end of the Sierra Nevada in California was established in 1908 and named in honor of the Cherokee scholar who helped his people learn to read and write. Other awards and honors were accorded the famed Cherokee linguist, both during his lifetime and afterward. He was often chosen to represent his people on important commissions and study groups, particularly where the Cherokee point of view needed emphasis. After participating in a delegation to Washington in 1827, where he was scrutinized with much curiosity and interest, he was promised $500 cash and a salt spring as a reward, although the government only paid $150 of the stipend plus a saddle and twenty-two salt kettles. The government also pledged to set up a western printing press. In like fashion, it reneged.

More meaningful to Sequoyah were the rewards given by his own people. In 1832, the Cherokee nation awarded him a $20 silver medal complete with an inscription of gratitude: "as a token of respect and admiration for your ingenuity in the invention of the Cherokee alphabetical characters" (Foreman, 8). The bas-relief on one side of the medal pictures two pipes crossed; the reverse features Sequoyah in profile.

Sequoyah's contributions have been immortalized in numerous other ways. Charles Bird King, painter of American Indians, captured Sequoyah in the only extant portrait. In 1885, George E. Foster wrote a biography, *Se-Quo-Yah, the American Cadmus and Modern Moses*, after the mythical founder of Thebes and the leader of the Hebrew people (Foreman, 57). The Creek poet Alex Posey honored Sequoyah's genius, which "shaped a dream into a deed" (Foreman, preface). Oklahoma, which is a major residence of the Cherokee nation, recognized Sequoyah's part in the state's early history in 1917 by selecting him as one of the state's two representatives in Statuary Hall in the Capitol in Washington, D.C. British collectors, who prize Sequoyah's contribution to the history of language, maintain the most representative file of the *Cherokee Advocate*, which is currently housed in the British Museum in London.

SOURCES

Cwiklik, Robert, and T. Lewis. "Sequoyah and the Cherokee Alphabet." *School Library Journal*, April 1990, 128-129.

Dockstader, Frederick J. *Great North American Indians*. New York: Van Nostrand Reinhold, 1977.

Foreman, Grant. *Sequoyah*. Norman, Okla: University of Oklahoma Press, 1938.

Foster, Lee. "Sequoyah: The Cherokee Genius." *American West*, November-December 1981, 24-25.

Traveller Bird. *Tell Them They Lie*. Los Angeles: Westernlore, 1971.

"Where an Alphabet Was Born: The Sequoyah Birthplace Museum, Vonore, Tennessee." *Southern Living*, April 1988, 33.

Wilkins, Thurman. *Cherokee Tragedy: The Story of the Ridge Family and of the Decimation of a People*. New York: Macmillan, 1970.

Chris Sizemore

Publicized in print, and in cinema by *The Three Faces of Eve* and Joanne Woodward's Oscar-winning screen portrayal, Chris Costner Sizemore's life of mental aberration fascinated millions in the late 1950s. Most people had heard of neurosis and hysteria; the popularized course in dissociative reaction syndrome was a first. By sharing her most personal agonies, Chris revealed the hell that had monopolized her life. Later, Chris gave a clearer account of her strange retreat from reality in three autobiographies. With these works, she helped many people learn to cope with their own and others' mental torments and opened the way to freer discussion of one of the dark recesses of human experience.

THE DISEASE

Multiple-personality syndrome is like a shadowy octopus reaching into all phases of a personality, rearranging and obliterating the normal order of memory, and creating a wearying chaos in an otherwise productive mind. Chris's suffering had gone on from early childhood, when she repressed memories of acts that brought inexplicable punishment. The resurfacing of these events in adulthood occurred spontaneously as well as through drug and hypnosis therapy.

With the aid of psychotherapy and a long sequence of self-healing conversations with her cousin, Elen Pittillo, Chris learned the causes of her malady and came to terms with the many faces that masqueraded as the real self. In her reflective autobiography, *A Mind of My Own*, she concluded: "My illness ... had estranged me from my *selves* and had estranged my family from me; but it had not caused me to view either my family or my friends as strangers. Instead, it had made *me* the stranger" (Sizemore, 17). Her courage not only reacquainted her with self but earned her the Clifford W. Beers and the National Mental Health Bell of Hope awards in 1982 for her advocacy of better mental health care.

A CLOSE FAMILY

Through painstaking self-analysis, Chris summoned the image of herself as seen by another self—a girl with fluffy red hair cut in bangs, freckles, blue eyes, and frail limbs. With the precision of a hobbyist assembling a jigsaw, Chris searched shreds of childhood, recalling her mother, Zueline Hastings, a sweet-natured, unassuming homebody, and her father, Acie Costner, a country boy who worked at the sawmill down the road from their house. Her memories of Wallace, North Carolina, depict a simple farmhouse heated with fireplaces where her mother churned buttermilk—a bucolic setting for the birth of her bizarre malady.

Chris was born on April 4, 1927. Because she was a two-pound breech baby and had difficulty nursing, she had a host of protective pseudoparents among her extended family and acquired nicknames such as Carrot Top and Teeny. Her most traumatic memories were her early confrontations with death—the drowning of a derelict in the irrigation ditch outside her house, the dismemberment of a sawmill worker, the death of an infant cousin. Her mind, through dissociation, tried to distance her from realities too stark for her child's reasoning to manage.

Chris was a curious, active toddler. She often caused a ruckus in the family by denying her participation in mischief, which she blamed on another little girl who remained invisible to her perplexed family. Discipline was lax for five-year-old Chris, who acted out frustrations at the birth of her cousin, Elen. Another crucial aspect of Chris's formative years was the overwhelming crush of aunts, uncles, and grandparents. To survive repeated buffets, "she splintered; she created other selves to endure what she could not absorb, to view what she could not comprehend, to do what she had been forbidden, to have what she had been denied" (Sizemore and Pittillo, 64).

ENCOUNTERING STRESS

After the birth of her twin sisters, Rebecca and Louise, in 1933, Chris's alter ego exerted itself in greater dissociative acts of jealousy and rage. Her parents, dismayed that their oldest refused to behave, increased their efforts to eradicate her naughtiness, especially when it endangered the infants. Chris, consumed by distress at second-class status, began to manifest other neurotic symptoms, particularly sleepwalking.

By the time she entered school in Edgefield, South Carolina, at age six, Chris was ready for the diversion. During that winter, another change occurred. The Costners moved to a large Victorian mansion to serve as caretakers and managers of a dairy. Offsetting the pleasure of a spacious home was the death of Acie's mother. Chris's aunt tried to force the child to kiss the corpse. Chris reacted in terror and over a six-month period suffered nightmares about that face stiffened with rigor mortis.

Throughout these formative years, Chris, under the manipulative influence of Anne, an aunt who was only a few years her senior, earned a reputation for mulishness, lying, thievery, and destruction of property. Other children taunted her for waywardness. Her first-grade teacher lectured her sternly. In addition to having problems with morality, she was discouraged from using her left hand for writing. Equally debilitating were the financial ravages of the depression era, which diminished the family's ability to provide adequate food and clothing.

WHERE TO CALL HOME

A shift in family structure increased Chris's emotional frustrations. The New Deal's Farmers' Rehabilitation Program supplied the Costners with a house. The move brought her even closer to her doting maternal grandparents; at the same time, the addition of more adults in her life lessened Acie's firm control. In time, her gentle father reached the breaking point because of his wife's close tether to her parents. He asserted his authority and cut the tie. This familial instability tore at Chris, pushing her further into dissociative behavior. When physical and mental pain clouded the picture, she withdrew into another being, a separate self.

For ten years, the Costners roamed about in search of tenant farms to work. As Chris reached the awkward teen years, one of her more aggressive personalities, Freckle Girl, emerged. Chris's erratic behavior zigged and zagged between her real self and that of her persona. In one hysterical outburst, she ripped to shreds a dress her mother had sewn for her. The undeserved whippings for the tomboyish shenanigans of Freckle Girl kept Chris on edge. With the death of her Uncle Ernest, a new self—Blind Girl—emerged, complicating Chris's fragmented ego.

More family woes increased Chris's tensions. To her already diminished sense of security came another change after Acie got a job with the highway department and moved his family to the county home, which Chris associated with extreme poverty. In addition, Rebecca fell ill with diphtheria, Acie contracted ptomaine poisoning, Lennie broke her arm, and then Aunt Mattie died and was embalmed on the premises, a procedure that overcharged Chris's imagination. She reacted with fainting spells, disabling headaches, and bouts of unexplained sightlessness. She also evolved another mask—Singing Girl. The only family member who recognized these psychic alterations was Fido, the family dog, who registered fear and confusion at the changes in Chris.

SEEKING SECURITY

On the day that Grandfather Hastings died, Chris succumbed to the Blind Girl and shoved sister Rebecca into the fireplace. On the day of the funeral, repression stole her memory of one more in a long line of family tragedies. As these terrorizing, denigrating experiences annihilated more of Chris's ego, she began relying more on school as a salvation, yet the academic setting proved just as intangible as her widely variant personalities moved in and out of control.

As a young woman, Chris defeated the negative influences for a short time with some positive achievements. In 1943, she published poetry in the *Edgefield Advertiser*. Her new status as poet elevated her above the designation "lying child."

Another boost to her self-esteem was a new friend, through whom she met Johnny, her first male admirer. Their relationship ended after Acie confiscated one of Johnny's letters and met with his father.

Chris, humiliated and histrionic, drank iodine and rubbing alcohol to end the psychic pain. Medics pumped her stomach and saved her life, but her spirit was badly deflated. Her senior year in high school was a fiasco owing to the appearance of Big-Eyed Girl, who replaced the previous year's Freckle Girl persona. Acie allowed her to quit school and take a job in the sewing room of a Greenwood uniform factory.

EMERGING MATURITY

Chris's reprieve from boredom came in the form of a proposal of marriage from Al Thorne, a stunt driver. They were joined in a hasty ceremony, then moved to Augusta, Georgia. From the first days of their union, Al assaulted and abused Chris. Freckle Girl tolerated Al's sadism; Big-Eyed Girl rebelled. Their homelife erupted in daily bouts of violence, and Chris returned to her family shaken and deeply demoralized.

After her divorce, a new romance renewed Chris's spirits. Engaged to Ralph White and looking forward to a normal future, she worked for a time for the telephone company. Her physical condition deteriorated from frequent fainting spells, unexplained contusions, and a close call with drowning. When Ralph returned from military service, he and Chris married. However, by the time of their daughter Taffy Acieline White's birth on January 9, 1948, their relationship had become dull and unfulfilling to Chris, who required inordinate amounts of love and attention to compensate for her emotional maladjustment.

Ralph moved his family into the Catholic rectory, where Chris, out of fear and ignorance of church teaching, resisted ritual and dogma as something sinister and insidious. A second pregnancy, ending in miscarriage, brought new physical and mental torment. Chris lost control of her bowels. The voices that inhabited her mind grew louder, more insistent. She repeatedly threatened her husband with his pistol. Ralph believed that his wife was losing her mind.

DR. THIGPEN

At Acie's insistence, Ralph sought psychiatric help for Chris at the Augusta University Hospital from Dr. Corbett H. Thigpen and his consultant, Hervey M. Cleckley, but Chris, fearful of electroshock treatment, signed herself out of their care. Schizophrenia wracked her mind. In a frenzy, she nearly strangled her daughter with a cord from a blind and plunged a second time into suicidal behavior. The rapid reemergence of Chris Costner, her rational self, prevented Chris White from self-destruction. Terrified, she returned to the hospital and treatment.

Ralph refused to pay Chris's bills, so she settled near Dr. Thigpen's office and took a job as a clerk at Davison's Department Store. Soon she was promoted to a receptionist's post. The struggle between Chris White, hard-working employee, and

Chris Costner, free-wheeling party girl, kept matters in a continual froth. Chris lost her job and endured another development in her mental odyssey—the emergence of Jane. An easier self to manage, Jane promised to help Chris and soon found a job as a bookkeeper under the name Jane Costner.

In 1953, there were hopeful signs in Chris's life. Her mental state took a sudden change for the better after she met Don Sizemore, an electrician. That same year, Dr. Thigpen lectured on her multiple-personality disorder to the American Psychiatric Association in Los Angeles. Chris, unable to get a job because of her illness, allowed Dr. Thigpen to publish case information in *American Weekly*, for which she received $1,000.

She continued in therapy yet repressed the most degrading event of her life, her relationship with the abusive Al Thorne. When circumstances forced her to face her dependence on others, she turned from doctor and husband, got a divorce, and agreed to marry Don. Freckle Girl and Big-Eyed Girl began to give way to the strongest personality, Jane, whom Dr. Thigpen deduced was an imitation of Chris's cousin Elen. To preserve the unique triad, Thigpen, employing the pseudonyms of Eve White, Eve Black, and Jane, made a film of the last phase of the trio of personalities, entitled *A Case Study of Multiple Personality*.

The final shaping of Chris's future self took place during the remaining months of 1953. To assure himself that Chris was going to be well cared for, Dr. Thigpen, wary of her choice of a third husband, interviewed her fiancé. In his opinion, the match bore signs of compatibility and trust. On December 19, 1953, Chris, with Jane's personality, married Don Sizemore.

A SECOND CHANCE

Life with Don lacked one necessity. Chris, to create a firm sense of self, required stability and security. Because of his nomadic job situation, Don never owned his own home. Chris, altering personae on a daily basis, maintained contact with Dr. Thigpen through a lengthy exchange of letters, detailing her most intimate thoughts and feelings about their many moves to apartments and trailer parks. The only other person fully apprised of her misery was her daughter, Taffy, who recognized when she was talking to the "other one" rather than her own mother.

Chris's third marriage turned into a nightmare. As more personalities struggled to emerge, her relationship with Don disintegrated. He threatened to leave her but opted to stay. To cope with daily crises, he moved nine times in an attempt to escape neighborhood gossip about Chris's psychic disturbance. Chris, equally terrified by the new rumblings in her identity, searched out a doctor to replace Thigpen. None of the twenty she consulted believed her avowal that she was the famous Eve.

Pressed for funds, Chris acceded to Dr. Thigpen's wishes that she relinquish rights to her biography so that Twentieth Century-Fox could film *The Three Faces of Eve* and McGraw-Hill could publish the book version. By the time the volume appeared, Chris had again changed, this time by eating her way to obesity from intense maladjustment. She longed to tell her story and replace the popularized tale that bore little resemblance to the truth: Whereas the public knew of three personalities, Chris was aware of thirteen.

THE LATER YEARS

After cutting ties with Dr. Thigpen and, under the pseudonym of Evelyn Lancaster, writing her own account of her illness, *The Final Face of Eve*, Chris struggled to control her mind. The ups and downs of her life continued in a steady alternation and included her treatment for endometriosis and the birth of Bobby in 1959. The family settled in Vienna, Virginia, outside Washington, D.C., where Chris located Dr. Tibor Ham, an understanding general practitioner who brought her some relief from self-destructive symptoms. The uprooting of the family for a move to Manassas rekindled her problems. This time, her parents, aged and facing their own crises, were unable to help.

More disruptions assaulted Chris's ability to cope. Her mother died, her father languished in a wheelchair, Chris's sewing business failed, a taxi struck her car and injured her, Taffy married, Don was hospitalized, Chris conceived another child and had it aborted. The maelstrom seemed to drag her to the bottom for the last time. A friend with whom she shared her personal concerns encouraged her to paint as a means of self-expression.

Referred to Dr. Tony A. Tsitos of Annandale, Virginia, in 1975, Chris maintained only a frail grasp on sanity. Elen, reunited with her cousin, watched in amazement the fragmented psyche that flashed in and out of control. Working through the mélange of twenty-two personalities that had gripped Chris over a period of forty-four years, Elen began writing a book—the book that Chris had longed to publish delineating the truth about her torment. Elen's surmise about the dissociative syndrome put Chris in touch with its purpose—she used splintered selves as a coping mechanism.

After Chris allowed herself to take responsibility for the segmented ego states, she began to relive some of the deeply repressed experiences that forced her to commit bizarre acts. With Elen's help, she probed the past that they had shared as children and young women. Recent traumas pushed out invasive personalities and revealed the real Chris for the first time.

A strong proof that Chris Sizemore possessed a true personality was her determination to be rid of the invasive selves. In breaking with past difficulties, she cleared up disagreements with Dr. Thigpen about the film he had made and gained possession of her medical records. In order to develop a useful pressure valve, she began painting as a regular self-guided therapy. A deluge of reporters printed interviews and recounted the Chris Sizemore story. After twenty-five years incognito, she admitted publicly that she was the famous Eve. As a survivor of years of misdiagnosis and inappropriate treatment, she continues to lecture, write, and support programs that aid similar victims and help families cope with the frustrations of dissociative mental illness.

SOURCES

Lancaster, Evelyn, with James Poling. *The Final Face of Eve*. New York: McGraw-Hill, 1958.

Sizemore, Chris Costner. *A Mind of My Own*. New York: William Morrow, 1989.

Sizemore, Chris Costner, and Elen Sain Pittillo. *I'm Eve*. Garden City, N.Y.: Doubleday, 1977.

Van Biema, David. "Three Faces of Eve Told Her Story." *People Weekly*, March 27, 1989, 79-82.

Gloria Steinem

Of the names associated with the liberation of women, none are more familiar than Gloria Steinem and *Ms.*, the name of the magazine she and others founded and the clarion word of U.S. feminism. At one time considered a lightweight because of her chic appearance—smooth blond tresses, aviator glasses, and miniskirts—and her association with frivolous causes, she evolved into a national legend with her soft voice of reason that generated hope for half the world's population. Named by *Harper's Bazaar* one of the ten most influential women in the country, Steinem, withdrawn from her earlier *Ms.* editorial role, continues supporting humanist causes in speeches, interviews, and debate in the public forum.

As advocate for complete and uncompromised liberation, Steinem models the ideal through her own well-rounded personality, which is neither strident, sex crazed, nor wimpish. In her revealing autobiographical bestseller, *Revolution from Within*, she spurns fears of advancing age and declines to slow down as new waves of interested women join a revitalized feminist movement, which is no longer pigeon-holed as a radical, hysterical fringe. Regretting that men do not accept a fair share of responsibility in the typical male-female relationship, she refuses to retire from leadership until fathers willingly embrace a full interest in child-rearing and husbands participate in every aspect of marriage and home life.

FEMINIST FROM BIRTH

Born the second daughter of antique dealer Leo Steinem and Oberlin graduate Ruth Nunevillar Steinem on March 25, 1934, in Toledo, Ohio, Gloria inherited a typically U.S. mongrelization. Her parents' religious backgrounds—Judaism and French Huguenot—plus her paternal grandmother's part in the 1908 International Council of Women equipped Steinem with melting-pot mores and a respect for other people's trials. Her mother, a former journalist, suffered chronic, disabling mental illness. Her father, an entrepreneur and the backbone of the family, at one time managed a resort and frequently moved the family's trailer to new territory, seriously disrupting his daughters' education.

Steinem was twelve and her sister, Susanne, twenty-two when their parents divorced. Gloria moved to a cheerless basement apartment in the Toledo slums, enrolled in school, and tended her ailing mother. Sometimes the two shared a bed for warmth. Less pleasant moments brought humiliation to Steinem, who was too ashamed of her home situation to invite friends in. The stress of serving as sole care-taker for an adult surfaced in later interviews and reflections, when she recalled constant insecurity, a need to suppress emotion, and the substitution of hamburgers and malteds for love. As she explained to an interviewer, "Obesity runs in my family; it's our way of coping" ("Feminist Takes Crusade," 7B).

Although Steinem professed no bitterness about neglect in her childhood, she felt distress and inadequacy at having to deal with so complex a dysfunction in her family. Her primary escape, fantasy, placed her in more traditional homes where parents carried their proper share of the burden and children could lean on them. Much later in her evolution as a feminist, she realized that the misery of serving her mother as full-time caregiver led to her own rejection of the motherhood role. As she worded her apprehension about bearing children: "I just don't have any faith in heredity" ("Gloria Steinem," n.p.).

Steinem's makeshift escapism extended to joining Girl Scouts, tap-dancing at the Elks Club, and entering talent competitions. Total relief from the confining apartment came in her senior year when she moved in with her sister in Washington, D.C. Free to explore possibilities, Steinem attended Smith College on scholarship and, for the first time, demonstrated the probing intelligence that became her hallmark. The awards for scholarly diligence—more scholarships, a junior year in Geneva, Switzerland, Phi Beta Kappa, graduation magna cum laude—climaxed with a degree in political science in 1956 and a Chester Bowles Asian Fellowship to Delhi and Calcutta, India, which she accepted in place of a proffered engagement ring, which many of her contemporaries considered the only form of feminine achievement.

A HUMANIST VOICE

The university experience in India did not work out as planned. Uninspired by impersonal coursework, Steinem began writing for southern Indian journals and published her first work, *A Thousand Indias*, a travel guide. She developed a sensitivity to the plight of poor Asians; supported by grant money, she allied with a radical humanist group, adopted native dress and customs, and associated with native activists. As a member of a peacemaking team during the caste riots, she developed keen sympathy for have-nots and a sense of urgency to alleviate the suffering of the world's poor. This will to do good permeated her entire career.

At twenty-four, Steinem returned to the United States and searched for journalistic work, which was usually at odds with her experiences amid the Indian underclass. To escape the welter of assignments on jet-set vacation playgrounds and the latest in haute couture, she migrated from New York to Cambridge, Massachusetts, and took a position in the Independent Research Service as a recruiter of students for left-wing European youth gatherings. Unknown to Steinem, her employer was the CIA; the association later caused her embarrassment.

Better jobs surfaced on Steinem's return to New York City in 1960. She rejected stereotypical women's assignments in fashion and beauty to coordinate cover stories and compose photo captions for *Help!*, a satiric magazine, and published the first of her outspoken stands for feminism in "The Moral Disarmament of Betty Coed" for *Esquire*. In free moments, she worked for the civil-rights movement. The separation between private humanitarianism and public frivolity left her alienated from her natural bent toward compassion and world betterment.

In 1963, a tongue-in-cheek exposé of a two-week stint as a cocktail-hustler, "I Was a Playboy Bunny," for *Show* magazine brought attention to Steinem's piquant style of reportage, which had not yet developed into more potent radical muck-raking. Of the experience at Hugh Hefner's pleasure emporium, she concluded: "I expected it to be more glamorous and better paid than it was.... Customers seemed to be there because they could be treated as superiors.... There is a real power differ-ence when one group is semi-nude and the other is fully-clothed" (*Contemporary Authors*, 444). More spirited writing and editing for *McCall's, Life, Esquire, Show, Glamour, Cosmopolitan, Seventeen,* and *Vogue* kept her name before readers. By 1964, she had moved up to scriptwriter for NBC's "That Was the Week That Was," followed by a job writing "The City Politic," a regular column for *New York* maga-zine, which she cofounded and edited. The magazine developed into a springboard for the Ms. Foundation for Women and its powerful offshoot, *Ms.* magazine.

DEVELOPING HER CAUSE

At first, Steinem gravitated toward the in-crowd. She dated elegant men, wore current fashions, danced at chic go-go clubs, and espoused appropriate causes, all of which changed in 1968 when she championed the migrant poor by joining forces with Cesar Chavez, spokesman for the Southwest's common laborers. Advocacy for left-leaners like Angela Davis, Norman Mailer, Adlai Stevenson, and Robert F. Kennedy put her in the populist spotlight, which brought out inherent sympathies that she had never before verbalized. Ultimately, she embraced a full spectrum of causes, from Vietnam-War tax evasion to legal defense for the indigent to aid for women in prison.

The end of Steinem's days as girl-about-town came in 1968 when she moved decisively toward radical feminism and joined the Redstockings, whose stand on abortion she shared because of her own decision to end an unwanted pregnancy. Her reasoning was simple: If one in four women ended a pregnancy, then there must be a need for safe, legal abortions at all levels of society, particularly for the very young and the poor. This epiphany led to her first major prowoman article, "After Black Power, Women's Liberation." Digesting hunks of feminist dialectic by feminist notables such as Bella Abzug and Betty Friedan, she developed into one of the divas of the movement, even though she had to steady her quailing voice when she addressed a large audience.

BECOMING AN ORIGINAL

Steinem earned her reputation for equanimity. A nonthreatening radical, she took part in the creation of the National Women's Political Caucus, Women's Action Alliance, Coalition of Labor Union Women, Voters for Choice, Women Against Pornography, Women U.S.A., and *Ms.* magazine. One of her most influential pieces for the magazine, a list of women who publicly acknowledged that they had undergone abortions, helped bolster the prochoice movement, which had begun to flag under persistent assault from right-wing groups, notably those led by Phyllis Schlafly. The response to editorial efforts, particularly the push for safe and legal abortions, brought Steinem immediate name identity with half a million readers and supporters.

A private person in her off-hours, Steinem utilized her fame in a push for the Equal Rights Amendment, which made its way through Congress, then stalled short of ratification. As a result, she received an honorary doctorate in human justice from Simmons College. In the 1970s, feminism in the United States bucked and swayed with the issues. Steinem, often at the forefront of controversy over pro-Left, pro-Right, and dead center, held steady during scathing criticism, particularly of her CIA ties. Support in the form of appointment by President Carter to a commission launching the International Women's Year and a Woodrow Wilson Scholarship in 1977 boosted her opportunities to do in-depth investigative reporting.

The Reagan years moved Steinem into the second stage of the feminist movement—a time when ideology gave way to confrontation, compromise, and realistic solutions. In 1983, she published a compendium of her best writings, *Outrageous Acts and Everyday Rebellions*, followed three years later by a controversial biography of Marilyn Monroe. The shaky outlook for *Ms.*, which passed into the ownership of Matilda Publications in 1987, reduced Steinem's role from editor to consultant. A second sale the next year led to a rebirth of *Ms.*, this time without advertising capital, the pursuit of which had been a regular drain on Steinem's energies. *Ms.*'s flagship issue contained "Sex, Lies, & Advertising," her demand for women's magazines that separate editorial concerns from a dreary rehash of chocolate cake recipes, eye makeup, and ideas for bathroom redecoration.

In two years, *Ms.* boasted a readership of 450,000, 90 percent of whom were women, including a sizeable proportion of nonwhites. The average female reader, aged thirty-one, was more economically empowered and better educated than her mother. The readership included 150,000 published authors. In keeping with Steinem's altruism, the magazine was sent gratis to women in prisons and crisis centers and on welfare. In the same spirit, the Ms. Foundation, with Steinem at the helm, spent over a million dollars annually to fuel activism in support of Native American craftswomen, Black housing developments, the Breaking Silence Project against incest, and all-women business pursuits.

THE PRIVATE PERSON

Steinem, who met the public celebration of her fiftieth birthday with grudging aplomb, remains fit and up-to-date. Her trim figure and beatific smile appear regularly in the national media. Her public shyness, which ceases to trouble her, has given way to an eyeball-to-eyeball candor. Neither feisty nor belligerent with detractors, gossipmongers, and anti-women's rightists, she projects a wholesome, pragmatic interest in movements aimed at bettering life for both sexes.

An avowed workaholic, Steinem avoids parties and lives centered in the sphere of work, which keeps her constantly on the move. She keeps no office, operates either out of her upper East Side brownstone apartment at Lexington and 73rd Street or from the *Ms.* conference room on Park Avenue and travels widely to fund-raisers and campus speaking engagements. Her compulsive productivity fills her calendar with projects, including books for Random House and Little, Brown and a stint replacing Jane Pauley, on maternity leave from the "Today" show. The television job gave Steinem opportunities to interview Robert Redford and Cher on deeper issues than the usual squibs from current movies. In a thoughtful tribute to Steinem, colleague Bella Abzug lauded her philanthropy: "She's a committed activist who has devoted a good part of her life to the cause of humanity both on the large scale and on a one-to-one basis" (Collins, n.p.). So dedicated is Steinem to these causes that she devotes much of her income to them, including the proceeds from *Revolution from Within.*

Steinem's personal philosophy remains upbeat. She acknowledges that an appreciation for women's rights did not come to her all at once but rather in small increments, such as the time she rebelled against the movie *Gentlemen Prefer Blondes* and walked out of the theater yet could not pinpoint the source of her rebellion. Much later in her evolution as spokeswoman for oppressed females, she verbalized distaste for the meat-market approach to women and the hasty push to link young women with marriageable men at whatever cost to individuality.

In a frank assessment of the "marriage or spinsterhood" mentality, Steinem registered a personal repugnance and expressed her feelings in terms of the generation in which she reached maturity: "You had to become what your husband was. You had to take his name and his identity and his profession. I never imagined it could be any other way. So marriage was the only life-changing mechanism that you really had" ("Gloria Steinem," n.p.). Neither iconoclast nor suffragette, she chose the single life for personal reasons and has stuck by her choice.

JUST BEING GLORIA

A sincere ascetic, Steinem maintains a firm grip on her beliefs and practices. She recoils at privilege, prestige, and inherited money. Her friends, including Marlo Thomas, are real buddies, not Hollywood connections. Where possible, Steinem keeps male friends out of the public eye, except on the evenings she goes dancing. Her relationship with real-estate magnate Mortimer Zuckerman, which ended in the late 1980s, brought adverse publicity because his sizeable wealth clashed with her alliance with nonaffluent America. On the political side, she continues crusading for women's rights yet divulges skepticism that U.S. women will ever win equality at the polls unless they form a creditable voting bloc.

The cerebral side of Steinem stays on course. Having spent fifteen years raising the U.S. public's consciousness about the needs of women, she has plunged whole-heartedly into the working stage of the women's revolution. She takes pride in having drawn attention to serious issues, particularly displaced housewives, date rape, sexual harassment, primary caregiving, glass-ceiling restraints, the "mommy track," Super Woman, pay equity, genital mutilation, and battered women. Her goals have moved on to men, whom she hopes to sensitize to become equal partners in family matters, and to the U.S. Constitution, which she envisions will one day apply equally to both sexes.

Rewards for Steinem's brash, but necessary, style come from all quarters. She has won the Penney-Missouri Journalism Award, the Ohio Governor's Award for jour-nalism, and the ACLU Bill of Rights Award and was selected as *McCall's* Woman of the Year in 1972. Additional honoraria came in the form of the UN's Ceres Medal, a Front Page Award, Clarion Award, and regular listing in the *World Almanac* as one of the United States' most influential women.

In a sketchy, introspective overview of her celebrated role in ridding the United States of prejudice, Steinem rejects heroine worship. As she describes herself, she has acted as facilitator for millions of women who want a simple opportunity—a chance to be: "I'm not a role model really, that isn't the nature of feminism. It allows you to be an individual, so it matters less what you decide, but just that you can decide" (Weldon, n.p.). Content as journalist and lecturer, she is pleased to be herself—a blend of conciliator and stand-up comedian. "I'm sure when I die and go to hell," she quips, "it will be a meeting that goes on forever and I am saying to each side, 'Now what do you think?'" (Weldon, n.p.).

SOURCES

Anderson, Walter. "Gloria Steinem Talks About Risk." *Cosmopolitan*, January 1989, 60-61.

Barthel, Joan. "The Glorious Triumph of Gloria Steinem." *Cosmopolitan*, March 1984, 216-224.

Collins, Marion. "Gloria Steinem Speaks." *New York Daily News*, November 30, 1986, n.p.

Contemporary Authors. New Revision Series, Volume 28. Detroit: Gale Research, 1977.

Current Biography. New York: H. W. Wilson, 1988.

"Feminist Takes Crusade Closer to Home." *Daily Record* (Hickory, North Carolina), January 19, 1992, 7B.

"Gloria Steinem: I Do What a Lot of People Do, React Instead of Acting." *Chicago Tribune*, January 11, 1987, n.p.

Orenstein, Peggy. "*Ms.* Fights for Its Life." *Mother Jones*, November/December 1990, 32-36, 81-83, 91.

Steinem, Gloria. "Sex, Lies, & Advertising." *Ms.*, July/August 1990, 18-28.

_____. "I'm Not the Woman in My Mind." *Parade*, January 12, 1992a, 10-11.

_____. *Revolution from Within: A Book of Self-Esteem*. Boston: Little, Brown, 1992b.

"An Unsinkable Feminist Sails into Her 50th Year Jubilant About Her First Best-Seller." *People Weekly*, November 21, 1983, 185-188.

Weldon, Michele. "Gloria Steinem a Reluctant Symbol of Feminism." *Dallas Times Herald*, August 7, 1987, n.p.

Charles Proteus Steinmetz

One of the world's electronics geniuses, Charles Proteus Steinmetz, the Wizard of Schenectady, was born with a cruelly deformed skeleton, yet he defied his informity to study magnetism and develop theories of power generation that undergird current theories of electrical power. With the encouragement of his mentor, Rudolf Eickemeyer, he tackled the basic problems that hampered engineers. By taming a snarl of mathematical data, Steinmetz established a place for himself among the noted scientists and inventors of his day.

FLEEING CONTROVERSY

Originally named Karl August Rudolf, Charles Steinmetz was born a diminutive hunchback in Breslau, Germany, on April 6, 1865. The only child of Caroline Neubert and Karl Heinrich Steinmetz, a lithographer for the railroad office, he and his two stepsisters, Clara and Marie, were reared by a grandmother after Caroline died in 1866. As a boy, he developed a mischievous sense of wit and curiosity. Because of his handicap and his lack of a mother, his father spoiled him.

In early childhood, Steinmetz was short and awkward in his movements as he endeavored with his spindly, crooked limbs to keep his balance in spite of his oversized head. He endured cruel jests and exclusion from the normal activities of his playmates. His father, also a hunchback, wisely counseled his son on how to cope with his affliction. "Don't think you can run away from it, son," he said. "Go ahead and live" (Markey, 25). Steinmetz, who was quiet and even-tempered with a piercing gaze and rare comprehension, took Karl's advice and developed into a startling prodigy. At first, an insensitive teacher misunderstood the boy's thought processes, labeled him a dunce, and suggested that special classes might suit him better than St. John's Gymnasium. As his intellectual pursuits broadened, his father opted to send him to the university rather than apprentice him to a tradesman.

UNIVERSITY DAYS

A professed liberal, Steinmetz, who evolved into a loner in his adult years, was in his student days a free-spirited joiner who loved to party to all hours, eat rich food, and discuss politics. Part of his urge to mix was compensation for the emptiness he suffered in early childhood, when children taunted and rejected him. At the University of Breslau, where he enrolled in 1883, he read a wide range of subjects and concentrated on ancient and modern languages, physics, astronomy, chemistry, electrical engineering, medicine, and higher mathematics. He astonished his classmates by scribbling an unheard-of number of notes in his own form of shorthand. He staved off boredom by enrolling in an array of extra courses in economics and classical literature and never missed a class in six years of college instruction, which he continued in Berlin and Zurich.

Steinmetz allied himself with the Breslau Socialist party and ghost-edited their paper, *The People's Voice*. In his editorials he criticized Otto von Bismarck's Prussian war machine, and in 1888 he received an urgent note from an anonymous faculty member pressing him to flee the country rather than face arrest by the German Social Democrats. His hasty departure saved him from a lengthy prison sentence but cost him his doctoral degree, for which he had completed his thesis.

Steinmetz found a haven in Zurich, Switzerland, where, as a poor working student, he gained entrance to the Polytechnic Institute despite the fact that he was considered a German criminal. In his year of exile, he survived financially by tutoring math students and writing articles on electrical engineering and astronomy for a German scientific journal. After his Danish roommate, Oscar Asmussen, received first-class passage to the United States from his rich uncle in San Francisco, Asmussen decided to cash in the ticket for two bunks in steerage so that both he and Steinmetz could establish a new life. As added inducement, Asmussen threw in free English lessons.

COMING TO AMERICA

Steinmetz accepted the generous proposal and migrated from Zurich aboard the French liner *La Champagne* in the spring of 1889, dropping his original name along the way. He anglicized Karl to Charles and replaced the two middle names with Proteus in reference to an ugly, misshapen sea god and prophet in Greek mythology, which was also the nickname assigned him by the campus mathematical society. He arrived in New York Harbor on June 1 and was nearly turned away because of his inability to communicate with immigration officials. Asmussen's quick talking convinced the gatekeepers that Steinmetz had much to offer the United States.

The new country brought a set of challenges—a new language and application for citizenship in addition to the need to locate a community of scientists. Temporarily, Steinmetz lodged with Asmussen's cousins on Atlantic Avenue in Yonkers while he searched for work. Carrying a letter of introduction, Steinmetz required only two weeks to land a position worthy of his talents. He was turned away from Thomas Edison's factory, then found work drafting schematics for streetcar motors at Eickemeyer and Osterheld Manufacturing, a small Manhattan electrical company that developed machinery.

On his first day at work, to Eickemeyer's amazement, Steinmetz did not require a slide rule for complex calculations. He did them in his head. The boss feared careless errors and tested his new draftsman with difficult computations. Steinmetz proved his skill by rattling off instant correct responses.

SETTLING IN

Settled at last in Yonkers, Steinmetz abandoned thoughts of marriage and family and channeled his energies into the practical problems of making electricity. His twisted frame failed to diminish his considerable energy and joy in the opportunity to express his genius. To accommodate his cramped organs and relieve fatigue, he stood up at his worktable and leaned against it for support. He wrote to his father of his satisfaction with the U.S. life-style, "where a reasonable man can live reasonably and succeed" (*The Steinmetz Era*, 6). When the death of his father brought unexpressed sorrow, he worked all the harder to fill the emptiness.

Quickly, his employers realized what a contributor he was to their operation with his grasp of mathematics and inventiveness. In a matter of months, he was communicating easily with his associates in English, which he mastered from scribbles in his notebook. Because of his expertise, he rose to the post of engineer.

Steinmetz also had a personal laboratory. Often forgetting to eat and sleep or light his ever-present cigars, he tinkered with alternating current, which varied from the mainstream direct-current system developed by Thomas Alva Edison and Charles Edison. Steinmetz's concentrated efforts helped to answer questions of his contemporaries about how to generate electrical power cheaply and more efficiently so that it could be harnessed to run ordinary laborsaving machines.

A SUBSTANTIAL BEGINNING

Within three years of coming to the New World, he delivered two distinguished addresses at the American Institute of Electrical Engineers in Chicago; he was able to place theories of transformer design within the grasp of most engineers. In 1892, after Rudolf Eickemeyer's retirement, Steinmetz moved to Lynn, Massachusetts, to oversee the calculations department of the neophyte General Electric, the nation's first major electrical company, which bought out Eickemeyer's holdings. GE, which evolved from the merger of the Thomson-Houston Company with Thomas Edison's Lighting Plant, employed 10,000 workers, made everything from dynamos, transformers, and generators to light bulbs, irons, toasters, and electric cars and grossed around $20 million annually. Wilbur Rice, company vice president, considered the acquisition of Steinmetz as vital to the budding firm as its patents. He convinced GE president Charles A. Coffin to follow Steinmetz's advice and establish a research laboratory.

The next year Steinmetz resettled at the GE plant in Schenectady and was employed there as consulting engineer the remaining thirty years of his life. He patented over 200 inventions, including the magnetite arc lamp for lighting streets and the aluminum lightning arrester. His services were so indispensable that the company allowed him to draw his salary of $100,000 per year whenever he wanted and, for him alone, lifted its ban on smoking.

As in his student days, he astounded coworkers with tireless dedication to sophisticated problems, such as how to develop turbines for the Niagara Falls power station. During this highly productive period, he refined his theories and published them as articles and textbooks for classroom use. Also to his credit, he staffed the GE lab with the finest young, inquisitive scientists to assure a bright future for the company.

CONTRIBUTIONS

One of Steinmetz's earliest contributions was his research on hysteresis, a phenomenon of lost power in motors. He worked out precise calculations of magnetic resistance, which led to his application of alternating current as a solution. For twenty years, he wrote formal explanations of his system and formulated tests to prove the law and demonstrate its applicability to laboratory situations. Because of his command of language, he enabled ordinary electricians and engineers to comprehend alternating current. His symbolic notation was adopted as the standard method of codifying schematic drawings of alternating current.

As a new citizen, Steinmetz took an active role in U.S. life. He joined the Illuminating Engineering Society, American Mathematical Society, American Institute of Electrical Engineers, and National Association of Corporation Schools. An outgrowth of his activism was his being appointed president of the American Institute of Electrical Engineers from 1901 to 1902. In response to his love of children and his concern for strong educational programs, in 1912 he was elected head of Schenectady's board of education, which he chaired for two terms. He then served as president of the common council in 1916. On his advice, the city added eight schools to its education system, created a public-parks network, and evolved a progressive attitude toward Schenectady's future.

In 1902, Steinmetz accepted a professorship of electrical engineering at Union College, which he held for twelve years. In this capacity, and later as professor of electrophysics, a position he held for another twelve years, he studied lightning and its effects on power-relay systems. To test his hypotheses about the creation of lightning, he crafted a small village on his worktable and ignited the tiny church spire with a bolt of artificial light from the simulated thunderclouds suspended above it.

From the studies of artificial lightning in his laboratory in 1921, Steinmetz was asble to formulate measures to protect high-tension power equipment from a chance strike. Interest in the information kept him in constant demand on speaker's platforms around the country; once in Hollywood he was the guest of Douglas Fairbanks. Touring sapped his diminishing energies. Upon his return from his last tour, he planned to revisit his home in Germany but took to his bed to rest his overtaxed heart.

A SOLITARY MAN

As a permanent mask, Steinmetz maintained the facade of the eccentric scientist as he contemplated his many projects, such as his study of the wireless and the rudiments of photography. He enjoyed pranks and jokes, particularly trick camera shots. His favorite pastime, fishing, gave him time to think. Some wags spread the rumor that he fished with unbaited hook so that he would remain undisturbed.

Steinmetz's personal life was low-key and private, partly from self-imposed isolation. Because of his evil-smelling and sometimes explosive experiments, he had difficulty renting lodgings. He never married, although he entertained the possibility of courtship with a young neighbor who later died, leaving him with bittersweet longing.

After establishing himself at the Schenectady lab, Steinmetz leased a home on Liberty Street and shared it with Ernst and Eskil Berg. The focal point of their new home was a zoo, which drew local children with its variety of animals, including a pet crow, a gila monster, snakes, a monkey, parrots, and a three-foot alligator. The men built a greenhouse, where Steinmetz grew prize ferns, cacti, and orchids. The Berg brothers found wives and moved away, leaving Steinmetz alone again.

As his assets accrued, he bought a boat, then built a one-room cabin on Viele Creek, which fed into the Mohawk River. On weekends, he worked on a dam, read from U.S. classics, and added a room to his dwelling. After the lab at his Schenectady home was lost to fire in 1901, he drafted plans for a rambling Elizabethan-style house, heated conservatory, and lab to occupy a bit of swampy land he owned on Wendell Avenue near Union College. He designed low shelves and a bed suited to his twisted body and built lily ponds to capitalize on the marshy ground.

To sublimate his desire for children, Steinmetz bankrolled deserving students and adopted a son, Joseph Le Roy Hayden. He invited Hayden and his bride Corinne, nicknamed Mousie, to share his home. In subsequent years, their children, Joe, Midge, and Billy, claimed Steinmetz as official grandpa. He shouldered tedious aspects of family life, from crying babies to bedtime stories before the great stone fireplace, and treated his adopted family to frequent frolics on the lawn, bicycle tours, and canoe trips.

Steinmetz's house filled with noted inventors, including Henry Ford, Guglielmo Marconi, Nikola Tesla, and Albert Einstein, whom Steinmetz praised for his theory of relativity. For discussions with colleague Tom Edison, who was deaf, Steinmetz tapped out words in Morse code that Edison could interpret from vibrations on a table. The lonely old scientist gave frequent parties, invited colleagues from GE, and put on a lavish spread of German food and folk music. For intimate dinners with close acquaintances, he cooked his favorite menu—terrapin soup, steak, and potatoes. He booby-trapped his house to amuse guests by giving them impromptu electric shocks or startling them with trick mirrors. When children visited, he created fireworks and other laboratory magic to delight them.

A LASTING MEMORIAL

Steinmetz's canon of published works is impressive. The titles indicate the depth of his scientific knowledge: *Theory and Calculation of Alternating Current Phenomena* (1897), *Theory and Calculation of Transient Electric Phenomena and Oscillations* (1909), *Engineering Mathematics* (1910), *Radiation, Light and Illumination* (1911), *Electric Discharges, Waves and Impulses* (1911), *Theoretical Elements of Electrical Engineering* (1915), *Theory and Calculation of Electric Circuits* (1917), *Theory and Calculation of Electrical Apparatus* (1917), and *General Lectures on Electrical Engineering* (1917). His single sociological treatise, *America and the New Epoch* (1916), expressed a belief that private ownership of business would give way to government ownership under private management.

In the final weeks of his life, Steinmetz contented himself with pencil-and-paper experimentation and frequent bedside visits from his family. At his death, his investigation of lightning remained uncompleted. Before he died on October 26, 1923, Steinmetz, the Wizard of Schenectady, earned frequent honors, including degrees from Harvard and Union College. The Franklin Institute in Philadelphia conferred on him the Elliott Cresson gold medal; Union College named its electrical-engineering lab Steinmetz Hall. Two major groups—the American Academy of Arts and Sciences and the American Philosophical Society—honored him with memberships.

Accolades from government and industry named Steinmetz's contributions to the United States. Herbert Hoover, then secretary of commerce, noted that "as a man he has set us all an example of physical courage and of devotion to our life work." R. A. Milliken, Nobel Prize winner in physics, stated in his encomium that "Dr. Steinmetz was extraordinary in his breadth of human sympathy, his devotion to ideals and in his continual effort to improve human society" (*The Steinmetz Era*, 69). Other tributes labeled him persistent, inestimable, and insightful.

A more important tribute to the solitary genius of Schenectady was the outpouring of love and respect from neighbors, colleagues, government officials, and family. Flags flew at half-staff in his memory. The General Electric Corporation compiled biographies detailing his work. However, as time passed, his name fell into oblivion, unrecognized by modern users of electricity. Most recognize the GE logo yet know little about its unassuming "little dwarf with the giant mind," Charles Proteus Steinmetz (Markey, 104).

SOURCES

Alger, Philip L., and Ernest Caldecott. *Steinmetz, the Philosopher*. Schenectady, N.Y.: Mohawk Development Service, 1965.

The Edison Era, 1876-1892. The General Electric Story: A Photo History, Volume 1. Schenectady, N.Y.: Schenectady Elfun Society, 1977.

Guy, Anne Welsh. *Steinmetz: Wizard of Light*. New York: Alfred A. Knopf, 1965.

Markey, Dorothy. *The Little Giant of Schenectady*. New York: Aladdin Books, 1956.

The Steinmetz Era, 1892-1923. The General Electric Story: A Photo History, Volume 2. Schenectady, N.Y.: Schenectady Elfun Society, 1977.

Jesse Stuart

To be labeled a hillbilly is not a great tragedy, particularly to someone who is proud of an Appalachian background, but to be classed among the ignorant rankled Jesse Stuart's self-esteem. With persistence and pluck, he shucked the stereotype of backwoods ignoramus and educated himself beyond the level of attainment common to his ancestry. Then, weaving the natural beauty of the Kentucky hills into his 55 books, 2,000 poems, 500 short stories, 260 essays, and myriad lectures, he did what Tom Sawyer is famous for: He made other people envy him.

As the local bard and oddity, Stuart, a peculiar blend of restless energy and sensitivity, chronicled the customs of hill people whom he admired as family and neighbors. More than he wanted to describe them, however, he wanted to lift their burden of ignorance. As he stated the challenge, "Illiteracy in my state was high. My portion of the state ... had remained static intellectually while the progress of a nation had swept around them like a great cyclone. If there was ever a man who wanted to obliterate illiteracy from the hill country, I was that man" (Blair, 225-226).

HOME IN W-HOLLOW

A native of W-Hollow, in the mountains five miles out of Riverton in the northeast corner of Kentucky, Jesse Hilton Stuart grew up in the Appalachian outback, where electricity and indoor plumbing were luxuries and kinship and friendship carried more weight than social class or wealth. Born one of seven children in a single-room rough-hewn rented cabin near the Big and Little Sandy rivers on August 8, 1907, he was the first of his family to seek an education beyond grade-school level. After him, four of his siblings obtained college degrees.

Stuart's father, Mitchell Stuart, an illiterate farmer of Scottish descent, tilled a fifty-acre spread and worked as a railroad section hand and coal miner, depending on the availability of jobs. Stuart's mother, Martha Hilton Stuart, completed second grade and did her share of the work by hauling drinking water from a neighbor's well and catching rainwater for washing. Jesse frequently centered his writings on his hard-pressed family. "What America Means to Me" is a tribute to his upbringing; "Clearing in the Sky" is a tender retelling of his father's determination to recover from heart disease.

In his early life, Stuart's own health was often poor, even though he grew into a sizeable, muscular man at 200 pounds and better than six feet tall. He contracted pneumonia in childhood and twice caught typhoid fever from drinking from polluted mountain streams. As a teenager, he developed tuberculosis but went on playing football and recovered without medical intervention.

Drudgery was the staple in greatest supply at the Stuart farm. Jesse and his mother earned a quarter a day for labor and housework; his father got $1.50 for the combined labor of man and horse. To increase family earnings, Mitchell plowed land and harvested his crops into the night by lantern light. Jesse arose before dawn to begin chores and ended the day with farm work that sometimes lasted beyond daylight.

When Jesse was five, his father sent him to Plum Grove Elementary School when he could be spared from fieldwork because he wanted his son to go into teaching, a profession with dignity and meaning. As a student, Stuart alternately studied and hired out as water boy for seventy-five cents per day and supplemented day work with nightly trapping for pelts and wildcrafting for medicinal roots. In his tenth year, despite the fact that his total schooling came to thirty months, he took an exam, passed eleven subjects, four of which he had never studied, and advanced to the seventh grade. During this period of growth and learning, he remained restless and unfulfilled as though some noble calling impelled him to further achievements, and he channeled his urge for greatness into composition.

The Stuart family engaged infrequently in recreation, some of which influenced his writings. Favorites in Appalachia during the depression were camp meetings and revivals, square dances, hunting and fishing, quilting bees, corn shuckings, and tale swapping. The influence of these episodes, rich in local folklore and music, appeared early in Jesse's scribblings on scraps of paper and poplar leaves. The gift of a collection of Robert Burns's poetry filled him with the desire to write poetry. His progress toward mature creativity, however, was often frustrated by the debilitating burden of poverty and a lack of opportunity. Once, after taking a date to a carnival, he returned and built a bonfire of his books to spare his brother James the anguish of trying to get an education.

THE VALUE OF LEARNING

Learning was the unquestioned goal of Stuart's life. Following his ragged, catch-as-catch-can grade-school education, he graduated from high school in 1926, worked for a brief time in the Auckland Steel Mills, in a blacksmith's shop, and in a traveling carnival, then trained for the army at Camp Knox before going to college. His sojourn among military people brought out his keen distaste for regimentation and petty rules, which reduced a soldier's humanity to a number on a dog tag. The only memorable moments of camp life were earning his sharpshooter's medal and spending free time immersed in the poems of Burns and Poe.

Doubting his credentials, Stuart longed to go to Harvard but settled instead for Berea. After hitchhiking to campus, he discovered that the school was full for the semester. He was delighted that a kindly teacher helped him enter Lincoln Memorial

University in Harrogate, Tennessee. He reported to campus with less than $30 and earned his tuition harvesting hay, carrying mail, washing dishes, and working in a quarry while finishing in three years. Among his credits were extra hours in English for editing the literary magazine.

Stuart advanced to graduate study at Vanderbilt University and Peabody College, where he wrote an autobiographical term paper that evolved into *Beyond Dark Hills* (1938). His strong point as a literature major was his love of poetry, especially that of Carl Sandburg, Walt Whitman, and Robert Burns, the Scottish plowman. Also evident in Stuart's style was the influence of the novels of Thomas Hardy and Thomas Wolfe. Still, under the mentorship of Donald Davidson, he rejected imitation and concentrated on original verse. He forced himself into a rigorous schedule of part-time work, classes, and writing, often going without food when he lacked the cash to buy it. One of the darkest periods of his life came the spring that a dormitory fire destroyed his thesis and other writings and cost him a master's degree. He was so wearied by work and disappointment that he lacked the stamina to start again.

Stuart began his teaching career in 1929 in Greenup County, Kentucky, the same year he began writing. *The Thread That Runs So True* records his perceptions of life from the point of view of a seventeen-year-old teacher. Stuart detailed the main character's determination to maintain his placement in that school district so that he could settle the score against his family. The character's persistence paralleled Stuart's own determination, which he demonstrated while trying to bring consolidation to rural students. As a result, he provoked threats from supporters of local schools, yet he refused to renege on his campaign to equalize opportunities.

Stuart started a family in October 1939 after he married teacher Naomi Deane Norris, the local girl he had courted in high school. They lived in the Stuart homeplace, which they remodeled, but they preserved its rustic exterior so that it would harmonize with the rural surroundings. They maintained the family farm, raised cattle and sheep, and cultivated corn, tobacco, and small grains. Stuart fathered one child, Jessica Jane, who married law professor Julian Juergensmeyer and produced two grandsons, Conrad and Erik. Stuart's family experiences served as the core of *Hold April*, which characterizes both his wife and daughter.

WRITING AND TEACHING

Stuart, who had begun composing poems at the age of eight, published his first collection of over 700 sonnets, *Man with a Bull-Tongue Plow*, in 1934. Immediately, because of the combination of writing and farming, he earned the nickname the American Robert Burns. Stuart followed this first collection ten years later with *Album of Destiny*, which took eleven years to complete. *Album*, which is divided into sections representing the four seasons and characterizes fifty people, uses John and Kathaleen, speaking in different dialects, as spokespersons. Through them, Stuart probed the lives of his trail-blazing forefathers and introduced a troubling contrast between early country life and the encroachment of urbanization, a key theme among the fugitive agrarian philosophers, who included his friends Robert Penn Warren and Allen Tate. Like these critical explorers from Vanderbilt's golden age,

Stuart expressed beliefs in the benefits of working the soil. A true southerner, he expressed a sense of wholeness resulting from contact with tradition, cooperation with neighbors, and the cultivation of independence, courage, self-reliance, honor, hospitality, and integrity. *Album*, however, failed to spark the critical and popular attention the poet felt it deserved.

In 1956, he returned for a brief stint as principal of McKell High School, where he served as superintendent in the 1930s. From there, his literary journeys took him to the University of Nevada in 1958 and to the American University in Cairo, Egypt, where he taught education and creative writing in 1960. Increasing fame brought him to the U.S. Bureau of Educational and Cultural Affairs in 1962 and to Eastern Kentucky University three years later. Overall, he shared his educational philosophies with colleagues in the Middle East and Orient as well as through symposia in the United States.

While thriving in public education, Stuart also began publishing the first of thirty-five books and submitting short stories, poems, essays, and articles to *Commonweal, Today's Health, Esquire, Woman's Day, Yale Review, Progressive Farmer, Christian Science Monitor, Audubon Magazine*, and *Harper's*. Critics like Mark Van Doren, William Rose Benét, and Malcolm Cowley praised his versatility, energy, and prolific outpouring, which averaged thousands of words per day. Contemporary and fellow poet Edgar Lee Masters described him as breezy, lively, and elemental and concluded: "He is not interested in theories, in gropings after the recondite, the vague thistle-wanderings of the imagination. By knowing life, and by devoted interest in it, he has all the criticism he needs.... He is a good tree and should be allowed to grow the way that nature wants him to" (Blair, 40). Another compatriot, William Saroyan, marveled that Stuart could be both nobody and genius and that he could capture natural wit without self-consciously reaching for it.

A MAN OF PRINCIPLES

Central to Stuart's original work was the question of values, which he saw as a cornerstone of civilization, whether in mountains or city. Even though he admired stalwart mountaineers, he disdained the label of regional writer or local colorist, pursuing instead a more universal view of native ethicist of his microcosm of W-Hollow and Greenwood County. He defended his stance by pointing to translations of his works into European, Asian, Middle Eastern, and African languages.

While editing the county newspaper, Stuart produced a short fiction collection, *Head o' W-Hollow*, then a second volume, *Men of the Mountain*, in 1941. He showed considerable talent in his novels, *Trees of Heaven* (1940), *Taps for Private Tussie* (1943), *Hie to the Hunters* (1950), *Kentucky Is My Land* (1952), *Mr. Gallion's School* (1967); and in his autobiographical works, *The Thread That Runs So True* (1949), and *The Kingdom Within: A Spiritual Autobiography* (1979). Likewise, he stressed mountain life in his young-adult works, *Mongrel Mettle* (1944), *The Beatinest Boy* (1953), *Red Mule* (1955), and *Old Ben* (1970), and his collected essays, *Lost Sandstones and Lonely Skies* (1979) and *If I Were Seventeen Again* (1980).

In his works, Stuart, like Thomas Wolfe and William Faulkner, fitted out his rural home with fictional place names and populace, featuring only a slight difference between reality and the literary copy. He showcased both rascal and neighbor, creating an organic connection between the people of Kentucky and the land they farmed. Frank H. Leavell characterized this living tie in these words: "A man draws his strength from the land. Its produce feeds his body as its poetry feeds his soul. He thrives when he is close to the soil; he withers when he forsakes it and sojourns in the city" (*Contemporary Authors*, 421). Fortunately, Stuart retained a close association with country life and avoided the atrophy brought on by cities.

In addition to more philosophical matters, such as an answer for poverty and coexistence with nature, Stuart stressed natural humor, particularly the incongruities of his small mountain community. His characters savor the pleasures of laughter and endear themselves to the reading public, enduring hardship and bad luck with grit and characteristic humor. Admirer Hal Borland commented that Stuart "[came] to accept and celebrate the humanity of people, even to cherish it" (*Something About the Author*, 237). It is this treasured accumulation of folkloric anecdote that set his writing above regionalism and put him in a class with Isaac Singer and other humanists.

The high point of Stuart's career, *The Thread That Runs So True*, gives a strong picture of the forces of ignorance and superstition that impeded the growth of education in the Appalachian hills. As a tribute to Stuart's literary acumen, critic Frank Levering of the *Los Angeles Times Book Review* compared him to a giant standing alone in the mountain forest. Levering praised Stuart's position as model for generations of mountain authors who followed, including Stuart's daughter, a scholar in Italian, English, and classical languages, who also returned to the hills to teach.

REAPING REWARDS

Though occasionally demeaned as a repetitive, unfocused, backwoods writer who rushed too much into print, Stuart never lacked for praise among fellow Kentuckians or more polished metropolitan readers. Critics compared his short fiction to the heartland glimpses of Bret Harte, Joel Chandler Harris, and Elizabeth Madox Roberts. He became poet laureate of his home state in 1954; scores of textbooks anthologized his short stories, essays, and poems as examples of the best in U.S. writing. His numerous awards include the Jeannette Sewal Davis Prize, Guggenheim Fellowship, Academy of Arts and Sciences Award, Thomas Jefferson Memorial Award, and NEA "best book" citation. In addition, he won a Berea College Centennial Award, $5,000 from the Academy of American Poets, and honorary degrees from numerous colleges and universities.

In 1954, at the peak of productivity, Stuart pushed too hard on the lecture circuit and crumpled in the aisles from the first of a series of heart attacks. With his wife's skillful nursing, he recuperated over two years' time, during which he grew more content with the rural values he learned in childhood. Fully rejuvenated, he served as Kentucky state chairman of the Heart Drive. An article in *Today's Health* characterized his joy in recovery: "I am so thankful I had a second chance, that I am above the ground and not under it. I cannot get too chummy with God. It is such a glorious feeling to return from the fingers of death and to live again" (Blair, 192-193).

Thirty years later, Stuart died of heart disease on February 17, 1984, in Ironton, Ohio. Eulogies recalled that he took pride in living on a farm, conserving the land, and remaining interested in education. He particularly enjoyed travel and visited forty-nine states and ninety-four foreign countries while spreading his gospel of individuality. Appropriate to his love of the Kentucky hills, he was buried in the Plum Grove Cemetery. After his death, a local school was named for him; his published works were assembled in the Jesse Stuart Room at Murray State University in Murray, Kentucky. Since 1967, the publication of *W-Hollow Harvest: A Magazine for Jesse Stuart Buffs* has paid tribute to his lasting appeal.

SOURCES

Blair, Everetta Love. *Jesse Stuart: His Life and Works*. Columbia: University of South Carolina Press, 1967.

Contemporary Authors. New Revision Series, Volume 31. Detroit: Gale Research, 1989.

Something About the Author. Volume 2. Detroit: Gale Research, 1972.

Stuart, Jesse. *The Thread That Runs So True*. New York: Charles Scribner's Sons, 1949.

_____. "What America Means to Me." *Reader's Digest*. August 1982, 33-36.

Mel Tillis

In his autobiography, Mel Tillis accounts for the cruel nickname, Stutterin' Boy, that has followed him since his bout with life-threatening illness in early childhood. He recounts the anguish he felt when he swallowed his tears and walked the levee, talking to himself and trying to halt the flutter in his speech. His parents, who lived close to the land and knew a life of manual labor, doubted their son's dream that he could tame his vocal handicap and make a living from music.

After working his way to stardom and instant recognition, Mel Tillis was able to discuss his malady objectively. He once said, "After a lot of years and more hurting than I like to remember, I can talk about it lightly—which eases things a bit. It's a way of showing people that it hasn't licked me, so it doesn't have to lick others" (Tillis, 228).

HARD TIMES

Born August 8, 1932, to Burma Magdalene Rogers and Lonnie Lee Tillis, Lonnie Melvin Tillis is a native of Tampa, Florida, and spent his first eight months near the Henderson Bakery, where his father worked as a master baker. To earn a living during the depression, the family, including older siblings Richard and Imogene, moved thirty-three times. The Tillises suffered poverty not only because of hard times but because Lonnie mismanaged family finances, refused to change his spendthrift ways, and often ran out on his responsibilities. At times, the family was forced to borrow money or move in with relatives.

At age three, Tillis contracted malaria and suffered high fevers. Doses of quinine plus Burma's constant care defeated the disease; then his ravaged body was attacked by colitis. Frail and battered from the two debilitating ailments, he began to put on weight again but found that the experience had left him with a stutter. He grew withdrawn, fearful, even refusing to answer the telephone. The family, unfamiliar with speech therapy and other methods of ameliorating the problem, waited for his stutter to subside on its own.

Life for the Tillises was unpredictable. Lonnie, a hard drinker, moved about, then abandoned his family and went to New Jersey and on to Puerto Rico. When Tillis was six, his father returned and settled his family in a house in Plant City.

Tillis entered Woodrow Wilson Elementary School in 1938, where taunting children made him feel like an outcast because of his speech impairment. The only way he could earn the right kind of attention was by singing, which he did without stuttering.

Because his parents' relationship often approached divorce, Tillis found ways to compensate for insecurity. He daydreamed, wandered the woods, and played with animals at a nearby farm. After seeing a puppet show at school, his first encounter with theatrical make-believe, he constructed a cardboard picture show fitted with actors and furnishings cut from a Sears Roebuck catalog. The first school year passed quickly, then ended with an unexpected blow when his teacher held him back at promotion time to break him of his stuttering.

In 1940, Tillis's Uncle Wiley invited Lonnie to move the family once more to Pahokee on Lake Okeechobee, where Uncle Wiley had started his own business, Tillis's Hometown Bakery. The security of a home and job lasted only three months, when Lonnie once more deserted Burma and the children. The family, uprooted and relocated at Turkey Creek, changed the rhythm of their days by following strawberry harvests. Tillis picked during the winter and went to school in summer. He earned a few dollars a day from gathering strawberries and later by shelling peas, especially when the draft took older male workers. In praise of the hard work he experienced in his childhood, he said: "Picking those strawberries on a cold winter morning ... sure taught me that a nickel was a nickel and some other realities of life. It's worth knowing that berries grow on bushes, but dollars don't grow on trees" (Tillis, 26).

DISCOVERING MUSIC

Tillis recalls that his family often sang, selecting music from their Scotch-Irish and Southern Baptist heritage. His first experience with a more varied music program came at a Pentecostal revival, where performers played banjos, fiddles, and guitars. Later, at the warehouse where the family was employed, he heard workers singing hillbilly songs and listened to disk recordings of the major country singers of his day, who became his idols.

In the mid-1940s, Tillis got a job as a soda jerk and learned to make cherry smashes and banana splits and other fountain treats. While working at the drugstore, he read *Country Song Roundup* and *Billboard* and kept up with his new heroes, particularly Bob Wills and the Texas Playboys, his favorite group. A few years later, Tillis delivered the *Miami Daily News* and *Palm Beach Post*, babysat, and parched and sold peanuts at ball games to earn money. Early each morning, he worked on a bread truck to pay for his first guitar, which he bought from his brother. Learning on his own, he was soon playing and singing so well that local clubs invited him to perform. While honing his talent, Tillis began developing himself in other ways. At age seventeen, he sought professional help for his speech defect at a free clinic at the University of Miami. Transported weekly via Red Cross station wagon from school to the clinic, he depended on volunteer drivers. The service proved so undependable that he gave up his visits to the clinic and resigned himself to stuttering.

In another attempt at self-improvement, Tillis joined the National Guard, which paid $50 per month. As a result of his performance with a country band at a company dance, he was invited to sing on a radio broadcast. Following graduation from high school, he enrolled at the University of Florida in Gainesville, even though his attempt at a football scholarship failed. School did not suit his needs, so he continued practicing his music and accepting small engagements, one at the Mayflower Hotel during Gator Bowl festivities in 1951. By Christmas of his freshman year, he had had enough of scholastics and joined the air force in hopes of better opportunities.

THE BIG TIME

Tillis, still eager to establish a musical career, hoped for a challenging military assignment, then was ordered to Fort Sam Houston, Texas, to serve as a baker. From there, he was shipped to Okinawa, where he worked as a cook and spent his off-hours playing rhythm guitar and singing for service clubs. The end of World War II had produced a ready audience for country music, which had languished in the early 1940s because stations and producers ignored its value. The mix of southern soldiers with young men from all sections spread the demand for Tillis's specialty—lively down-home music.

When he returned to his family home in Florida, Tillis gave up music and made a living at odd jobs, picking vegetables and fruit and painting houses. He worked as a fireman on a diesel engine for the Atlantic Coastline Railroad but lost his job because he was unable to call out signals in time. His family, particularly his father, badgered him to find a regular job and give up dreams of becoming a singer.

Determined to try his luck in Nashville, he joined two other men in the summer of 1956 and made the rounds of the city's three publishers. One official ridiculed his stammer: "Don't see how anyone could record you as a singer.... With a stutter like that, the record would have to be as big as a washtub" (Tillis, 87). Tillis ignored the jest and kept trying. Through careful networking, he got Webb Pierce to record his first song, "I'm Tired." Then he recorded his own hit, "It Takes a Worried Man." At the end of his first six years, he had written 350 songs. From that point on, he was on his way to a full-time career in the music industry.

HOME AND FAMILY

Signed to sing for Columbia Records, Tillis recorded "Honky-Tonk Song," then moved over to Cedarwood Publishing. Independent and unlikely to listen to reason, he married his first steady girl, seventeen-year-old Doris Duckworth, moved to Woodbine, outside Nashville, and started writing country songs, mostly for Webb Pierce to record. Sick from early pregnancy, Doris grew homesick and returned to Florida. Tillis had to renegotiate his home life to get his wife back and his singing career off the ground.

About the time of Tillis's first road tours, more difficulties struck his family. His father, never faithful in the past, decided to divorce his wife and remarry. Tillis, unwilling to abandon music, surmounted his parents' problems and his own impending fatherhood and joined Minnie Pearl's summer road show. He took along another beginner, Roger Miller, as backup musician. With Minnie's help, Tillis began venturing into comedy roles as a means of taming his stutter.

The milieu of the 1950s proved beneficial to country music. About the time Tillis's daughter Pam was born, his singing career was gaining ground. He took a bit too much pleasure in carousing with other entertainers, who drank heavily and partied late. His marriage faltered, then reestablished itself with the birth of his second daughter, Connie Lynn. Problems with his partner, Buck Preddy, tied up his royalties in litigation. To support his wife and two daughters, Tillis returned to Florida and drove first a cookie truck, then a milk truck until the lawsuit was settled.

GAINING EXPERIENCE

When Tillis got the business side of his career worked out, he had won a major battle. He stopped writing songs for other singers, who usually turned the material into hit records and kept a major portion of the proceeds for themselves. As he became more familiar with the country-music market, he began guarding his own interests and gradually outgrew a dependence on Webb Pierce, who had given him his start in the recording industry. Tillis longed to sell a song to Colonel Tom Parker for Elvis Presley to record yet never made the connection. Instead, his luck brought him another singer, Burl Ives, who was the impetus for Tillis's calypso numbers.

Lacking a thorough grounding in road tours or a string of hit records, Tillis expanded his audience recognition by appearing on Mike Douglas's television show, which Jimmy Dean cohosted, and singing "Detroit City," a plaintive original song about a factory worker longing to return to the South. A second television experience as a regular on Porter Wagoner's series boosted Tillis's name recognition, although the job ended after Wagoner became jealous of Tillis and another new star, Charlie Pride. Tillis, convinced that television benefited his career, appeared on Johnny Carson's "Tonight Show" and joined the "Glen Campbell Good Time Hour." It was during this phase that he formed his own band, the Statesiders, twelve unusually well-dressed men with a combination of drums, synthesizer, piano, guitar, steel guitar, bass, and three fiddles, and began performing independently of other big names in country music. His group received invitations for the "Tony Orlando Show," "Grand Ole Opry," "Dinah!," "Love American Style," "Hee-Haw," and the "Dean Martin Show." Tillis also appeared alone on "Love Boat" and "Dukes of Hazzard," made commercials for Whataburger and Purina Dog Chow, and cohosted a summer replacement show, "Mel and Susan Together." In all, he gave 250 performances per year.

SUCCESS AT LAST

One reason for Tillis's success was his appreciation for those who helped him rise to stardom. If Mel did well, so did his backup. He paid his band members a hefty portion of the proceeds and dressed them in spiffy outfits. Another factor that enabled him to worry less about details and concentrate on artistry was the financial management by his brother, nicknamed Breadman, who attended to the sale of tapes and T-shirts. With Breadman's help, he supervised his crew's behavior, firing any who drank, took drugs on stage, or misbehaved in public.

By 1966, Tillis had reached a notable point in his rise to fame. He wrote "Ruby, Don't Take Your Love to Town," a multimillion-dollar hit recorded by Kenny Rogers. The mournful lyrics depicted the life of a man who lived near Tillis's home — a self-pitying war veteran bent on curtailing his wife's adulteries. Because listeners interpreted the song as a protest against the Vietnam War, Tillis felt moved to deny the connection. In his autobiography he declared, "Well, I've never written any kind of political or protest song in my life, intentionally. I've got my views on politics — being a man who cares about what happens in the world he lives in — but I've never put them into my songs" (Tillis, 166).

MAKING CHANGES

Tillis, who understood the waste that permeated the lives of many great names in country music, particularly Hank Williams, who died young from overindulgence, tried to rid his own life of negative influences. Before alcohol engulfed him, in 1967 he stopped drinking and remained sober even when friends around him drank. Another challenge that affected singers on the road was separation from family. He stayed closer to home and experienced good times with the birth of his fifth child, Carrie April, and the purchase of his lake house at Groveland near Orlando, Florida. However, the shift away from the road robbed him of contact with the public. Bored and unchallenged, he started two publishing businesses, Sawgrass Music and Sabal, in a one-room office behind Cedarwood.

Tillis's workaholic ways alienated him further from Doris and the children, weakening the family structure and leading toward a permanent breakup. His teenage children rebelled by being unruly. His occasional flings with women admirers did not help matters at home. Then he fell in love with Judy Edwards, an unsophisticated mountain woman who worked as a secretary in his office. The resulting uproar with Doris led to his filing for divorce, moving to a motel, and contemplating suicide.

Tillis salved his hurt ego by living with Judy, whom he married on March 21, 1979. They set up housekeeping on a picturesque farm twelve miles from Henrietta, Tennessee. To flesh out their new spread, they stocked poultry, dogs, horses, and cows. To cement their new family, Judy worked her way into the role of stepmother and Mel took on his role as grandfather to Pam's and Connie's two boys, Ben and Phillip.

ENJOYING THE MOMENT

Today, the "stutterin' boy" makes his home in Ashland City, Tennessee, at Sycamore Acres, a 1,400-acre farm outside Nashville complete with ponds, rustic house, farm machinery, and pool. The walls of his home, shaped out of logs a century and a half old, display hit recordings and photographs of famous people whom Tillis has known, such as Ronald Reagan, Senator Howard Baker, and Governor Frank Clements. Still active in country music, Tillis appears on television talk shows, operates three radio stations and a film company, and owns a turboprop jet named *Stutter One*.

Lanky and affable, Tillis has won a number of awards for his unique brand of entertainment, including Music City News Comedian of the Year in 1975 and Entertainer of the Year in 1976 and 1978, and he holds a place in the Songwriter's Hall of Fame. He has acted in several movies: *Every Which Way But Loose, Smokey and the Bandit II, W. W. and the Dixie Dance Kings, Murder in Music City, The Villain, Uphill All the Way,* and *Cannonball Run*. His current bookings take him to Las Vegas and Atlantic City casinos and hotels rather than the auditoriums, clubs, and county fairs of his early tours.

One of his major accomplishments was a confrontation with his father shortly before Lonnie's death. The two were estranged by time, distance, and Lonnie's remarriage, but Tillis, longing to gain his father's approval, convinced him to visit the family and acquaint himself with the life he had built from his musical success. At last, he received the acceptance that he had longed for in boyhood.

Looking over his life as a speech-handicapped person, Tillis takes pride in being able to set an example for others fighting the same malady. He believes that stutterers can enjoy a satisfying life if they give themselves the chance. In recent performances and interviews, Tillis has spoken candidly about his career and where he hopes to take it. In a standard opening remark, he said, "One reason I'm here tonight is to d-d-dispel those rumors going around that Mel Tillis has quit st-st-stuttering. That's not true. I'm still stuttering and I'm making a pretty good living at it t-t-too!" (Stambler and Landon, 740).

SOURCES

Adair, Don. "Old Hands." *Spokesman-Review* (Spokane, Washington), February 5, 1988, n.p.

Goldsmith, Thomas. "Mel's Loved Country All Along." *Tennessean* (Nashville), July 27, 1985, n.p.

Mikia, Pete. "Mel Tillis Likes Being an Author." *Review Journal* (Las Vegas), December 5, 1986, n.p.

Romine, Linda. "Mel Tillis 'I've Done Just About Everything,'" *Daily News* (Tempe, Arizona), February 27, 1987, n.p.

Sharpe, Jerry. "A Discouraged Mel Tillis Ready to Split with Nashville." *Press* (Pittsburgh), July 25, 1986, n.p.

Spatz, David J. "Mel Tillis Claims Country's Still Cool." *Press* (Atlantic City, New Jersey), September 21, 1986, n.p.

Stambler, Irwin, and Grelun Landon. *The Encyclopedia of Folk, Country & Western Music*. New York: St. Martin's Press, 1983.

Sullivan, Elizabeth. "He Comes to Play, Not Fiddle Around." *Plain Dealer* (Cleveland, Ohio), February 17, 1987, n.p.

Tillis, Mel, with Walter Wager. *Stutterin' Boy*. New York: Rawson, 1984.

Dalton Trumbo

During the late 1940s, the United States faced an inner threat from the McCarthy era, notorious for the cold war's reckless red-baiting. As the gung ho post-World War II period came to a close, the frenzy to sniff out "commies" and ascertain loyalties cost teachers and social workers their jobs and brought under public scrutiny compulsory loyalty oaths required by unions, colleges, and other organizations. People on both sides of the loyalty question debated the issue of who supported the United States and who advocated its downfall. In 1953, at the height of the witch-hunt, Julius and Ethel Rosenberg were executed in Sing Sing for allegedly selling atomic secrets to the Soviets.

Accusations, media-inspired degradation, and counterclaims of slander, libel, and perjury mounted as vulnerable groups sought to prove their innocence in the face of innuendo and outright lies. The furor against un-American activities stifled and, in some cases, devastated promising careers, including those of Paul Robeson, Charlie Chaplin, Bertolt Brecht, Lillian Hellman, Elia Kazan, Arthur Miller, José Ferrer, Sterling Hayden, Ring Lardner, Jr., Gail Sondergard, John Garfield, and Zero Mostel. Some of the 300 victims, whose only crime was to have Eastern European forebears or to have shown compassion for the downtrodden, languished for decades in obscurity and suffered loss of credentials, suicidal urges, divorce, alcoholism, drug addiction, and despair.

One of the central group of nineteen victims, known as the Hollywood Ten after being whittled down to the handful who refused to be intimidated, was novelist and screenwriter Dalton Trumbo, famed for his versatility and skill. Journalist Charles Daggett and writer Martin Berkeley and others labeled him a subversive. Because Trumbo refused to cite his political history or answer questions concerning whether he had ever been a Communist, he was labeled a hostile witness, then convicted of contempt of Congress and jailed. The concentrated character assassination, under-girded with media sensationalism, truncated his initial rise to fame. He and other blacklisted professionals, who surrendered to federal officials, were ostracized in Hollywood.

For thirteen years, Trumbo continued fighting for his reputation, defeated his persecutors, and eventually heaped notoriety upon himself because he refused to give in to an illegal inquisition. His explanations usually stated the same notion, that ethics outweighs expedience. In his own words, "I affirm the basic constitutional principle that men may be questioned and prosecuted for their acts, never for their thoughts" ("Reclaiming a Name," 98).

PIONEER STOCK

A native of Montrose, Colorado, James Dalton Trumbo, descendant of fighters in the American Revolution, Indian Wars, and both Union and Confederate armies, was a scion of the "Westward Ho" movement and grandson of a crusty frontier sheriff. The son of seamstress Maud Tillery and Orus Bonham Trumbo, a grocery clerk, Dalton was born December 9, 1905, in his parents' apartment above the Montrose Public Library. Along with sisters Catherine and Elizabeth, he grew up in Grand Junction, in the far west of the state on the Colorado River. As a student at Grand Junction High, he avoided athletics, took on a huge paper route, and began his writing career at the local newspaper, the *Daily Sentinel*.

In 1925, during Trumbo's first year at the University of Colorado, his family completed the trek west by moving to California. After his father's death, he was forced to quit school and take jobs as car washer, section hand, bootlegger, then bread wrapper and night-shift estimator at Davis Perfection, Los Angeles's largest bakery, where he worked for nearly ten years. In his leisure time, he wrote six novels and eighty-eight short stories but found no buyer for his work. He managed to squeeze out two more years of training at the University of Southern California from 1928 to 1930 and wrote for a trade journal as a movie critic.

A PROFESSIONAL CAREER

In the 1930s, Trumbo, who had moved to Los Angeles, began selling some of his essays and stories to popular magazines, including *Vanity Fair, McCall's, New Masses, North American Review, Masses and Mainstream, Nation, Theatre Arts, Playboy, Saturday Evening Post, Liberty*, and *Forum*. From a post as managing editor of *Hollywood Spectator*, in 1934 he moved up to reader and then screenwriter for Warner Brothers. The next year, he published a novel, *Eclipse*, a fictionalized view of his hometown. It was followed in 1936 by *Washington Jitters*, which the Theatre Guild produced in play form. His later works include *The Remarkable Andrew* (1941); *Harry Bridges* (1941); a three-act comedy, *The Biggest Thief in Town* (1949); and the screen versions of *Jealousy* (1934), *A Man to Remember* (1938), *A Bill of Divorcement* (1940); and *We Who Are Young, The Man with the Shovel*, and *Thirty Seconds over Tokyo* (1944). One film, *Kitty Foyle* (1940), won an Academy Award for actress Ginger Rogers plus nominations for Trumbo and his associate, Donald Ogden Stewart, along with nominations for best director and best picture. During the war years, he also chaired Writers for Roosevelt, directed the Screen Writers Guild, founded *Screenwriter* magazine, and served as war correspondent for the U.S. army air force.

Trumbo took pride in his contributions to U.S. movies. He rejected the notion that all scriptwriters are inconsequential hirelings and jeopardized himself more than once by balking at assignments that demeaned his talents. One such standoff cost him a twenty-day suspension of pay for insubordination. He also supported trade unions and decried censorship boards because he wanted the U.S. moviegoer to have a full range of intellectual choices. In his words, "The American people should be · able to exercise their democratic right to approve or disapprove the pictures Hollywood gives them" (*Current Biography*, 873).

Early on, Trumbo, an egalitarian and a man of principles, wanted to give up his hard-drinking past and establish a family. He met photographer Cleo Beth Fincher at McDonnell's Drive-In, where she worked as a waitress. They were married March 13, 1938. Eighty-five miles from Hollywood in a mountain ranch, he made a home for his family. During this idyllic period, to acquaint his children, Nikola, Christopher, and Melissa with Hollywood's heyday, he kept a photographic record for future study.

THE McCARTHY ERA

The idyll ended in the McCarthy era, which halted the careers of Trumbo and nine other dissenters who were blacklisted for refusing to cooperate with the House Un-American Activities Committee, chaired by J. Parnell Thomas of New Jersey. The original blacklisting committee, converging in 1947 at a New York conference of the Motion Picture Association of America at the Waldorf-Astoria, targeted 300 victims—mostly writers, musicians, actors, directors, and cinematographers—suspected of maintaining close ties to Communism. In their original wording, "We will not re-employ any of the ten until such time as he is acquitted or has purged himself of contempt and declares under oath that he is not a Communist" ("Reclaiming a Name," 98). The list also named those who had invoked the Fifth Amendment during House-committee grilling. For all its ballyhooed importance, the list was never published in its entirety and eventually came to nothing, except to the people it victimized.

At first, the committee asked only one question—had Trumbo belonged to the Screen Writers Guild or the Communist party? Then the committee scrutinized RKO's production of *Tender Comrade* (1943), one trivial story among Trumbo's voluminous works, about a war bride working as a welder. Congressional inquisitors were particularly critical of the term *comrade* and picked apart Trumbo's script in search of evidence of an attempt to overthrow the United States government. Ironically, the committee failed to locate Communist propaganda or complicity with anarchists in this or any other Hollywood product.

Additional testimony threw doubt on Trumbo's loyalty in April 1940, when his story "Johnny Got His Gun" was serialized in the *Daily Worker*. Because Communist bookshops sold the book and Communist magazines synopsized it, the committee concluded that Trumbo was a sympathizer. Other incriminating data linked him with Harry Bridges, a known Communist, as well as with the American Peace Crusade, a rally held at the Shrine Auditorium, and other Communist gatherings, where Trumbo often spoke. In self-defense, he riposted: "You have produced a capital city on the eve of its Reichstag fire. For those who remember German history in the autumn of 1932 there is the smell of smoke in this very room" (Vaughn, 320).

Until the government probe of 1947, Trumbo, the only defendant who sprang from proletarian roots, had earned his niche among the highest-paid of Hollywood's scriptwriters. At his career peak, he received as much as $4,000 per week or a one-time fee of $75,000 per script from Metro-Goldwyn-Mayer. After being identified as a Communist sympathizer and worse, he earned only subsistence wages because Hollywood film moguls like Eric Johnston feared to have their names listed alongside his. Many associates and friends turned against Trumbo and his family. He faced lawsuits, bankruptcy, and the narrowmindedness of right-wingers in what he termed a "nauseous quagmire of betrayal" (Trumbo 1972, 25).

For his stand on First Amendment rights, he was ruled in contempt of Congress, and served a ten-month prison sentence at the Federal Correctional Institution in Ashland, Kentucky, from 1950 to 1951. With typical tongue-in-cheek humor, he quipped about his incarceration: "I was there for a misdemeanor called contempt of Congress. Try as I might I could not repent of the crime of contempt for an idiotic Congress" ("Dalton Trumbo," 22). During this period, J. Parnell Thomas, the committee chairman, was also serving a sentence for a felony, embezzling from the government. The irony afforded Trumbo more than a few chuckles.

Under these unpromising circumstances, Trumbo kept working. Two years before leaving for jail, he published *The Time of the Toad: A Study of Inquisition in America, by One of the Hollywood Ten.* During his term, while working as a storeroom trustee, he completed a screenplay for *Gun Crazy* (1950) and sold it on the black market. Most of his cellblock writings reveal what *Newsweek* termed a "modest, humane, utterly decent man of principle" ("Reclaiming a Name," 98). Upon his release, he found the political climate still ruled by reactionaries, yet he refused to be daunted by indiscriminate labeling. As a gesture of defiance, he rejoined the Communist party in 1954 until other blacklisted victims were exonerated.

Trumbo's steely First Amendment defense, based more on idealism than on philosophical expertise, brought hardship and ignominy on his family. Forced to sell his ranch, he moved to the Imperial Hotel in Mexico City, where he wrote for B films for some of the same people who conspired against him. In self-imposed exile, he assumed the pen names Sam Jackson and Robert Rich. For the eighteen screenplays produced during this nadir in his career, he earned an average of $1,750 each, a paltry figure compared with his literary worth.

A mild-mannered, balding, and comfortably balanced man who knew his own value, Trumbo refused to fall victim to hard times, which, he declared, "passed beyond the control of mere individuals" (Schickel, 16). He maintained his sense of humor, continued writing, and returned to California, settling this time in Highland Park. By 1960, with the help of Otto Preminger, who publicly welcomed him back to the Hollywood establishment, Trumbo reemerged under his own name.

REESTABLISHING A CAREER

The return to normalcy was hard for all the Hollywood Ten. While still writing under the pseudonym Robert Rich, Trumbo produced the screenplay *The Brave One*, a humanistic story of a boy who rescues a pet bull. For this work, he won an Academy Award in 1957, to the chagrin of those supporters who clung to the ideals of blacklisting. Witty, devoid of bitterness, and eager to broadcast his travail, he published *The Devil in the Book* (1956), *Additional Dialogue: Letters of Dalton Trumbo, 1942-1962* (1970), "Honor Bright and All That Jazz," and *Night of the Aurochs* (1979), his supreme antiwar novel, which Robert Kirsh completed and published posthumously. His other triumphs include his screen rewrite of Leon Uris's *Exodus* (1960), which won an Academy Award for music and two additional nominations for photography and acting. By this point, he was officially deleted from the blacklist.

That same year, Trumbo wrote the screen version of *Spartacus*, a Roman-era spectacular starring Kirk Douglas, Laurence Olivier, Charles Laughton, Tony Curtis, Jean Simmons, and Peter Ustinov. The movie won two Academy Awards and received a third Oscar nomination for music. During this project, he formed a friendship with Douglas, who starred as Spartacus. Douglas spoke on behalf of the Hollywood Ten, particularly for Trumbo, whose talents had been stymied by unjust accusations. Another fan, President John Kennedy, attended a showing of *Spartacus* in obvious defiance of a boycott led by the American Legion.

Trumbo's later screenplays, written under the pseudonym Robert Rich, were for *The Last Sunset* (1961), starring Kirk Douglas and Rock Hudson; *Lonely Are the Brave* (1962), also starring Douglas, as well as Gena Rowlands and Walter Matthau; *The Sandpiper* (1965), part of the Richard Burton-Elizabeth Taylor canon; and *Hawaii* (1966), which won an Academy Award for music and nominations for cinematography and supporting actress. In his sixties, Trumbo continued his string of screen successes with *The Fixer* (1968), the film vehicle that netted star Alan Bates an Oscar nomination; *The Horsemen* (1970), starring Omar Sharif; *Johnny Got His Gun* (1971); and a multi-award winner, *Papillon* (1973), which showcased Steve McQueen and Dustin Hoffman and won an Academy nomination for music. It was during this last film that Dalton's cancerous lung was removed, resulting in his first heart attack.

While living his last years on St. Ives Drive in Los Angeles, Trumbo actively pursued his career. During his lifetime he won a National Book Award for *Johnny Got His Gun* plus honors from the Teachers Union of New York, an Atlanta Film Festival Golden Dove Peace Prize, the Golden Phoenix for Best of Festival, a Belgrade Film Festival Audience and Director's Award, the Writers Guild Laurel Award, a Cannes Film Festival Special Jury Grand Prize, the International Critics Prize, an Interfilm Jury World Council of Churches Prize, and a Japanese International Festival of the Arts Grand Prize. Most of these honoraria dating to the 1970s were for the film version of *Johnny Got His Gun*, a cult classic that proved unsuccessful at the box office.

THE TRUMBO LEGACY

Trumbo died of a second heart attack at the age of seventy on September 10, 1976, at his home in Los Angeles. The reading of his will revealed that he had donated his body to the UCLA Medical Center—a uniquely human gesture from a man who suffered imprisonment rather than abandon his right to free speech. Morsels of his ready wit and charity surfaced during the mourning period. The *New York Times* obituary, for example, quoted his wry rejoinder about membership in the Communist party, whose meetings he typified as "dull beyond description, about as revolutionary in purpose as Wednesday evening testimonial services in the Christian Science Church" ("Dalton Trumbo," 22).

An even greater legacy lay in Trumbo's speech to the Writers Guild, which he titled "Only Victims." Flourishing his cigarette holder, sporting a fluffy mustache, and sharing his cheerful outlook, he noted that the zeitgeist of the McCarthy era provoked many people to respond inappropriately to the House Un-American Activities Committee witch-hunt. Some proved selfless, some opportunistic; some were wise, some stupid. In a noble, altruistic overview of one of Hollywood's most difficult periods, he concluded, "Some suffered less than others, some grew and some diminished, but in the final tally we were *all victims*" (Schickel, 11).

SOURCES

Capouya, Emile. "Review of *Additional Dialogue: Letters of Dalton Trumbo, 1942-1962.*" *Saturday Review*, October 31, 1970, 29.

Contemporary Authors. New Revision Series, Volume 10. Detroit: Gale Research, 1983.

Cook, Bruce. *Dalton Trumbo.* New York: Charles Scribner's Sons, 1977.

Current Biography. New York: H. W. Wilson, 1941.

"Dalton Trumbo, Film Writer, Dies." *New York Times*, September 11, 1976, 22.

"Douglas Honored for Helping End Hollywood's Blacklist." *Variety*, December 14, 1988, 85.

"Reclaiming a Name." *Newsweek*, November 9, 1970, 98.

Rowe, Frank. *The Enemy Among Us: A Story of Witch-hunting in the McCarthy Era.* Sacramento, Calif.: Cougar Books, 1980.

Schickel, Richard. "Return of the Hollywood Ten." *Film Comment*, March/April 1981, 11-17.

Trumbo, Dalton. *Additional Dialogue: Letters of Dalton Trumbo, 1942-1962.* New York: M. Evans, 1970.

_____. *The Time of the Toad: A Study of Inquisition in America, by One of the Hollywood Ten.* New York: Harper & Row, 1972.

Vaughn, Robert F. *Only Victims.* New York: G. P. Putnam's Sons, 1972.

Tina Turner

A jangling, driven rocker, Tina Turner, with her fright wigs, undulating diaphragm, long throbbing legs, and double-barreled sensuality, introduced her name and style to the music scene, then endured twenty years of physical and spiritual abuse from Ike Turner before reviving her career in the 1980s. From her debut with Ike's Kings of Rhythm through her devastating, Svengali-esque marriage, Turner had one description of their brutal relationship: "a horror movie, with no intermissions" (Turner and Loder, 120). Divorced and returning even more revved up, but with just the right touch of older-but-wiser vulnerability, she surpassed Ike in her revival.

COUNTRY GIRL

A farm girl from Nut Bush, a minuscule mountain community outside Brownsville, Tennessee, Anna Mae Bullock, the child of Zelma, offspring of Black, Navajo, and Cherokee blood, and Floyd Richard Bullock, Baptist deacon and resident manager of the Poindexter cotton plantation, was born in the Black section of Haywood Memorial Hospital on November 26, 1939. The family situation was typical of working-class southern Blacks—intense fundamentalist Bible-thumping and even more intense family feuding and accusations of adultery. From the grandparents on her mother's side, Turner found love and nurturance; from the Bullock side, suspicion and alcoholic rancor.

The second child of the family, Turner lived in a four-room shotgun shack with sister Alline, three years her senior. Turner had no difficulty discerning Zelma's disinterest in her or her preference for Alline. Still, Turner idolized her .45-toting, cigar-smoking mother. Often lonely and alienated, Turner willingly hoed and weeded, then grew to despise fieldwork, which provided her family with fresh vegetables and extra funds from harvesting cotton and strawberries. If given a choice, she preferred hunting with her father for rabbits and squirrels or fishing the ponds for perch.

LOCAL RHYTHMS

She accepted responsibility for herself while she was still a child. In 1941, after her parents succumbed to the lure of easy money by taking jobs with the Oak Ridge atomic plant, she remained with her Bullock grandparents. Two years later, she and Alline rejoined their parents in Knoxville. While in the care of a babysitter, Turner experienced her first Holy Roller service and revelled in the ecstatic clapping, singing, and celebrating that later influenced her stage performances.

More riotous experiences colored her childhood after the family moved back to hill country. She accompanied her mother to weekend juke joints, thrilled to the flirting and dancing, and ran from scenes of random violence, often initiated by a brawl over an unfaithful lover. During these growth years, she got attention for her mimicry—gasping, she succumbed in a movie-style death scene—and imitations of stars. In her mind, she replaced the drabness of home with the glamor of Hollywood.

Turner quickly allied herself with the Baptist Church choir, her main vocal outlet. Because of others' responses to her singing, she realized early that her ability to duplicate any musical form—from rock to soul to opera to blues—was her ticket out of the agricultural South and its squalor. Through her imagination flitted the stereotypical femme fatale: "I had an image in my head of how a star was—somebody with a star on the door and a lot of chiffon dresses. I wanted that" (*Current Biography*, 410).

FAMILY DISINTEGRATION

Life in the Bullock household supplied no model of starry-eyed lovers and, even worse, promised no security. Turner's mother ran away for good in 1951. Turner rebounded from the shock but found herself in a seamier situation after her father married a city woman, who stabbed him on two occasions to halt his beating her. Eventually, he moved to Detroit and left the girls in the care of relatives.

Turner looked to her grandmother for security. Her self-esteem began to improve during her stint as a cheerleader at Lauderdale High. On the basketball court, she met her first love, Harry Taylor. As teenage pleasures opened doors for her, she blossomed into a leader, played basketball, and organized outings, dances, and get-togethers. After her grandmother's death four years later, she was devastated by a sense of rootlessness and loss. She considered working for a local white family and finding a small room to rent when her mother reentered her life.

The Bullock girls reunited with their mother in East St. Louis and attended Sumner High School. During this period of tenuous teenage emotions, they danced to radio rhythm and blues and created a second home in juke joints and nightclubs, where music let their spirits run free. One of the big draws, especially for Black women, was Ike Turner's Kings of Rhythm. Turner thought him short and ugly but tuned in to his music.

LITTLE ANNA, THE SINGER

Her professional career began in 1956, when she wangled a place with Ike Turner's group at the Club Manhattan, a St. Louis beer hall. For her debut, she sang "You Know I Love You," "Love Is Strange," and "Since I Fell for You." Ike, who had a feel for emerging talent, made a keen and opportunistic assessment of her gritty, jolting, gospel-erotic style and signed her for weekend performances under the name Little Anna. He convinced her mother, who at first disapproved, then wowed Turner with tawdry glamor—glitzy beaded dresses, rings, dangly earrings, long gloves, sling pumps, seamed hose, and a fur stole.

In 1957, the absence of the regular headliner opened the way for Turner. Ike, who had difficulty keeping band members because of his tightfistedness, hired her as a last-minute replacement and featured her at a fraternity party in Columbia, Missouri. Her success fed his dreams of breaking out of the St. Louis cycle and moving on to national fame. That year, Turner lived with Raymond Hill, who played saxophone with Ike's band. Only a senior in high school, she conceived a child, graduated with her class, then gave birth to Raymond Craig. Hill moved on, leaving her to raise their son alone.

Turner got her own apartment and made a home for Craig. At night, she sang with Ike's band; during the day, she labored as a nurse's aide in the Barnes Hospital maternity ward. When two jobs and the care of an infant sapped her strength, she gave up hospital work and moved in with Ike and his common-law wife in a loosely defined brother-sister arrangement.

Earning $25 per week, she made her first local recording, "Box Top," which received little recognition. Her platonic relationship with Ike continued during her apprenticeship as she observed his business deals and learned his style of operation. At length, Ike and Turner became lovers; then, his former girlfriend reappeared. Turner, out of place with the twosome, moved into a small house in St. Louis and contemplated the birth of her second child, fathered by Ike.

FIRST HIT

Her 1960 hit on the Sue label, "Fool in Love," which sold 800,000 copies, kept her voice before rockers for thirteen weeks in the top 100 recordings. At the insistence of underwriter Juggy Murray, Ike centered his act on her and renamed her Tina Turner from his childhood fantasies of Sheena, Queen of the Jungle. On the brink of matrimony, Tina felt divided—she thrilled at a chance to succeed but hesitated to marry the father of her unborn child. Then, on a casual jaunt to Tijuana, she decided to risk it.

The Turner road show expanded with the Ikettes, a three-girl backup group, plus a full complement of eight musical instruments. Billed as the Ike and Tina Turner Revue, the entourage made its way across the country, one packed house at a time. At $450 a performance and eighteen appearances per week, they kept up a frenetic pace.

From the first, Turner's marriage lacked compatibility and trust. She acknowledged her husband's womanizing and vitriolic temper, and she knew that he was under investigation for defrauding a bank. After she disobeyed Ike's order to accompany him to California, he beat her into submission. Fear for herself, her son Craig, and her unborn child shackled her to Ike, even though she recognized that divorce was inevitable. Meantime, son Ronald was born in Los Angeles.

HANGING TOUGH

In the next decade, she and Ike performed their down-and-dirty mélange of Black rock, sensual grind, and hurtin' soul for Black, white, and mixed audiences. Turner accidentally ruined her hair through overprocessing and covered her scalp with a wig. The look, which the Ikettes duplicated, caught on and became her trademark. Underneath the surface of her appeal, however, lay the insidious secret that kept her in line: Ike was an out-of-control batterer who showered unpredictable blows with any handy object, they polished off his tyranny with sex.

By 1964, the Turners had bought a three-bedroom ranch house in the View Park Hills section of Los Angeles. They formed a family with her son Craig, his two sons, Michael and Ike, Jr., and their son Ronald. Closeness and motherhood were impossible, so Turner found a housekeeper to keep order while the Revue traveled. To enable her to overcome hoarseness on these tours, Ike forced her to swallow bennies.

Turner's pungent brand of raspy, soul-stirring song kept dancers on their feet, rocking to her rhythms, swaying to her beat on sixty singles and fifteen albums. The group's hits, on Warner, Liberty, and Blue Thumb labels, moved across the charts at a steady pace—"It's Gonna Work Out Fine," "I Pity the Fool," "I'm Blue," "I Idolize You," "Poor Fool," "Tra La La La La," "I've Been Lovin' You Too Long," "Bold Soul Sister," "The Hunter," and "River Deep, Mountain High."

The Turners, like other Black artists of the 1960s, felt more at home on British stages, where they formed a tight bond with Mick Jagger, even teaching him to dance the Pony. As an opener for the Rolling Stones, the Revue pulsed across the stage, revving up from instrumental to the Ikettes to Ike on bass guitar to Turner's explosive appearance in full swing. Crowds thrilled to her wild, hyperkinetic sexuality. The draw held in Germany, but in France it soared even higher.

The offstage reality of these good times was a Jekyll-and-Hyde story of beatings, infidelity, and alienation. To Ike, she was a commodity to feed the Revue money machine. During their off-hours, she didn't count for much. She revived her flagging self-esteem by shopping. To answer her inner questions about how much longer she could keep up the charade, she turned repeatedly to seers and palm-readers. Ike found his own answers in mounting viciousness and cocaine.

The first half of the 1970s, with its rhythm-and-blues Grammy for "Proud Mary," brought assurance to Turner, who had no difficulty talking about her pumping, nonstop delivery. In an interview, she promised, "We never, ever do nothin' nice and easy.... So we're gonna do it nice—and rough" (*Current Biography*, 411). Without a hitch, the Revue cranked out hit albums—*Workin' Together, Blues*

Roots, Nutbush City Limits, The Gospel According to Ike and Tina—and their greatest hit, *Gimme Shelter*, a re-creation of the Rolling Stones' tour of the United States. Their rewards came in accolades from peers like Janis Joplin, in regular invitations to appear on talk shows, and in acceptance by middle-class whites.

MAKING A HOME

Marriage to a self-promoting, violent rock star presented Turner with her most serious challenge. At first, they denied themselves nothing in their Los Angeles home, which boasted a garage filled with Ike's Rolls Royce and Cadillac and Turner's Jaguar. Ike set the group's pace, masterminded each tour down to the last encore, and handed out a pittance of an allowance for Turner's use. Her response to his tyranny was first an abortion followed by an overdose of valium, then near collapse from tuberculosis. Fans sent flowers; Ike ignored her illness and fumed over canceled show dates. Only with homeopathic medicine did she recover. Later, she discovered Buddhist chants to help her cope with Ike's rages.

To success and money, Ike had one response—accommodate himself. He bought his own double-chambered recording studio, Bolic Sound, on La Brea Avenue. He added a maximum-security pleasure room in back, complete with a pornographic mural. In his petty kingdom, he could fine-tune his recordings and fondle the myriad female fans who were drawn to him.

In her mid-thirties, Turner—for all her glitter and much-touted success—saw the futility of life with an abusive drug addict. As she described it: "It wasn't even *my* career—it was *Ike's* career. And it was Ike's songs, mostly, which were about Ike's life—and I had to sing them. I was just his tool" (Turner and Loder, 155). What she preferred was her own show. At length, she established her own success: Her parts in the movies *Tommy* and *Acid Queen* as well as her solo albums, *Tina Turns the Country On* and *Let Me Touch Your Mind*, assured Ike that his wife was capable of succeeding without him.

The cataclysm came suddenly in July 1976, twenty years after she first met him. While touring in Dallas, Ike beat her for the last time. Despairing to the point of self-denigration, she grasped her remaining shred of dignity and, with a Mobil credit card, thirty-six cents in her pocket, and a pile of debts against her name, ran away. Feeling strong for the first time since she met Ike, she rebelled against his physical and emotional brutality by flying to Los Angeles.

ON THE RISE

For a year, she lived in a rented house and relaxed in a setting filled with peace and freedom. She relied on friends and lawyer Arthur Leeds to handle negotiations with Ike, who by that time was deep into underworld involvement. Divorce, finalized in 1978 with few compromises from Ike, left her little money, but her relief at being away from Ike was worth the loss. Still, he continued harassing her and threatening bodily harm. However bizarre his vengeance, she refused to return or to perform with him.

For three years, Turner, under new management, performed in an era marked by taste changes. She accepted foreign club dates with band and backup so that she could provide for her staff and four sons. She first moved north into Canada to avoid competing with Ike or riling his surly bodyguards. With costumes by Bob Mackie and with Mike Stewart's management, her career took on a new aura.

Turner, ever a ball of energy, moved on toward more varied challenges. Her cloak of glamor and allure masked the scars of harder times as she teamed with Mick Jagger and the Rolling Stones in 1981 for a U.S. tour followed by television appearances with Rod Stewart and Olivia Newton-John and bumptious Las Vegas club dates with Ann-Margret. A team-up with Mel Gibson in *Mad Max: Beyond Thunderdrome* left little doubt that Turner did not need Ike.

Within three years, she inaugurated a European tour and paired with Lionel Richie. In 1985, she swept the Grammies with a platinum album, *Private Dancer*, which established her as a survivor of the decade. The list of songs with her personal stamp of raw-edged sizzle includes "Let's Stay Together," "I Can't Stand the Rain," and "What's Love Got to Do With It?" her first popular title to hit the top of the charts.

At rest in her oriental-style four-bedroom house in Sherman Oaks, California, Turner became more solitary, more contemplative. She continued to meditate and corresponded with her sons, Craig, Ike, Jr., Michael, and Ronald, who went through hard times with drugs. She dated occasionally and cultivated a select group of close friends, especially Ann-Margret and Roger Smith. Self-discovery worked. With the rough times firmly shoved aside, she was at last sure that Tina Turner was an entity in her own right.

SOURCES

Collins, Nancy. "Tina Turner: The Rolling Stone Interview." *Rolling Stone*, October 23, 1986, 46-52.

Current Biography. New York: H. W. Wilson, 1984.

Fissinger, Laura. *Tina Turner*. New York: Ballantine, 1985.

Ivory, Steven. *Tina!* New York: Putnam, 1985.

Johnson, Brian D. "The Comeback Queen of Rock 'n' Roll." *Maclean's*, July 22, 1985, 44-46.

Kamin, Philip. *Tina Turner*. Milwaukee, Wis.: H. Leonard, 1985.

Koenig, Terry. *Tina Turner*. Edited by Howard Schroeder. Mankato, Minn.: Crestwood House, 1989.

McGuigan, Cathleen. "The Second Coming of Tina." *Newsweek*, September 10, 1984, 76.

Norment, Lynn. "Rich, Free and in Control: The 'Foreign Affairs' of Tina Turner." *Ebony*, November 1989, 166-170.

Sporkin, Elizabeth. "Tina Turner: Her Most Candid Interview." *Ladies' Home Journal*, April 1987, 34-38.

Turner, Tina, and Kurt Loder. *I, Tina*. New York: William Morrow, 1986.

Wallace, David. "Tina Turner: A Success Story You Won't Forget." *McCall's*, August 1985, 16-20.

Hervé Villechaize

Dwarfism is a condition that can be caused by Down's syndrome, thyroid deficiency, Turner's syndrome, achondroplasia, or pituitary malfunction. The last two of these conditions differ from others in that they shorten or stunt the extremities but do not distort the skeleton or deter normal brain functions. Victims of these diseases live normal lives, so far as their miniature bodies will allow.

Far into the backdrop of history, dwarves have always dominated the position of court jester and friend to the mighty. However, their personal lives have remained a daily struggle with compromise, both regarding physical compensation and emotional self-esteem. Not so different from Princess Floy, Tom Thumb, General Mite, Billy Barty, Johnny Puleo, and other noteworthy little people, Hervé Villechaize, his body scarred from repeated chores normally done by men of greater height and weight, has overcome the barrier of diminutive size to create his own niche as television and film actor, photographer, and artist.

BEGINNING SMALL

Born in Paris on April 23, 1943, Hervé Jean Pierre Villechaize, the youngest of four sons of Eveline Rechionne and André Villechaize, a Toulon surgeon, was the only abnormal member of his family. He lived part of his childhood in southern France and attended Paris's famed Beaux Art School. An astute, perceptive learner, he nevertheless hated academics, dropped out of classes in 1954, and relied on his zest for do-it-yourself projects to replace formal education.

Choosing to emigrate to a more promising location, Villechaize arrived in the United States at age sixteen and learned to speak English from watching western movies on television. He lived in a rundown midtown hotel in New York City and recoiled from casual street violence, which was far more threatening to an undersized person than to people of normal size. He was sensitive about his height, disliked being photographed or looking in a mirror, and resented snide remarks people made to the normal-sized women he dated.

Villechaize had the right physical attributes to further a career on television and in movies. His body, sturdy and well proportioned, was adequate for most demands. His round face and narrow, slanted eyes lit up quickly with passing bursts of emotion. His short arms and stubby fingers seemed always in motion, always gesturing. His voice, irrepressibly sudden and urgent, added to the overall impression of involvement. With small, neat ears, wide smile, and a generous crop of dark hair, he appeared alert and filled with joie de vivre, a necessary adjunct for a man who must take three steps to keep up with an average-sized stride.

BEING HIMSELF

Villechaize's first wife, Anne, a diminutive artist at five feet four inches, won him with her appealing brown eyes, long lashes, and pale complexion. While attending Manhattan's Art Students League, she met him at a laundromat, where he strained to place his coin in the slot above his head. She helped him out with the laundry and became his steady girl. A native of New Jersey, she loved plants and quiet pleasures but relied on him to protect her from harsh economic realities. Their relationship thrived on her patience and long-suffering with his collecting and hoarding guns and knives.

In 1970, the Villechaizes shared a low-rent loft at Foreplay Studios on Greene Street in the Soho section of Manhattan, known for defunct factory buildings and run-down streets. Villechaize knew how to scrimp and prided himself on his survival skills. Living among other aspiring artists, he and Anne managed with a freight elevator and no heat at night and on weekends. Their furnishings, culled from rejects, discount stores, and lumber left on the street, were meager.

The Villechaizes moved to a sixth-floor loft in a former button factory on Broadway in the summer of 1971. It took them two years to clean the buttons from the rooftop and refurbish the twenty-by-seventy-foot space into livable quarters. Because they did not have the cash to hire decorators, he and Anne completed the remodeling themselves. A master at a variety of trades, Villechaize tackled plumbing, carpentry, floor refinishing, and painting and often supplied himself with bits of salvage from Canal Street.

DEALING WITH DISCONTENT

By late 1972, discontent marred the marriage. The following year, Villechaize, eager to expand to relationships with other women, grew demanding and restless, sometimes driving his wife to despair at their mutual misery. To create a change, they journeyed to Paris. Shortly, he returned to his New York loft, leaving Anne to cope in France alone. Soon, she was exulting in her independence in a Paris apartment near the Eiffel Tower.

The separation lasted until mid-winter, when Villechaize was hospitalized for kidney failure. His illness resulted in a forced reconciliation. His response was a serious depression, arising in part from the stifling repression of the New York lifestyle. To escape, he spent time apart from Anne with Scott and Sandy Seldin in Shady, a rural village near Woodstock, New York. By this point in his marriage, he was determined that Anne learn to manage without him. From this same urge for separation came his desire to collaborate with Seldin on an autobiography. The resulting book, *Yes, Boss* (1982), was seriously flawed by Seldin's urge to tell of his relationship with Villechaize.

In 1973, following an uneasy truce with Anne, Villechaize joined the Seldins in opening the Soho Loft, a four-way antique cooperative. He participated fully in the enterprise, from ad copy to purchasing and layout, but zeal was not enough to keep the dealership solvent. As the partnership ended, his marriage again foundered and he sold his loft, vowing to quit Manhattan for good. Anne left, glad to part with what she saw as his faults—cruelty, violence, and narcissism. In 1978, their eight-year marriage ended in divorce.

With an eye toward furthering his acting career, Villechaize reestablished himself in Los Angeles, at times sleeping in cars until he could make contacts in Hollywood. Within three years, his health, stamina, and outlook had improved. He seemed more serene, less critical of himself. Even more important, he was gaining a firmer hold on his career. His only regret about past losses was his acrimonious break with Anne, whom he continued to miss. He blamed himself for the fact that she no longer wanted to correspond with him.

CARVING OUT A CAREER

In contrast to his relationship with his ex-wife, Villechaize's grasp on acting was more promising. In his early twenties, he enrolled in the Art Students League. In 1966, as a free-lance photographer, he met Conrad Rooks, who gave him a start in film with a small role in *Chappaqua* followed by bit parts on stage and with the New York City Opera. Eleven years later, however, Villechaize had achieved little. He nearly drowned after falling into a pool on the set of Norman Mailer's *Maidstone*. Later, his part in the movie was cut to small glimpses of his hands on the keyboard of a piano. Still, he refused to quit, even when the demands on his body threatened his health without advancing his on-screen worth.

At three feet eleven inches, Villechaize had more to offer than a tiny body. Originally a painter represented in numerous U.S. galleries, he has also written children's literature, taken professional-quality photographs, sketched, and played the harmonica. For a time he set his hopes on the theater. As a member of the Hartford Stage Company, he appeared in *Carry Nation, Ubu Roi, Rosencrantz and Guildenstern Are Dead,* and *Scuba Duba.* For Theatre, Inc., he acted in *Elizabeth the First* and *Gloria Experenza.*

As a cinema actor, Villechaize appeared in *Guitar, Hollywood Boulevard No. 2,* a Mafia spoof called *The Gang That Couldn't Shoot Straight* (1971), a U.S.-Italian film, *Crazy Joe* (1973), *Seizure, Forbidden Zone,* and *Greaser's Palace.* A promising part in *The Man with the Golden Gun* (1974), starring Roger Moore as Agent .007, revitalized Villechaize's hope that he could return to France and succeed in his native language, but the endeavor failed to materialize.

In 1977, he found work in an underground film entitled *Hot Tomorrows*, which was featured at the New York Film Festival and earned a cult following among film aficionados. Afterward, to gain recognition as star material, he posed with starlets at

Joe Allen's Bar. The ploy landed him an agent and a role in Henry Winkler's senti-
mental farce, *The One and Only* (1978).

"FANTASY ISLAND" AND BEYOND

. As an actor, Villechaize maintained his pride. He rejected demeaning parts such
as elves and Santa's helpers. In 1976, he made his television debut costarring opposite
Ricardo Montalban's Mr. Roarke as the midget Tattoo on "Fantasy Island," a weekly
episodic series for ABC in a prime Saturday slot. The filming demanded strenuous
activity but required one-dimensional acting skills. In this contrived romance, he
played factotum to "the boss." The popular show, which followed the equally successful "Love Boat," was filmed at the Arboretum, a public park twenty-five miles
from Los Angeles, and remained a hit until 1983. Villechaize earned a wide following
for his lisping French-flavored dialogue and officious, intrusive character. From stardom came invitations to appear on "Tomorrow," "The Johnny Carson Show," and
"The Merv Griffin Show," photos in the *Hollywood Reporter*, articles in the *National
Enquirer* and *Mad Magazine*, and investment opportunities.

During his rising fame in the 1970s, Villechaize and a couple shared a large two-
story house in a seedy section of Los Angeles. Under contract agreements with ABC,
Burbank Studios supplied him with a trailer, a driver and station wagon, and a
female bodyguard from James Investigation Agency. In addition, his staff included a
business manager, wardrobe attendant, and speech therapist. In exchange, the studio
demanded that he guard his health and not take chances with his livelihood by flying
in planes or meeting with accidents, which were frequent because of his size.

THE REAL HERVÉ

After his rise to fame on "Fantasy Island," the public's curiosity about him
burgeoned. Once, a fan snatched him up off the sidewalk, forced him into a vehicle,
took him home to meet his family, then returned him to the streets. He bridled at
such crude treatment and indiscriminate labels, such as "Whatsisname" or the
"midget from TV." In his entry in *Who's Who*, he spoke frankly about his size as it
applied to success: "I never thought of my life on a small scale. For my self-worth and
respect, money and success is not my bible. My achievements in the past and my
goals in the future can only be achieved by melding will with love (*Who's Who*,
3334).

In June 1978, about the time the studio was receiving telephoned kidnap threats
to its free-spirited dwarf star, Villechaize bought a ranch in the San Fernando Valley
outside Los Angeles, where he protected himself with a ready revolver and can of
Mace. He shared the two-story brown shingled house with Scott and Sandy Seldin,
who occupied the second floor. The inside was sparsely furnished, but there was a
large assortment of cats. The acre and a half of grounds featured a barn, rabbit hutch,
chicken house, stables housing two horses and three ponies, pool, garage, and understated landscaping. He later added goats, an owl, and a raccoon to his menagerie.

A major advantage of the new house's location was the neighborhood children, who helped him groom and show his pony, Lady. He enjoyed equestrian activities so much that he considered ordering a stallion from France and going into serious breeding. To complement his newfound identity, Hervé bought boots and cowboy outfits and rode frequently, preferring to leave his bodyguard behind.

For a time, he seemed to thrive on solitude and the warmth of the Seldins' friendship. On one occasion, however, he was taken to the hospital to ease shortness of breath. Later physical symptoms of stress included nosebleeds, headaches, and stomach spasms, which occurred during emotional lows. Other indications of unrest were his frequent abrupt firings of bodyguards, whom he resented for intruding on his privacy and independence.

A rebel, bon vivant, and romantic, Villechaize radiated enthusiasm. Determined and aggressive, he defied his handicap by denying its existence. To retain a degree of normalcy, he rode horseback and drove a pickup truck. While building his home, he disregarded size and tackled jobs that would daunt a normal person. With his deftness and drive, he was constantly busy, often compulsive in his perfectionism and drive to succeed. He banked on natural creativity to fuel his many projects, especially his new interest in dressage. Thrifty from leaner times, he clipped coupons, fed a compost heap, and kept meticulous records of household expenditures. In some respects both shy and melancholy, he countered the frequent low spots during the rise in his career with dynamism and ambition.

At the crest of Villechaize's popularity on "Fantasy Island," Alan Glickman directed a documentary segment of "Comeback" based on his life. The show, filmed on location at the ranch, featured Villechaize at his easel, then outdoors near the pool in the company of a gang of children. Other high spots of the time included a trip to Maui in August 1978 to film a segment of "Fantasy Island." Shortly before departure, Anne returned for a tender reunion with her ex-husband, whom she affectionately dubbed Irving Dwarf. The return from Hawaii, however, plunged him into despair. Following his arrival at his California ranch, he made a decisive break with the Seldins. Shortly afterward, he and Anne separated once more, this time for good.

DOWNS FOLLOWED BY UPS

In 1980, Villechaize briefly courted twenty-three-year-old Camille Hagan, a statuesque stand-in on *Charlie's Angels* whom he met in 1976, took to France in April 1980, then married in September. In an article in *People Weekly*, he reported that the curious made cruel taunts about the twenty-one-inch difference in their heights and started rumors about his physical deformity. His plea to the public was to be allowed to live a normal life. He admitted to joining a UCLA research program in Torrance, California, probing health problems connected with dwarfism. One of the results of this study was that dwarves' lives can be shortened by trying to keep up with normal people.

In the 1980s, Villechaize developed an interest in public service in the Burbank area. He took part in the Venice Anti-Crime Committee, MacLaren Hall, a halfway house, and Sunland Lakeview Terrace Little League. He served on the board of directors for Hathaway House for Children and the Sheenway School and Cultural Center. On the national level, he supported the International Wildlife Federation, Save the Seals, National Wildlife Association, and Save the Whales. As a member of AFTRA, the Screen Actors Guild, Actors Equity, and the American Film Institute, he maintained an active part in his profession and received some awards for activism and artistry. For the horses from his stables he earned ribbons from the Tri-Valley Horse Show Association. From the city of Paris he received an art award.

In an intimate self-assessment, Villechaize, who is often inexplicably moody, summed up his true character: "There are three Hervés. One is the public Hervé, the TV star 'Tattoo.' Another is the Hervé my friends know. No one knows the third Hervé. That's the one that keeps me alive. It's a candle burning inside me. No one has a chance to blow it out" (Seldin, back cover).

SOURCES

Jackovich, Karen G. "We Are as Normal as Anyone." *People Weekly*, October 13, 1980, 135-138.

Seldin, Scott. *Yes, Boss.* Croton-on-Hudson, N.Y.: Blythe-Pennington, 1982.

Who's Who. Detroit: Gale Research, 1984.

Bob Welch

From lead pitcher for the Los Angeles Dodgers to all-star to alcoholic, Bob Welch made the classic slide in his twenties. What began as teenage drinking developed into full-scale substance dependency. Like other drinkers, Bob went through stages of denial, anger, manipulation, and broken promises to quit drinking. Only professional treatment at the Meadows was able to set him free of alcohol's grip.

In retrospect, Welch realized that he had only one choice. To George Vecsey, his friend and collaborator on his autobiography, he confided the truth about his decline: "I'm sober today.... That's what counts. I can't make any promises about tomorrow, but I'm sober today. If I follow the things I've been taught, I know I won't die of alcoholism" (Welch and Vecsey, 18).

CITY BOY

The youngest child of Lou-Nell Welch, a part-time floral arranger, and Rupert Welch, a lathe operator in an aviation-parts factory, Robert L. Welch grew up in Hazel Park, Michigan, a working-class neighborhood on the outskirts of Detroit. He, his brother, Donnie, and sister, Diane, came from a picture-book U.S. home, where the family consumed alcohol as a natural accompaniment to good times. In scholastics, Welch was a good speller and all-round reliable student. On the playing field, he demonstrated the stamina, verve, coordination, and muscle to become a professional athlete in whatever sport he chose.

Welch sometimes endangered his health for foolish reasons. Once he sneaked a parrot across the Texas-Mexico border and suffered forty-two days of hospitalization from an unnamed disease. Doctors feared that he had parrot fever. Oftentimes, he hurt himself and broke bones in trying to get the most attention. In later years, he connected his daredevil attitude to a fear of death, which gripped him when he faced the loss of someone close.

In his preteen years, Welch won a sportsmanship award. His academic growth failed to keep pace with his physical acumen, however, as his grades dropped from outstanding to acceptable. He remained competitive in all phases of school but performed best at sports. For a hero, he selected Bob Russell, Boston Celtics center, but his fantasies of future team play focused on baseball, especially the Detroit Tigers.

Welch and his brother and male cousins shot hoops or played ice hockey or whiffleball in the coldest weather. Because he was undersized and usually the last one chosen for a team, his friends named him the Heckler. Later, as a professional athlete, he took pride in having his parents root for him and see him play his best.

League play drew Welch away from all-white teams to the West Side Cubs, the most competitive nonwhite group. In looking back over his development, he credited these hard-driving teammates with improving his skills. From learning experiences with the Cubs, he avoided local racism and developed strong relationships with Black players, who became his best friends in professional play.

BECOMING AN ALCOHOLIC

As sports formed the core of Welch's life, consumption of alcohol became a regular feature. His first overindulgence came at age fifteen on the way to a football game. Bolting a bottle of Mogen David was his introduction to manhood. He used alcohol and sports for the same purpose — to set him apart from others and bolster his self-esteem. One of his keenest memories from school days was his first starring role, pitching his team to second place in a Class A tournament. In his autobiography, he confessed, "My whole personality was based on being a star" (Welch and Vecsey, 42).

Scouted in high school, Welch was drafted by the Chicago Cubs and offered $5,000. He rejected the low bid and opted instead for college. He liked the idea of passing up factory work, which dominated people in his family's social class, and seeking something better, more substantial. The choice took commitment: As a university student, he would not be eligible for the draft for three years; if he chose a junior college, the time span was one year. After a three-hour visit to Ranger Junior College in Texas, however, he realized that a four-year college closer to home was more to his liking and registered at Eastern Michigan University.

Academics remained distant among Welch's goals. He attended classes but often cut lectures when he wouldn't be missed and cheated as a means of maintaining passing grades. One subject that did hold his interest was psychology, which came in handy during his treatment at the Meadows. More important to Welch, however, was the fact that he was a starting pitcher his freshman year and ultimately earned a Most Valuable Player award.

To quell his timidity around girls, Welch turned to liquor and occasionally to marijuana and tranquilizers in his early teens. By college age, he was addicted to alcohol as a means of coping. He drank on most occasions, ranging from loss to success. Boredom and fear also caused him to reach for the bottle. By clowning for a superficial crowd, he covered up the fact that he needed a drink to survive.

A knee injury in December 1976, his sophomore year, gave Welch some cause to worry. Fortunately for his athletic career, therapy restored him to team play by spring. In August, *The New Yorker* described him as a promising new face on the mound. Overconfidence from this minor accolade caused him to break team rules and carouse after hours, despite warnings that he would be put off the team. The coach backed down, enabling Welch to avoid punishment for his destructive behavior.

During his sophomore year, Welch took part in an all-star tour to Japan, where his drinking got out of control at a hotel and coach Red Dedeaux chastised him for unacceptable behavior and called him a drunk. It was the first time anyone had ever labeled him an alcoholic. In Welch's words, "He could see that my personality changed when I drank, that I abandoned all pretenses at being civilized" (Welch and Vecsey, 68). Other hints from friends and family remained repressed in his memory until much later, when he had to face how the disease was ruining his life.

THE DODGERS

Good times came in 1978 after Welch signed with the Dodgers to replace Rick Rhoden. Welch had missed much of his junior year because of an elbow injury, but he still filled a slot in a professional club. For the moment, he forgot college and moved toward his dream — professional baseball. From the beginning of his career in the major leagues, he wore the blue-edged logo with pride. Impressive at six feet three inches, he bore his height with the bounce and control of a natural athlete. His winning qualities boosted the Dodgers from a downward spiral after his initial win against the Giants.

Fitting in with the big league put additional stress on the insecure Welch. At first, he missed the camaraderie of his college team. In the professional league, there was more jealousy, less friendship. Eventually, his short comebacks fit in with the witty, peppery repartee of the jock inner circle, where he finally found a place. His after-hours drinking helped smooth over personality clashes and other rough spots. Still, commentators were not fooled and stereotyped him as immature and nonverbal. When his drinking stymied his mental faculties, teammates dubbed him Spaceman.

MARY ELLEN

Welch dated numerous girls, yet he always returned to Mary Ellen Wilson, a sweet-natured, well-meaning girl with high standards who had been a cheerleader at his high school and continued her education at Western Michigan University at Ypsilanti. During the first low days of professional play, he telephoned her for solace and invited her to visit him on weekends. He felt at home with her and could confide his problems, especially his drinking habits. After college, she followed the league circuit and lived wherever Welch did, even though he made no firm commitment to marriage.

One of his worst memories of their relationship was a New Year's Eve celebration where he lost control. He began the evening with two bottles of wine before he came for her. Their date deteriorated rapidly and ended with his passing out on the toilet, then wandering around in below-freezing weather and vomiting. A friend's photograph of him was a permanent reminder of the squalid celebration.

As Welch began the recovery ordeal, he was forced to examine ways in which he had wronged people while he was under the influence of alcohol. Mary Ellen had suffered extreme abuse, usually from the harsh words he heaped on her to hide his sensitivity and confusion. He also blamed professional sports for overtaxing him, but he learned early that Alcoholics Anonymous rejects excuses. The blame lay on him alone.

STARDOM

Sports stardom, as a rule, comes at somebody else's expense. For Welch, stardom came in front of a crowd of 56,000 fans the day he struck out Reggie Jackson during the ninth inning of a World Series game against the New York Yankees. It was the event that he returned to repeatedly in writing his autobiography. Yet, the momentary thrill paled beside the round of congratulatory parties, speaking engagements, interviews, and other congratulations that poured in. Soon, Welch was swept up in his own fame; he neglected his health and deadened his emotions with drink. When he returned to his old neighborhood, he couldn't get enough of visits to the Rainbow, his longtime hangout, where the applause continued for a favorite son.

Welch had a usual human mix of bad habits: He was restless and introverted, bit his nails, kept a pinch of Copenhagen in his cheek, and drank to excess. The escapades resulting from drunkenness caused him to brawl, drive recklessly, wreck a golf cart at spring training, and overturn his Bronco at the beach, endangering himself and two companions. He lied about numerous scrapes, made no attempt to curb his insults, and often cultivated enmity where he might have made friends. When baseball officials pressed him to curb his childish shenanigans, he complained that everyone blamed him unjustly.

Ultimately, Welch got careless with his career. He drank before practice, then started sneaking beers in the weight room during games. To cover infractions of league rules, he tried to enlist others in his shady behavior. The scout who discovered his duplicity wrote him a long letter pointing out where his recklessness was leading. Welch reacted with casual concern, then anger that anyone would label him an alcoholic.

In 1980, after he arrived drunk at batting practice, a caring but stern management refused to let a twenty-three-year-old player destroy himself with alcohol. Club officials ordered him back to Los Angeles, where consultant John Newton, himself an alcoholic, delivered a four-hour lecture. The ball club had allied with an alcoholism-awareness program. The candidate that first came to mind was Bob Welch. He had a choice: Dry out or else.

THE MEADOWS

For intense psychotherapy and medical treatment for his dependency, Welch signed himself into the Meadows, a former dude ranch in the desert near Wickenburg, Arizona, one hour from Phoenix. The Meadows staff provided hospital-issue pajamas and robe for the first few days and expected him to make his own bed and follow the rules like every other patient. None of the inmates catered to a baseball whiz—in the hospital, he was just another alcoholic.

The shock of hospitalization brought Welch to a crisis. Huddled under the running shower, he wept and longed to withdraw completely. He plotted to escape and hitchhike back to Phoenix. He tried to comprehend the stereotypes that society had taught him about being young and enjoying life. Most definitions of a good time included a few drinks, but alcoholism was not fun. It was hell, and it was going to kill him.

By helping Welch assert his own strengths, tough-talking counselors spurred him to accept his addiction and overpower it. Among his realizations during counseling was that his family members had never communicated well with each other and that well-meaning friends had helped him manipulate, deny, and cover up his blackouts and binges. Further insights came from group sessions. In these mutual self-help discussions, fellow alcoholics goaded im to full disclosure of his faults.

STRENGTHS

In his autobiography, subtitled *A Young Man's Battle with Alcoholism*, Welch described his dependence on Mary Ellen, revealed in the deluge of letters to her during his weeks at the Meadows. When he concentrated on her, the nursery rhyme "Mary Had a Little Lamb" filled his thoughts, making him see his relationship in an unfavorable light. He recalled using dates with her as an excuse to polish off a bottle of wine, assuring himself that the meal and their friendship were more enjoyable with alcohol. As a soulmate, she perceived his anguish and gave him the backing he craved as he fought the disease.

During family week at the Meadows, Welch sat through a lengthy grilling with his sister and brother, parents, girlfriend, colleagues, and even Tommy Lasorda, manager of the Dodgers. The revelations of their hurt, embarrassment, anger, and rage helped him vent his frustrations. He saw himself as the family star and as little Bobby, the family pet. By the end of thirty-six days of treatment, he was able to admit that he had never been honest in relationships with loved ones.

Returning to normal life was not easy for Welch. Friends were supportive, but temptation remained close, beginning with a stewardess offering drinks on the flight out of Arizona. He stayed sober and played well for the team until a pulled groin muscle in 1980 plunged him into despair and self-pity. He avoided alcohol, then succumbed to Valium, which he obtained from a friend. Loosened from pain and sobriety, he caused a highway accident, then sank into deeper despair because of his return to the old pattern of dependency.

A call to the Meadows restored Welch to the right train of thought. He forgave himself one failure and set out to live one day at a time. His life began to come into focus. Mary Ellen got a job counseling alcoholics; he joined Alcoholics Anonymous. When he gained control of his behavior, he bought his first home, a two-story condo at Huntington Beach, California. The purchase helped him grow up and work toward mature goals, such as furnishing rooms and landscaping the yard.

A SETTLED LIFE

The 1980s brought monumental changes in Welch's life. After a two-year separation and some deep soul-searching, he married Mary Ellen on January 19, 1982, and fathered his first child, a son, Dylan. He was named one of the ten outstanding young Americans in 1986 and was traded to Oakland five years later. While living temporarily in a stucco house on Beach Street in San Francisco on October 17, 1989, the family survived the earthquake that demolished part of the neighborhood. The setback put off completion of their new condo in the marina section, which suffered even worse tremors.

Welch demonstrated a new maturity as he comforted his wife and explained the waiting period for their house to be completed. Having lost his mother to pancreatitis on July 28, the day after Dylan was born, Welch hid his grief and went on with team play against the Seattle Mariners. Moving between home and the hospital, he got to Kentucky too late to say good-bye to his mother, then returned to the funeral home to place photos of his infant son in her hand.

Other difficulties hit Welch during the World Series after Dave Stewart and Mike Moore replaced him as starting pitcher in the third and fourth games. Colleagues, who nicknamed him Wile E. Coyote, rewarded the more stable Bob Welch for his self-control and his ability to face loss without going back to the bottle. The next November, after his twentieth win, he received a major honor—the Cy Young Award. As celebrators popped corks and toasted his win, he remained dry—and proud of it.

SOURCES

Fimrite, Ron. "One Pitch at a Time." *Sports Illustrated*, September 17, 1990, 58-62.

Gammons, Peter. "Their Ride of Terror." *Sports Illustrated*, October 30, 1989, 28-30.

Stier, Kit. "Welch Garners Cy Young Award." *Oakland, California Tribune*, November 14, 1990, n.p.

_____. "Welch Gets Historic 26th." *Oakland, California Tribune*, September 27, 1990, n.p.

Welch, Bob, and George Vecsey. *Five O'Clock Comes Early*. New York: William Morrow, 1982.

Elie Wiesel

To have outlived Hitler's concentration camps and overcome the bitterness of the Holocaust is a major accomplishment. For Elie Wiesel, victory lacked the taste of glory because survival cost him a mother and sister on the first day of incarceration and, after months of hardship and torture, his beloved father, who was beaten to death by an SS officer wielding a truncheon. In his retelling of his family's agonies, he proclaimed: "Never shall I forget those moments which murdered my God and my soul and turned my dreams to dust. Never shall I forget these things, even if I am condemned to live as long as God Himself. Never" (Wiesel 1960, ix).

From Wiesel's experience has come a lifetime of commitment to Judaism and world peace. As a mythic figure, one of the most beloved and revered human-rights activists, he sets an example of civilized behavior and strikes out against hate, war, torture, persecution, deprivation, and other barbarities. To an ecumenical gathering in Charlotte, North Carolina, he stated the personal and compelling philosophy that spawned his activism: "The opposite of love is not hate, it is indifference.... The opposite of life is not death, but indifference to life and death" (Williams, n.p.).

FROM SIGHET TO HELL

Eliezar Wiesel, third child and only son of grocer and community leader Shlomo and Sarah Feig Wiesel, was born on September 30, 1928, in Sighet, the provincial Romanian home to 15,000 Jews in the Carpathian Mountains on the Russian border. From early childhood, Elie demonstrated keen intellectual curiosity, which impelled his father to plan for the boy's education in psychology, astronomy, and modern Hebrew. Elie's mother, of a more traditional bent, encouraged a regimen of Torah, Talmud, cabala, and Hasidic lore.

Against the backdrop of *Kristall Nacht*, the "night of broken glass," the invasion of Poland, pogroms and deportations, and the first gassings of undesirables with Zyklon B, Elie was developing into a pious student, filled with delight in the mysticism of cabala. In 1941, as deportations began in Eastern Europe and 33,000 Jews were machine-gunned at Babi Yar in Russia, he lived in innocence of the coming catastrophe. Near the end of that year, Elie came under the influence of Moshe the beadle, a minor parish official who perceived that a child who weeps as he fervently prays possesses more than the usual understanding of the divine. A year later, as Wiesel described in *Night*, his autobiography published fifteen years after the war, Moshe returned from being kidnapped by the Gestapo to Transnistria. He warned the neighborhood that Nazism held more terror for Jews than the Babylonian captivity, the Spanish Inquisition, or any other persecutions of the past. His prophetic words, like those of Homer's Cassandra, went unheeded.

By 1944, Elie's father, a knowledgeable spokesperson for local Jews, could not ignore the menace that was about to strike yet rejected any notion of emigrating to another homeland to begin again. News from Budapest indicated that anti-Semitism was rampant—synagogues closed and temple leaders were arrested. Elie's mother had a premonition of evil after noticing German officers in the ghetto. Still, optimism prevailed. Germans moved into Sighet and lived peaceably alongside Jews. Without warning, during Passover week Jewish leaders were arrested. New laws deprived Elie and his family of civil rights and required them to live in ghettos and wear an identifying marker—a yellow star. The Saturday before Pentecost, Shlomo attended a council meeting and returned with terrible news—Jews were to be deported.

On June 13, a week after the Allies stormed the beaches at Normandy, Elie and other Jews of Sighet were ordered to line up in the street at 8:00 A.M. Five hours later, the first of a series of train cars loaded with deportees departed from the station. The Wiesel family, which was not selected, was housed temporarily in a synagogue. The process continued until the last roundup on June 20, when Elie and his father, mother, older sisters, Hilda and Beatrice, and baby sister, Tzipora, were forced into a cattle car. The two-day journey in wretched, cramped quarters took their convoy northwest to Birkenau-Auschwitz, deep in German territory. Along the way, Madame Schächter, a Jewish matron, rent the night with shrieks of doom and visions of a demonic burning.

SURVIVING A DEATH CAMP

Immediately separated from the women, Elie and his father moved on to a Gypsy camp, then escaped assignment to the crematory, which belched smoke and flames into the night sky. Healthy men reported to work camps. As Shlomo and Elie watched, a truck delivered babies to be burned alive in a pit. Elie was shocked into the realization that Moshe's prophecies and Madame Schächter's hellish dreams had foretold his future.

Elie and his father managed to stay together. They resided in meager barracks and slept on wooden slatted bunks stacked four layers deep. Their heads were shaved; they were issued ill-fitting work clothes. *Kapos*, or trustees, beat and intimidated them. Separated from skilled workers, Elie and his father went to a stone barracks and then by a half-hour march to another camp, where treatment was more humane. Elie's arm was tattooed with the number A-7713.

A DIET OF BRUTALITY

At the end of three weeks, prison conditions became more brutal. The 100 remaining unskilled workers were marched for four hours to the electrical warehouse at Buna, which was nearly deserted. Following a three-day quarantine, the group was examined by three doctors. A band played a march as Elie and other prisoners trudged to the warehouse to work. He and other Zionist youth decided that if they survived, they would leave Europe and emigrate to Haifa, where Jews were creating a new Zionist state.

Greater trials awaited Elie, who by then was fifteen years old. The camp dentist attempted to remove his gold crown. The boy lied to save it from confiscation so that he could use it later as a bargaining point, but Franek, the foreman, forced him to part with his tooth. In another brutal episode, Idek, a crazed *Kapo*, beat Elie. A French Jewess who passed as an Aryan soothed Elie's bloody face. Years later, he saw her again and renewed their acquaintance with reminiscences of Buna. The worst of Elie's mistreatment came after he laughed at the sight of Idek lying with a young Polish girl. For his indiscretion, Elie received twenty-five strokes with the lash.

A WORSENING SCENE

One Sunday, U.S. planes bombed Buna for over an hour. Elie and his father were cheered, even though prisoners were forced to remove an unexploded bomb. A week later, the assembled prisoners watched the hanging of a man who stole during the alert. A later incident in which three people were hanged left a dismal memory in Elie's mind. He wondered why God did not intervene in their sufferings.

Feeling was strong in the fall at Rosh Hashanah. Jews prayed together, but Elie could only accuse God of forsaking him. On Yom Kippur, formerly fastidious in his piety, he did not fast and interpreted his act as rebellion against God. The SS, members of Hitler's elite corps of 750,000 fanatical henchmen, began the selection process of weeding out the weak for extermination. Elie ran past Dr. Joseph Mengele, death-camp doctor, to demonstrate his strength. Days after the selection, Elie's relief proved short-lived when Shlomo was called up for a second examination. Fearful that he faced the gas ovens, he bequeathed to Elie a pitiful inheritance—his knife and spoon. Later that day, a jubilant Shlomo returned to claim his belongings.

In January 1945, Elie underwent surgery on his right foot, which was filled with infection. A kindly doctor soothed his fears and praised his bravery. Before Elie was fully recovered, the camp was evacuated. Elie was forced to limp on his bandaged foot. He and his father trudged through snow toward an unknown destination as the SS shot all who fell behind. Shlomo forced Elie to fight sleep so that he would not freeze to death.

Arrival at Gleiwitz brought little relief. For three days they received no food or water. Again, Shlomo fell victim to the selection process, but Elie rushed to save him and in the scramble brought his father back among the survivors. The next leg of their journey was by roofless cattle wagon, each filled with a hundred prisoners. Elie feared that his father was dead, then managed to revive him. The prisoners lived on snow for ten days of travel through Germany. Elie's despair deepened.

THE FINAL SEPARATION

At Buchenwald, while Shlomo and Elie awaited the obligatory delousing bath, Shlomo collapsed. An alert sounded and Elie was driven to the block, where he slept until daylight. He realized that he had abandoned his father. Hours later, Elie found Shlomo begging for water. The old man was feverish from deprivation, cold, and the wasting effects of dysentery, which rapidly depleted his strength.

As rumors of rescue by the advancing Red Army fell on unbelieving ears, Elie stayed at Shlomo's bunk for a week. The head of the block advised Elie to think of himself and leave Shlomo to die. On January 28, Elie went to sleep in his bunk above Shlomo, who was transported from the barracks during the night. On the morning of January 29, only two-and-a-half months before liberation, another inmate occupied the bunk. Elie feared that Shlomo might have been thrown alive into the gas ovens. His last memory was his father's final word — "Eliezar." Unable to weep, the boy was further tortured by feeling relieved at no longer having to care for Shlomo. At the same time that Roosevelt, Churchill, and Stalin were discussing an end to the war at Yalta, Elie, blaming himself for failing his father, reached the depths of hopelessness.

RESCUE AND REPATRIATION

About the time that Allied troops were reaching the Rhine, Elie was transferred to the children's block. On April 5, organized camp resistors refused the Germans' orders to assemble. No more food was distributed to the 20,000 inmates for the next five days. They subsisted on grass and discarded potato peelings until April 10, when the resistance took control of the camp. At 6:00 P.M., U.S. tanks arrived at the gates. He recalled later the soldiers' response to their plight: "They were the first free men to see the world of horror. I'll never forget their eyes, the rage, the anger. Their reaction was so profound. We became each other's witnesses" (Williams, n.p.).

Elie and his fellow prisoners, sick with a variety of camp diseases and unable to think of anything but food, relieved their hunger. Three days after liberation, badly undernourished, he fell ill with food poisoning. After two weeks of serious illness, he recovered enough to look at himself in the mirror. The haunting memory of the cadaverous reflection never left him.

After liberation, Elie refused to return home to Sighet and was sorted out along with 400 other orphans bound for Normandy. As he described his late teens, "I was not 18. I was an old man. What I knew then, the teachers of my teachers never knew. What I lived in an hour, people don't live in a generation" (Freedman, n.p.). Unable to understand a spoken offer of French citizenship, he remained stateless until 1963, when he became a naturalized U.S. citizen. His older sisters, Hilda and Beatrice, survived imprisonment and rejoined their brother after the war.

At eighteen, Wiesel migrated to the Sorbonne in Paris, read deeply of existential writers Camus and Sartre, and studied philosophy in order to better interpret the events that he had witnessed. Working as a reporter for a Tel Aviv journal, he interviewed and became a protégé of François Mauriac, Nobel Prize-winning French author. Mauriac, grieved to learn that Wiesel was one of the children victimized by the SS, embraced him and wept. He helped him publish *Night*, which began as an 800-page handwritten manuscript. Wiesel traveled from France to Africa, South America, India, and Israel, where he lived for a time and covered the events that marked evolving Jewish statehood. After 1960 he covered United Nations activities for an Israeli newspaper.

WRITING AS A CAREER

Two years after the publication of Anne Frank's diary, after resurfacing from ten years of self-imposed post-Holocaust silence, Wiesel began telling his story. He has made writing and speaking about the death of 6 million Jews his life's work. In 1970, he noted the reason for his obsession with writing about the Holocaust and its aftermath: "I write in order to understand as much as to be understood" (Wiesel 1982, iii). At first, he was unable to find a willing publisher. After Hill and Wang agreed to distribute his first descriptions of Nazi atrocities against the Jews, the public embraced all that Wiesel has put into print. As he looks out on Central Park from his study window, he hammers steadily at his task. He describes himself primarily as storyteller rather than as philosopher or theologian. He composes in French, his adopted language; his Austrian-born wife, Marion Erster Rose, a Holocaust survivor he married in 1969, translates some of his work into English.

The most significant of Wiesel's early prose—*Night* (1960), *Dawn* (1961), and *The Accident* (1962)—informed much of the world of the savagery of Auschwitz. The trilogy was followed by four major novels—*The Gates of the Forest* (1964), *The Town Beyond the Wall* (1964), *A Beggar in Jerusalem* (1970), and *The Oath* (1973). His nonfiction and dramatic works include *The Jews of Silence* (1966), *Legends of Our Time* (1968), *One Generation After* (1970), *Souls on Fire* (1972), *Ani Maanin* (1973), *Zalmen, or the Madness of God* (1974), and *Messengers of God* (1976).

A prolific writer and scholar, Wiesel continues to produce timely lectures, interviews, and commentary. The most recent of his thirty-plus works are *A Jew Today* (1978), *Four Hasidic Masters* (1978), *The Trial of God* (1979), *Images from the Bible* (1980), and a three-volume work, *The Fifth Son* (1985). A successful and influential spokesman on behalf of humane treatment, Wiesel currently holds the Andrew Mellon Chair in the Humanities at Boston University and lives near Central Park in New York City. His son, Shlomo Eliezar, named to honor both Elie and Shlomo, the boy's grandfather, gives his life new meaning and purpose.

WORLD-CLASS HUMANITARIAN

Elie Wiesel has received much public acclaim. His honorary degrees come from an array of colleges and universities: Jewish Theological Seminary, Hebrew Union, Manhattanville, Yeshiva, Boston, Wesleyan, Notre Dame, Anna Maria, Brandeis, Bar-Ilan, Hofstra, Talmudic, Marquette, Simmons, St. Scholastica, and Yale. Numbered among his honors are the American Liberties Medallion, Eleanor Roosevelt Memorial, Prix Medici, Congressional Gold Medal, Martin Luther King, Jr., Award, and the Nobel Peace Prize, awarded in Stockholm in 1986 with his sister Hilda present. Among those who petitioned the Nobel committee on his behalf were Mother Teresa, Henry Kissinger, François Mitterrand, and Lech Walesa. Along with the medal, Wiesel collected a stipend of $287,769.78.

A gentle, sad-eyed, tousled man, Wiesel, who before he began writing considered suicide on more than one occasion, continues to bear his burden and celebrate the triumph of survival. He challenged Ronald Reagan concerning Reagan's state visit to an SS cemetery in Bitburg, Germany; in 1987, he testified on the inhumanity of Nazi prisons at Klaus Barbie's trial in Lyons, France. To help other victims, he interceded for Ethiopian famine victims, Nicaraguan Indians, Cambodian boat people, Soviet refuseniks, missing Argentine children, battling factions in Northern Ireland, and Iraqi refugees. As a messenger for peace, human dignity, and atonement, he continues to probe the Holocaust, the world's most extreme episode of religious prejudice, as a means of honoring the dead and warning the living that such an atrocity must never happen again.

SOURCES

Abrahamson, Irving. *Against Silence: The Voice and Vision of Elie Wiesel.* New York: Holocaust Publications, 1985.

Berenbaum, Michael. *Elie Wiesel: Messenger to All Humanity.* South Bend, Ind.: University of Notre Dame Press, 1986.

Freedman, Samuel G. "Bearing Witness." *New York Times Magazine*, October 23, 1983, n.p.

Greene, Carol. *Elie Wiesel: Messenger from the Holocaust.* Chicago: Childrens Press, 1987.

Wiesel, Elie. *Night.* New York: Bantam Books, 1960.

_____. *One Generation After.* New York: Schocken Books, 1982.

_____. "What Really Makes Us Free." *Parade*, December 27, 1987, 6-8.

Williams, Ed. "Editorial Notebook: The Enemy Is Indifference." *Charlotte Observer*, March 15, 1990, n.p.

Index